NANO
CONSPIRACY

Dr. James Orrington

ISBN: 978-1-965663-09-7
LCCN: 2024922962

First printing, edition 2024
Orrington publishing
7931 S. King Dr.
Chicago, IL 60619
www.apdminis.com
info@airguardhealth.com

Disclaimer: *This book is a work of creative nonfiction. Names, characters, businesses, places, events, and incidents are either the products of the author's imagination or used in a fictitious manner. Any resemblance to actual persons, living or dead, or events is purely coincidental.*

---

i

Dedication

For those who stand for the truth in the shadows of government cover-ups. May this tale illuminate the darkness that emanates from the government and the military. To the relentless pursuers of justice and the victims who never found peace, this is for you.

Individuals who remain unaware of the implications of nanomaterial weaponry, particularly in conjunction with Wi-Fi and 5G technologies, may undermine their physical and mental well-being. This represents a concerning new dimension of oppression. The book 'Harness the Power of Water: A Revolutionary New Approach to Achieve Success' and ' Hints for Discerning Our Reality: Clues to Understanding Our Reality" gives insights that can illuminate these issues and foster a deeper understanding of the truth.

Table of Content

Dedication ii

Table of Content iii

Introduction vi

Chapter 1 1

Chapter 2 14

Chapter 3 20

Chapter 4 26

Chapter 5 33

Chapter 6 51

Chapter 7 58

Chapter 8 67

Chapter 9 82

Chapter 10 89

Chapter 11 98

Chapter 12 111

Chapter 13 122

Chapter 14 138

Chapter 15 162

Chapter 16 173

Chapter 17 180

Chapter 18 208

Chapter 19 238

Chapter 20 246

Chapter 21 257

Chapter 22 269

Chapter 23 277

Chapter 24 285

Chapter 25 290

Chapter 26 302

Chapter 27 306

Chapter 28 315

Chapter 29 328

Chapter 30 331

Chapter 31 339

Chapter 32 346

Chapter 33 352

Chapter 34 359

Chapter 35 364

Chapter 36 373

Chapter 37 381

Chapter 38 389

Chapter 39 395

Chapter 40 410

Chapter 41 421

Chapter 42 425

Chapter 43 432

Chapter 44 434

Chapter 45 440

Chapter 46 447

Chapter 47 457

Chapter 48 472

Chapter 49 484

Chapter 50 489

Chapter 51 508

Chapter 52 525

Chapter 53 533

Chapter 54 541

Chapter 55 546

Chapter 56 550

Chapter 57 569

Chapter 58 580

Real World Applications 587

Introduction

This is the description: A Dentist's Journey into Nanomaterial Weaponry and Social Injustice In a world where scientific advancements often collide with ethical considerations, a dentist's unexpected journey reveals a troubling narrative. This tale explores the unsettling intersection of nanomaterials and systemic oppression, particularly affecting marginalized communities. As I delved deeper into my practice, I began to notice a disturbing trend: the disproportionate impact of certain medical technologies on people of color. My initial focus was oral health, but the implications of my findings extended far beyond the dental chair. Through meticulous research and patient interactions, I uncovered evidence suggesting that nanomaterials, initially developed for medical purposes, were being weaponized in ways that perpetuated inequality and harm. This narrative is not merely about scientific discovery; it is about accountability and justice. The silence surrounding these issues is as alarming as the technologies themselves. Cover-ups and systemic neglect have obscured the reality faced by vulnerable populations. My commitment as a healthcare provider now extends beyond treating individuals to advocating for those affected by these hidden dangers. As we navigate the complexities of innovation and ethics, it is crucial to confront uncomfortable truths and ensure that advancements in science serve to uplift all communities rather than oppress them. This journey has transformed my understanding of my role as a dentist, highlighting the urgent need for vigilance, advocacy, and change within the healthcare system.

Chapter 1

The hum of dental equipment mixed with the sterile aroma of the office, a familiar backdrop to Dr. Richard James. He was in his element, focused, methodical. Years of experience made his work efficient, almost mechanical. But today, something was different.

"Open your mouth wide," Dr. James said as he looked into the mouth of his patient, a middle-aged man reclining in the dental chair. The man's calm eyes looked at the ceiling, trusting in the usual routine.

But this was not routine.

Dr. James narrowed his eyes and leaned closer. Something along the patient's gum line glistened under the bright light. He frowned. At first, he thought it was just buildup, perhaps some dental material left over from a previous procedure. He grabbed a small tool hoping to scrape it off. However, when the instrument touched the spot, the material seemed to move, almost... repelling the metal.

Dr. James froze, his instincts alerting him. This was not normal.

"Is everything okay, doctor?" the patient asked, his voice tinged with concern.

Dr. James stepped away, hiding his confusion behind a practiced, reassuring smile.

"Yes, of course," he said, forcing calm into his tone. "Just a little buildup on the gum line. I need to grab a different tool to clean it properly."

He leaned back in his chair, pushing up his magnifying glasses, his mind racing. This was not any kind of buildup I had seen before. In fact, he wasn't sure what he had just found.

****

Dr. James left the exam room, his mind full of questions. Walking down the hallway, he noticed his assistant, Lucy, talking to Dr. Sam Taylor near the break room. Their laughter faded as they saw him approach.

"How did it go with Mrs. Malone?" Lucy asked Sam. "Are you still complaining about his gums?"

Sam chuckled. "Have you complained about that before?"

But Lucy's attention quickly shifted to Dr. James. He noticed the slight tension in his posture, the crease in his forehead.

'Dr. James, is everything okay?

He paused, not knowing how to respond. His thoughts returned to the strange specks on the patient's gums. Maybe it was nothing, but he couldn't shake the feeling that something was wrong.

"Yes, I'm fine," he finally said, although his tone was less convincing than he expected. Just... when was the last time Mrs. Malone was here?

Lucy raised an eyebrow, surprised by the change in conversation. —Uh, about a month ago. He complained that his gums were always itchy.

Dr. James's eyes narrowed. —Who did you see?

"Not me," Sam said quickly.

"Dr. Evans," Lucy said. I was covering for you while you were on vacation.

Dr. James nodded, although his mind was elsewhere. It wasn't just the patient who was in the chair today. Mrs. Malone's complaint suddenly seemed more significant.

"You look like you've seen a ghost," Sam said, half-jokingly. "Are you sure everything is okay?"

Dr. James forced a smile, trying to play it off. "It's probably just a reaction to some dental work," he said, although the explanation didn't sit well with him.

He walked quickly past them, leaving Lucy and Sam exchanging glances. Something about their behavior wasn't right, and they knew it. But they let it go and continued with their jokes.

****

Back in his office, Dr. James was sitting at his desk, staring at his computer screen. His thoughts were stuck on what he had seen. Shiny spots at the gum line? Repelling your tool? It was absurd. He had never encountered anything like it in his career.

He pulled out the patient's file and looked through it for any clues. The man's medical history was unremarkable: he had had no recent surgery, no new medication, nothing that could explain the strange material.

It bothered him. I needed a second opinion, or at least some clarity.

His fingers hovered over his phone. He hesitated for a moment before dialing a familiar number. The call rang several times before a voice on the other end answered.

"Dr. Connors".

"Mike, it's Richard," he said, trying to sound casual, although his mind wasn't at all. "I need your opinion on something."

"Richard, hello! What's going on?"

"I had a patient today... There's something unusual about his gums. I can't explain it. There were some shiny specks... I tried to remove them, but they seemed to repel the instrument."

A long pause followed.

"Repel the instrument?" Dr. Connors repeated, his tone skeptical but intrigued. —That doesn't sound like anything I've heard. Did you get a sample?

'Not yet. I wasn't prepared.

'You should take one. Whatever it is, it's worth investigating.

"I thought the same thing," Dr. James agreed, although something about the idea of taking a sample made him uneasy. Still, he knew he needed answers.

"I'll call you when I have something," Dr. James said before hanging up. He leaned back in his chair, staring at the ceiling. The more I thought about it, the more disturbing it became. What was he dealing with?

****

The next day, Dr. James felt strange

Dr. James had a sense of anticipation as he prepared for the patient's follow-up visit. He had asked the man to come back and take another look, but he honestly wasn't sure what he expected to find.

When the patient arrived, Dr. James led him back to the exam room.

"Thank you for coming again," he said, trying to keep his tone light. "I just want to take another look at your gum line, make sure everything is clear."

The patient nodded and relaxed in the chair while Dr. James adjusted his gloves and glasses.

Bending over, Dr. James gasped. The bright specks had spread. Where there had been only a few specks the day before, there was now a thin, interconnected web of the substance, weaving along the gum line like an intricate pattern.

His stomach turned. How had he grown so fast? What was it?

Doctor James hesitated and then picked up a tool. I needed a sample. Slowly, he scraped along the gum line, but the substance clung stubbornly, resisting as before. He applied more pressure, trying to loosen a chunk. Finally, a small fragment broke off, and he carefully captured it in a small jar.

The patient winced in pain, but said nothing, trusting in the doctor's experience.

"There," Dr. James said, trying to sound casual, even though his mind was racing. "I'm going to send this in for analysis, just to be sure."

The patient nodded, unaware of the growing concern in Dr. James' mind.

****

After the patient left, Dr. James quickly prepared the sample for analysis. His fingers moved deftly, but his thoughts were elsewhere. Something wasn't right. The speed at which the material had spread, the way it resisted his tools, all pointed to something unnatural.

While he was saving the sample, his phone vibrated. It was a message from Dr. Connors.

"Let me know when you have the sample. I'll run some tests on it. It might be nothing, but it's better to be sure."

Dr. James quickly wrote: "I will send it today."

He leaned back in his chair, looking at the jar on his desk. The small fragment inside seemed harmless enough, but he couldn't shake the feeling that it was far from benign.

What had started as a routine date was turning into something much more disturbing.

****

As the day progressed, Dr. James couldn't concentrate. His mind kept going to the patient's gums, to the way the material had spread so quickly. He found himself staring at the clock, waiting for the moment when he could send the sample to Dr. Connors.

But even as he tried to calm himself, a nagging feeling of dread settled in his chest.

Dr. Richard James left his office feeling more uneasy than usual. Although he tried to convince himself that everything had a logical explanation, something in his gut kept screaming at him that what he had seen was not normal. He had overlooked many details in his career, but this would not be one of them.

Arriving home, fatigue hit him all at once. He slumped into his favorite chair and closed his eyes, hoping the tiredness would bring him some peace. He couldn't stop thinking about what he had seen during the day: that strange glow on his patient's gums, the feeling that something was moving, alive, beneath the surface. Although he had spoken to Dr. Connors, the answers he sought still seemed far away.

Finally, after a light dinner and a shower, he lay down in his bed. Sleep came slowly, but with it, the restlessness of his day seeped into his subconscious.

The nightmare began with a feeling of confinement. Dr. James was in his office, but everything felt different. The walls were oppressive, and the usual hum of dental equipment sounded more like a roar. He looked around, feeling a growing sense of unease. He knew something was wrong.

Suddenly, the doors swung open, and in walked several men dressed in hazmat suits. Their faces were hidden behind dark visors, but their movements were steady and controlled, as if they knew exactly what they were looking for. Each wore a symbol on their suits, a strange insignia that Dr. James didn't recognize, but that made him feel even more scared.

One of the men approached him with a cold seriousness, and before Dr. James could react, he was handcuffed.

"What are you doing?" he shouted, his voice echoing in the small room. "I haven't done anything!"

The men didn't respond. They lifted him from his chair and dragged him out of the office. Outside, the light was blinding, and when his eyes adjusted, he saw something even more disconcerting: his office building was surrounded by government vehicles, with more agents around, all wearing those suits. It looked like a massive containment operation.

He tried to resist, but his movements felt heavy, as if he were trapped in an invisible sludge. His body was unresponsive. He tried to scream again, but the words stuck in his throat. He didn't understand why he was being arrested. What had he done wrong?

As he was led to one of the vehicles, he noticed something even more terrifying: the agents' suits were covered in a material that was painfully familiar to him. It was the same strange sheen he had seen on his patient's gums. Only now, that sheen seemed to move like some kind of liquid that covered every surface of the suits, as if it were part of them, living and breathing.

"No!" he screamed desperately, struggling to free himself from the handcuffs. "This isn't real!"

One of the agents looked at him through the visor, but didn't say anything. Instead, he pressed something on his suit, and suddenly, everything around him began to melt. Buildings, people, even vehicles, crumbled as if they were made of wax melting under intense heat.

Panic gripped him. He was trapped in a world that was crumbling around him, unable to do anything to stop it. He felt the suffocating heat of something approaching, but just when everything seemed lost, something changed inside him. As if a spark of lucidity passed through him, he realized he was dreaming.

"This is a dream," he told himself forcefully, trying to take control.

The world around him continued to distort, but now, instead of being carried away by fear, he tried to focus. He knew that if he could control his mind, he could control the dream.

With a titanic effort, he imagined himself free, uncuffed. He imagined the agents retreating, and slowly, the scenery began to change. The agents faded away one by one, and the strange material covering their suits began to dissipate into the air like smoke.

Finally, he found himself alone in a vast, empty space. There were no buildings, no agents, just him standing in the middle of nowhere. He took a deep breath, trying to calm his racing heart. He knew the dream had been a manifestation of his fear, but that didn't make it any less terrifying.

Suddenly, a voice echoed in the void.

"Dr. James..."

He spun on his heels, searching for the source of the sound, but there was no one in sight.

"Dr. James..." the voice repeated itself, louder and louder.

The dream was beginning to crumble again, but this time not from fear, but from the growing awareness that something was waking him up.

James' eyes snapped open, his breathing ragged and his heart hammering in his chest. It took him several seconds to realize that he was in his bed, safe. But the feeling of The nightmare still hung over him like a shadow he couldn't shake.

He sat up in bed, rubbing his face with his hands. He glanced at the clock beside his bed. It was three in the morning. The silence of the night surrounded him, but his mind was still filled with noise. He couldn't stop thinking about what he had dreamed, how those agents seemed so real, how the foreign material seemed to be alive.

He knew he wasn't going to get back to sleep that night.

He got out of bed, put on a robe, and walked to the kitchen. He needed to clear his mind, but what he really needed were answers. The dream had been a warning, or at least, that's how it felt.

As he poured himself a cup of coffee, he decided that the next day he would take a sample of the material he had seen in his patient's gums. He needed to know what he was dealing with. And if there was more than just dental work at play, he would find out.

Chapter 2

The silence of the night enveloped the house of Dr. Richard James. In his office, barely lit by the screen of his laptop, the doctor flipped through the digital pages of scientific articles, desperately searching for answers to what he had discovered. The blue light from the monitor accentuated the shadows under his eyes, the product of poorly slept nights and accumulated hours of restlessness.

In front of him, on the desk, lay stacks of papers: medical records, medical reports, and a reference book open in the middle. His already cold cup of coffee accompanied him as a silent witness of his exhaustion. The article on the screen captured their full attention: "Nanoparticles in medicine: potential and risk." His fingers moved quickly, searching for more information, but nothing seemed to offer any concrete clue as to what he had found.

Dr. James exhaled slowly, rubbing the bridge of his nose. The word "magnetic particles in human saliva" appeared on the screen after his hasty search, but the results were discouraging: "No known studies found."

This was unprecedented. His gaze then went to the small vial that he had placed on his desk, the same one contained the sample taken from the patient that same afternoon. He knew something strange was happening, something beyond any conventional medical explanation, and every minute that passed only fueled his sense of entering uncharted territory.

He stood up, grabbing the jar carefully. The weight of the small sample seemed almost symbolic to him, as if it contained answers that he was not yet able to understand. He walked to the other corner of his office, where there was a microscope, ready to take a closer look at the mystery he had discovered in his patient's mouth.

****

Leaning over the microscope, Dr. James adjusted the lens and placed the specimen. The silence of the office was interrupted only by the faint hum of the device. He looked down at the particles, and what he saw left him momentarily breathless.

Under the lens, the particles moved. Not like normal cells or debris he had ever observed would. These particles seemed to have a life of their own, grouping and separating in almost...deliberate patterns. They formed into shapes, dispersed, and then reorganized. For a moment, they seemed like traces of something structured, a system or an intelligent form. But then, they grouped together again in apparent chaos.

—What the hell is this? —he murmured, incredulous.

He turned away from the microscope, rubbing his eyes wearily. The implications of what he was seeing were disconcerting. It was as if these particles had a kind of autonomous behavior, something that did not belong to any disease or allergic reaction. It was as if they were active on their own, and that only made the situation more terrifying.

Dr. James stood up suddenly, needing air. He walked to the window of his office and opened it, letting the cool night air wash over him. He looked out into the dark garden, trying to gather his thoughts. Something inside him knew that what he had found was not only strange, but potentially dangerous.

His mind returned to the patient, to the first man who had shown these symptoms. He wondered if he had gotten worse since the last visit, if the particles were expanding in the same way inside his body.

The ringing of his phone brought him out of his trance. He took it from the table and looked at the screen. It was a message from Dr. Connors, his colleague to whom he had sent the sample for independent analysis.

"Richard, I received your sample. I reviewed what you sent. This is very strange. It doesn't appear to be organic, but I can't identify it with the team here either. I need more time, but this could be more serious than we thought. Keep the patient under close observation and tell me if you find anything else."

The message only confirmed his fears. Something out of the ordinary was happening, and the worst part was that, for now, he had no answers.

****

The next morning, Dr. James arrived at the clinic with the same weight on his shoulders that he had carried all night. He knew he had to go about his normal work day, but the particles were the only thing on his mind.

Lucy greeted him when he entered, as usual.

'Good morning, doctor. —His carefree tone contrasted with Richard's mental storm—.' Did something happen to you? Yesterday I noticed you a little... distant?

"Yes, everything is fine, just a little tired," he replied, faking a smile.

She looked at him with a mixture of concern and curiosity, but did not insist. He had learned over the years that when Dr. James was engrossed in something, it was best to let him process in his own way.

Dr. James headed to his first appointment of the day, but his mind was still stuck on the sample, on the particles he had seen moving under the microscope. As soon as he had a free moment, he would have to review them again.

However, his day did not allow him that luxury. Patient after patient, his mind had to return to routine. It was what he knew how to do best: efficient, fast, precise work. But it all felt like a distraction as I waited for answers.

Finally, after lunch, the moment I had been waiting for arrived: the sample patient was returning for his checkup.

****

The man sat back down in the same chair, oblivious to the gravity of what Dr. James had discovered in his mouth. Dr. James tried to maintain his composure as he adjusted his gloves and prepared for another inspection.

"Thank you for coming so soon," the doctor said as he leaned over him with the dental mirror. I just want to see if everything is in order.

But as soon as he looked inside the man's mouth again, he knew that it was not in order at all.

The particles had grown. What were once small specks now formed a kind of network, thin but visible, extending from the gums to the nearby teeth. Richard was overcome by a wave of anguish. It was like these things were expanding, and they were expanding fast.

Everything okay, doc? —the patient asked with a slight grimace, noticing the long pause.

"Just… give me a second," Richard said, staying calm. Quickly, he finished the exam and stepped away, forcing a smile. Everything seems fine. Let's follow up on this, okay?

The patient nodded, confident in the doctor's professionalism. However, Dr. James' mind was racing. I knew this wasn't normal. I knew the clock was ticking.

Chapter 3

Sitting in his office, Dr. James mentally reviewed the images he had seen that day. The particles were clinging to the gums of the elderly woman, a patient who had come for a routine checkup. Her children had accompanied her, joking about the need to take better care of their teeth in old age. But when Dr. James had examined his mouth, he had seen the same metallic sparks, like tiny flashes of some strange material alien to human biology. His heart had raced. It was the second time he had seen something like this in less than a week.

The next patient was a middle-aged man, with a confident smile as he entered the office. He had no apparent symptoms. However, the particles reacted to Dr. James' dental equipment in a way that left him stunned. The vibration of the tool caused the tiny specks to move as if charged with energy, grouping and dispersing with the precision of something beyond the natural.

"Everything okay, Doc?" the man asked, uneasy at the prolonged silence.

"Yes, of course. Just a moment," Dr. James replied as he carefully took a sample.

Each patient who came to his office brought with them new confirmation of what he already feared: what he had found was not an isolated case. Something strange was happening in town, and it didn't seem to have an easy explanation.

****

That afternoon, Lucy walked into the exam room with Dr. James as they attended to a little boy no older than seven. The little boy fidgeted in the dental chair, swinging his feet around as Dr. James adjusted his gloves. The boy's parents waited in the reception area, unaware that anything out of the ordinary was going on.

"It's not going to hurt at all, I promise," Lucy told the boy, with a reassuring smile.

When Dr. James shined the light on the little boy's teeth, there they were again. This time, the particles weren't just shining on the gum line, but were covering part of his teeth. A faint metallic glow seemed to emanate from his mouth. Dr. James exchanged a quick glance with Lucy, who also seemed to have noticed the strange glow.

"It's all right, little one." "I just need you to stay still for one more minute," the doctor said, trying not to alarm the boy.

Lucy frowned at him, clearly confused. Something in Dr. James' expression put her on alert.

"Is this…?" Lucy started to ask, but stopped, unsure of how to phrase what she was seeing.

"We'll see about that later," he replied curtly, as he finished the exam.

After dismissing the boy and his parents, Dr. James leaned over his desk, propping his elbows up and running his hands through his hair, frustrated. Lucy watched him from the doorway.

"Doctor… what's going on?" she finally asked, with an unusual seriousness in her tone.

He didn't answer right away. There were things he couldn't explain yet, not even to himself.

"I don't know, Lucy. Something's not right. Whatever we saw today… it's not normal."

Lucy crossed her arms, worried.

"Do you think it's contagious?" Something in the air?

Dr. James shook his head.

"I don't know. But I've seen it in several patients already. And it seems to be getting worse."

The silence between them was tense. Neither of them knew for sure what to do next. Should they inform the health authorities? Their colleagues?

"Let's keep this between us for now," the doctor finally decided. "I need to do more research before jumping to conclusions."

Lucy nodded, though she was clearly not calm.

****

That night, in the solitude of his home office, Dr. James sat in front of his microscope again. The sample he had taken from the boy revealed the same disturbing behavior: the metallic particles clustered and separated, as if they had some kind of communication with each other. They seemed to respond to external stimuli in a way that defied the laws of biology. What were they doing in the bodies of his patients?

Every time he thought about the implications, he felt a mix of fascination and terror. It wasn't something that could be explained with conventional medicine. Hours passed as he took meticulous notes, recording every behavior, every reaction under the microscope. His mind was
He ran in a thousand directions, searching for possible answers in the medical literature, but every search on his computer resulted in dead ends.

He tried different combinations of search terms: "metal particles in saliva," "gum abnormalities," "metal reactions in the human body." None of the articles that appeared on the screen offered a plausible explanation. It was as if what he was observing had never been recorded before in modern medicine.

A frustrated sigh escaped his lips. "No known studies found," read on his computer screen for the umpteenth time. Dr. James dropped his head into his hands, feeling the weight of uncertainty. He knew that what he had discovered went beyond his specialty as a dentist. This was something new, something that required deeper research and resources that he did not have at his disposal.

His phone vibrated on the table, bringing him out of his reverie. A message from his colleague, Dr. Connors, appeared on the screen:

"Richard, I checked the sample you sent me again. The particles aren't organic, but they don't seem to be entirely inert either. It's like they're... responding to something. We need to talk, this is more serious than I thought."

James' heart raced as he read the message. It wasn't just his intuition that was guiding him into this abyss of uncertainty; his colleague, someone he trusted completely, had also noticed how strange these particles were. Something was going on, and they couldn't ignore it any longer.

****

The next morning, Dr. James called a private meeting with Lucy before her shift started. She walked into his office, still worried about what she'd seen the day before.

"Lucy, I need us to keep watching the patients closely." Every case that presents something unusual, every strange symptom, everything has to be documented," the doctor said as he paced nervously around the office.

"And what are we going to do when we start gathering more evidence?" she asked, aware that the problem seemed to be growing.

"I don't know yet," he admitted. "But for now, we can't alarm anyone. Not the patients, not our colleagues. This has to stay between the two of us until we know more."

Lucy nodded, though the worry didn't leave her face.

"Do you think it could be something contagious?" she asked cautiously, touching on the subject that worried her the most.

Chapter 4

Dr. James' office was unusually quiet that morning. Patients came and went, chatter between the staff flowed as usual, but he felt a weight in the air, an eerie silence that only he seemed to notice. Sitting in his office, his gaze was lost through the window. The cloudy sky seemed to reflect his mood, cloudy, dark, with a storm brewing on the horizon, a storm he didn't know how to stop.

Lucy entered his office, a folder in her hand.

"Dr. James, I have that patient's file for you," she said, interrupting the flow of his thoughts.

He didn't answer immediately. His eyes remained fixed on the gray landscape, lost in the tangle of worries he couldn't verbalize. His mind was trapped in the particles, in the patients, in the mystery that had settled in his office like a shadow.

"Dr. James!" —Lucy insisted, more firmly this time, worried about his distraction.

James suddenly sat up, coming back to reality. His gaze focused on her, but not completely. He nodded slowly, trying to maintain his composure.

'Everything okay? Lucy asked, with a mix of concern and curiosity.

Dr. James forced a smile. One of those that didn't quite light up his eyes, but that served to reassure whoever saw it. He knew Lucy was observant, and that she wouldn't be easily fooled, but he didn't want to alarm her more than necessary either. He was carrying something that he didn't fully understand himself.

'Yes, everything okay he answered in a calm voice, although his mind was still buzzing with unanswered questions.

Lucy left the file on the counter, but before she could leave, something prompted him to stop her.

'Lucy! he called her, his tone more urgent than he intended.

She stopped short and turned slowly to look at him.

"Have you seen anything strange on any of the patients?" he asked, his voice lower this time, but laden with tension. "Anything that looks… metallic."

Lucy frowned, confused.

"Like a filling?" she replied, searching her mind for some reference.

"No, not fillings," he replied quickly. "More like little specks. Particles. Like they were coming out of the person."

The silence between them was heavy. Lucy watched him closely, trying to process what he had just said. Dr. James' tone, the concern in his voice, was not something she was used to seeing from him. She had worked with him for years, and she had never seen him so distraught.

"Maybe... you need a break, Dr. James," she suggested, softening her voice, worried about the growing tension in her boss. "You've been working a lot lately."

James nodded slowly, trying to hide his frustration. He knew she was just trying to help, but he couldn't take a break. Not now. Something was up, and he had to find out what it was.

"Yeah... maybe you're right," he said, but his words rang hollow. He knew he wasn't going to rest. Not while those particles kept showing up in his patients' mouths.

****

Later, James was looking over the patient file Lucy had left him. It was a routine case, nothing out of the ordinary in history. However, when he got to the exam notes, he saw something that made him uneasy: "Tender gums. Possible inflammation, recommends follow-up."

He stared at those words, wondering if the patient was also infected with those foreign particles. Without further testing, he could only speculate, but every patient who showed any sign of tender gums now made him suspicious.

The phone on his desk rang, startling him. He looked at the caller ID: it was Dr. Connors. He took a deep breath before answering.

"Richard, do you have a moment?" "Yeah, sure. Have you found anything?" James asked, more hopeful than he expected to sound.

"I've looked over the samples you sent me. And honestly, I don't know what the hell those particles are," Connors said, his voice gravelly. "They're nothing I've ever seen before. They don't appear to be organic, but they're not completely inert either. There's something about them… like they're responding to some kind of stimulus."

James' heart raced. He wasn't alone in his concern. What he'd been seeing wasn't just his imagination.

"Do you think they might be interacting with the human body in some way?" James asked, sensing that this conversation might be the first step toward an answer.

"I'm not sure. I need to run more tests, but there's something unsettling about all this. I recommend you keep taking samples and documenting everything. This could be something big... and not in a good way."

James was grateful for the advice, but anxiety continued to build inside him. If Connors, someone with so much experience, was alarmed, then there was more to worry about.

****

That same afternoon, as James prepared for his next patient, he noticed his hands shaking slightly. Every time he approached someone, he felt a twinge of anxiety. He didn't know if he would find those shiny particles or not, but what he did know was that the chances were getting higher and higher.

The patient, a young man in his thirties, sat in the chair, showing no apparent symptoms. As James performed the exam, he held his breath, looking for any sign of those metallic flecks.

Nothing. The gums were clean, with no sign of shine or foreign particles. He took a deep breath of relief, but the calmness was short-lived. The next patient might be different.

When the day was over, James returned to his office. He was exhausted, but he knew his work wasn't done. He sat down at his computer, determined to continue his search for answers. Every time he investigated, he found more questions than answers.

He knew he couldn't keep this up for much longer. The mystery of the particles was beginning to consume him. The nights were getting shorter, and fatigue was building up in his body. Yet he couldn't stop. Every day, more patients were showing signs of those particles, and he couldn't ignore it.

He opened a new file on his computer and began to type up a detailed report of what he had seen so far. He knew he would have to share this with someone, but he wasn't ready to make what he knew public yet. He needed more tests, more data. But most of all, he needed time.

****

The days went by, and Dr. James's behavior was beginning to change. Lucy noticed him growing more distant, more reserved. He no longer shared jokes with the team like he used to, and his absences from staff meetings were becoming more frequent.

One afternoon, Lucy decided to confront him. She knocked on his office door, and when she received no answer, she walked in.

James sat, staring at his computer screen, his eyes bloodshot from exhaustion. He barely noticed she had entered.

"Doctor…" Lucy began, her voice soft. "You need to rest."

James didn't answer right away. He was engrossed in what he was reading on the screen, an article he had found about metals in the human body, but it offered no clear answers. Finally, he looked up.

"I can't, Lucy," he answered honestly, his voice cracking with fatigue. "This is bigger than we imagined."

Lucy looked at him, concerned by the depth of his obsession. She knew something was going on, but she didn't understand the scope of what her boss was facing.

"Then let me help you," she said, firmly. "You don't have to carry this alone."

For the first time in days, James felt like maybe he wasn't completely alone in this. Lucy had proven to be a constant ally, and maybe, just maybe, trusting her could be his salvation.

Chapter 5

Dr. James stood at the front of the American Dental Society boardroom, feeling all eyes in the room on him, assessing every word he was about to say. The large, shiny table in the center of the room was surrounded by several board members, all of them wearing expressions of stiffness and professionalism. Among them were Dr. Paulson, the Society's director, and Dr. Shaw, a renowned dentist whose impeccable reputation preceded him.

He held a stack of notes and slides, but he wasn't sure how to begin. He looked slightly disheveled, as if he hadn't slept in days, with a stubble that he hadn't had time to shave. His mind, however, was sharper than ever. He knew what was happening, but the thought of sharing it filled him with a desperation and urgency he hadn't felt before. He took a deep breath before he began to speak.

"Gentlemen, what I am about to share with you is not just a medical concern, it is something that could change the way we understand dentistry... and science," he began, his voice firm but charged with palpable tension.

The attentive gazes of the board members did not intimidate him, but he felt that every second was a struggle to maintain his composure.

"I have been observing an alarming pattern in some of my patients," he continued, unfolding one of the first slides on the screen. "In their gums, specifically in the gingival tissue, metallic flecks are appearing. Small particles that do not behave naturally."

Dr. Shaw crossed his arms and raised an eyebrow.

"Metallic particles? Are you suggesting that these particles are being ingested somehow?" he asked with a mixture of disbelief and skepticism.

James paused, aware of how unusual all this sounded. He didn't have all the answers, but he knew what he'd seen wasn't normal.

"I don't know how they get there, but these particles aren't something we can ignore. They react strangely to dental instruments, seem to respond to magnetic stimuli, and don't correspond to any material commonly used in dental procedures."

The board members exchanged awkward glances, as if evaluating the credibility of his words.

"Look, Dr. James," Paulson interjected in a condescending tone, "we appreciate you bringing this to our attention, but we need more concrete proof. These patients, is there anything that connects them? Any common factors?"

James nodded quickly, sliding over another slide that showed a series of images of mouths with the particles glistening under the examination light.

"Three of my patients, all of different age groups and health conditions, have shown these particles. I've examined them carefully, and I can't find a clear link between them. They don't share medications, they don't live in the same area... but they all exhibit the same phenomenon. This is not a coincidence."

Dr. Shaw leaned forward, visibly intrigued despite his initial skepticism.

"And what have you done with these particles?" he asked, his eyes narrowing. "Have you analyzed them?"

James nodded again, pulling out a small box with several sample containers he had brought with him. He placed it on the table in front of the board members.

"I've conducted some preliminary analysis," he explained, lifting one of the sample jars. "The particles don't seem to be completely inert. They clump together in unusual ways, and under the microscope they behave as if they have some sort of magnetic charge."

The atmosphere in the boardroom grew more tense. Some of the members leaned forward, interested, while others maintained a stiff posture of disapproval. It was hard for them to believe that something so strange was occurring in something as mundane as a patient's mouth.

Paulson let out a sigh and crossed his arms.

"Dr. James, have you considered the possibility that this is simply a contaminant? Perhaps something in the water or food of these patients...

Before James could respond, the lights in the room flickered briefly, interrupting the flow of conversation. It was a minor detail, but odd enough to make James turn his gaze toward the window. The storm in the distance had already arrived.

"We can't rule out any possibility," James replied finally, "but these particles don't seem to be simply a contaminant. I've investigated and there's nothing in the food or water that would explain this behavior. In fact..."

He paused, knowing that what he was going to say next might sound even more alarming.

"In fact, these particles are similar to those described in some papers on nanotechnology. I think they're not a problem."
Specifically, in research related to Charles Lieber.

Hearing that name, several of the board members looked at each other. Lieber had been a prominent figure in nanotechnology, but his recent arrest for ties to the Chinese government had caused a stir in the scientific community. What James was suggesting sounded impossible… but also dangerously plausible.

"Lieber?" Paulson repeated, his tone incredulous. "Are you suggesting that Lieber's research is related to this?"

"I don't know," James admitted. "But I can't ignore the similarities. Lieber was arrested for developing nanoparticles with both medical and military applications. And what I've seen in my patients… it's not far from what his research describes."

Dr. Shaw, who up until that point had remained silent, spoke in a calmer but firmer voice.

"This is too much to ignore, but it's also something that needs to be handled carefully. We can't go around making claims without conclusive evidence." We need more evidence, more analysis… and maybe someone who can corroborate their findings.

James nodded slowly. He knew he couldn't go forward alone, but every minute that passed without a clear answer filled him with more uncertainty. How much longer could they hide what was happening before it became something no one could ignore?

****

That night, Dr. James was back in his home office, surrounded by papers, samples, and research articles. He had gone over the day over and over in his mind, but he couldn't find peace. The connection to Lieber had left him uneasy. Everything pointed to this being bigger than he had imagined. And if Lieber was involved in something as sinister as the news suggested, then the threat those particles posed was real.

The soft murmur of the television in the background barely caught his attention, until he heard a name that made his body tense: Charles Lieber.

He looked up at the screen. A news anchor was talking about the scientist's recent arrest. The footage showed Lieber being escorted by federal agents, his face expressionless as he was led in handcuffs toward a prison.

"Lieber, a leading nanotechnology researcher, is accused of accepting millions of dollars in secret payments while collaborating with Chinese military officials," the anchor said, his voice cool and businesslike.

Dr. James leaned forward, eyes wide, listening to each word intently. The implications of what he was hearing began to settle in his mind.

"Lieber is believed to have been involved in covert research projects funded by the Chinese military, potentially developing advanced weaponry using nanotechnology. Sources say his work could have significant implications for national security," the anchor continued.

On the screen, a headline ran across the bottom: "Dr. Lieber Reportedly Received $2 Million from China for Research."

James couldn't believe what he was seeing. Not only was Lieber involved in nanotechnology, he had been developing something that could be related to weaponry. Could the particles he had found in his patients be related to this type of research?

Quickly, he turned to his computer. He typed "Charles Lieber Nanotechnology Research" into the search engine, and the answers began to appear in front of him. Several articles detailed Lieber's work on nanoparticles with potential medical and military uses.

He read quickly, his eyes scanning each word. The terms "medical devices" and "weapons" appeared again and again, reinforcing his worst fears. The puzzle pieces were beginning to fit together, but the picture they formed was terrifying.

He picked up one of the sample containers from his desk and held it up to the light. The metallic particles glowed faintly. If what he was thinking was true, then these particles weren't just a medical mystery. They were something far more dangerous.

He had to make them see what he had discovered.

"These nanoparticles," he said, his voice shaking slightly, "are reacting in ways I've never seen before. I've been finding them in several of my patients." None of them were vaccinated, all with the same foreign material sticking out of their mouths.

Dr. Paulson sighed and leaned back in his chair.

"Dr. James, with all due respect, we don't engage in conspiracy theories."

James felt frustration rise in his chest, but he tried to remain calm. He cleared his throat and continued.

"This is not a conspiracy theory, Dr. Paulson. I've run the tests. I've collected the samples. I've done the research. These particles are not a common occurrence. And I think… no, I'm sure that Dr. Charles Lieber's nanotechnology research is involved in all of this."

Lieber's name seemed to cause discomfort in the room, but not in the way James expected. Instead of surprise or concern, he saw skepticism in the eyes of the others. Dr. Shaw was the first to speak.

"You're suggesting that a scientist's research in nanotechnology is related to particles he's found in his patients' teeth," he said incredulously. "Do you hear how that sounds?"

"I hear how it sounds, but I've reviewed the papers on his work, and there are clear similarities in the types of nanoparticles he developed to what I'm finding in my patients," James replied, struggling to maintain control.

Dr. Shaw paused before shaking his head.

"What you're describing sounds like an isolated incident, contamination perhaps. No other dentist in the country has reported anything similar."

"This isn't contamination!" James exclaimed, finally losing his cool. "This is advanced nanotechnology! I'm not imagining it. I've seen how these particles react to magnetic fields, I've seen how they behave under controlled conditions. There's something bigger going on here, something that's happening right under our noses."

Dr. Paulson stood up, making it clear that the meeting was over.

'We appreciate your enthusiasm, Dr. James, but without concrete evidence, we cannot commit to a formal investigation. If you find anything substantial, we will revisit it. Thank you for your time.

The board members began to rise, gathering their notes and politely bidding farewell. James watched them leave, feeling frustration gnawing at him inside. He couldn't believe they were ignoring something so obvious, something that could have global consequences.

As the door closed behind them, he slammed his fist on the table. He was alone, again, with no one else seeing what he saw. But he wasn't going to give up. He couldn't.

****

Days passed, and the atmosphere in the lab grew tense. Dr. James, who had once been the beating heart of the team, was now a shadow of himself. Lucy, who had worked side by side with him for years, noticed the alarming change. The sparkle in his eyes had faded, and his laughter had turned into a distant echo. He no longer told funny anecdotes or shared the joy of small achievements. His absences from meetings became more frequent, and the team murmured in his absence.

One afternoon, Lucy felt she could wait no longer. She decided to confront him. She knocked softly on his office door, and when she received no answer, she cautiously pushed it open.

"Dr. James…" she began, her voice soft, seeing his figure hunched over the computer, his eyes bloodshot from exhaustion. "You need to rest I am saying this again."

James did not respond immediately. He was engrossed in the screen, in an article that seemed to consume him. The search for answers about metals in the human body had led him into a maze of confusing data and disturbing theories. Finally, he looked up, fatigue visible on his face.

"I can't, Lucy," he replied, his voice cracking, as if each word cost him a monumental effort. "This is bigger than we imagined i thought i could do this all by myself."

Lucy's concern grew as she saw the depth of his obsession. Something dark and disturbing lurked in his mind, and she didn't know how to help him.

"Then let me help you," she said firmly, taking a step toward him. "You don't have to carry this alone what are friends for."

For the first time in days, James felt a glimmer of hope. The idea that he wasn't completely alone touched him in an unexpected way. Lucy had proven to be a constant ally, and maybe, just maybe, relying on her could be his salvation.

"I don't know if I can, Lucy." I don't know if what I'm facing can be shared," he said, his voice shaking slightly.

"Whatever you're discovering, I'm here to support you. You don't have to face this alone." Lucy looked at him, and in her eyes he saw a flash of determination.

James felt the pressure in his chest begin to ease. The warmth of her support was comforting, but the shadow of his discoveries still kept him wary.

That night, as he prepared to sleep, restlessness haunted him. As he closed his eyes, thoughts of the investigation and Evelyn's death intertwined in his mind. He fell into a deep sleep, but this time it wasn't a peaceful sleep.

In his vision, the world was falling apart. Images of chaos and despair filled his mind. He walked through the streets of a city he had known, but everything was shrouded in smoke and rubble. The buildings were in ruins, and the air was heavy with the smell of rusty metal and hopelessness.

Suddenly, a group of men appeared before him. They were dressed in hazmat suits, with masks covering their faces. Their movements were agile and precise. They were arresting people emerging from the sea, with a lost look in their eyes. The scene was surreal, as if the end of the world had suddenly arrived.

James felt a chill run down his spine as he watched the men in suits forcefully lead people away. Their bodies were dragged away, and their screams echoed in his mind, distorted by the sound of the raging sea.

"What's going on?" he shouted, but his voice was drowned out by the roar.

The waves crashed against the shore, and the water was dyed a dark red, as if nature itself was crying out for help.

As he watched the chaos, he noticed that there were familiar faces among the crowd. He saw Lucy, his colleagues, Evelyn. They were all trapped, all staring in terror as the men in suits surrounded them.

"No!" he screamed, reaching out for them, but it was as if an invisible wall separated him from reality.

The men came closer, and James felt a wave of helplessness. In that instant, he realized he couldn't save them. The vision went dark, and he fell to the ground, trapped in an endless abyss.

Suddenly, he woke up, sweating and with his heart racing. The darkness of the bedroom enveloped him, and the images of the nightmare still danced in his mind.

"What was that?" he muttered, trembling. Reality and dream merged, and he felt a deep fear that this was not just a dream.

He got out of bed, feeling that the real world was as disturbing as what he had seen in his dream. He knew he had to talk to Lucy, he had to share what he had experienced.

Yet he couldn't shake the feeling that the nightmare was an omen. Something was coming, something that threatened to destroy everything he knew. He quickly dressed and left his room, determined to find answers.

When he arrived at the lab, sunlight was beginning to filter through the windows, but the atmosphere was still gloomy. Lucy was already there, looking over some reports.

"James, I'm glad you're here. I was worried," she said when she saw him.

"Lucy, we need to talk," he said, the urgency in his voice evident.

She looked at him with concern, putting the documents aside.

"What's wrong?"

James inhaled deeply, preparing to tell her about his dream and his concerns.

"I had a dream. It wasn't normal. There were men in suits, arresting people from the sea… and among them were our colleagues, even Evelyn. I felt it was a warning.

Lucy became serious, feeling the gravity of his words.

"It may just be a dream, James. But it may also be a reflection of what we're facing."

"Exactly. I can't ignore it. I feel like the danger is closer than we think." James fidgeted, the anxiety in his chest rising. We need to investigate more about BioCore and what they're really doing.

Okay, but we need to be cautious. If we're in danger, we can't act impulsively Lucy warned, but her gaze showed a hint of acceptance.

James nodded, feeling the urgency inside him being a driving force. He had to find out the truth. Not just for himself, but for Evelyn and everyone he loved.

Then let's get to work. Determination filled his voice as he approached the computer. We need to dig deeper into his research, and this time, we can't hesitate.

They both dove into their work, the sound of keys echoing around the room. Time faded away as they searched for answers, each second more intensified by the pressure of what was at stake.

As they searched through documents and digital files, James felt the nightmare still following him. The threat was real, and the clock was ticking. They had to act before chaos broke out.

****

As the days passed, the research became more intense and the atmosphere in the lab became charged with unspoken tensions. Lucy became the support James needed, and together they began to uncover a disturbing truth about BioCore.

Each new discovery seemed to bring them closer to the darkness lurking in the shadows. As they reviewed confidential files, they realized they were dealing with more than just experiments; there were implications of social control, data manipulation, and a plan that went beyond their understanding.

"James, look at this," Lucy said, pointing to a line in a document. "It talks about a project called "Controlled Immunity."

James read quickly, his heart pounding.

"They are trying to create a way to control people through nanomaterials. This is what Evelyn was researching."

"That means her death wasn't an accident," Lucy concluded, her voice shaking. "They knew what She was doing."

James felt the air drain out of him. The connection between his investigation and Evelyn's death was deeper than he had imagined. Each answer seemed to lead to more questions.

"We have to do something, Lucy. We can't just stand by while BioCore continues this."

"But what can we do?" she asked, fear creeping into her voice. "We don't have enough evidence, and they have unlimited resources."

James paused for a moment, remembering

his dream. The chaos, the men in suits. It was a warning, and he knew they had to act quickly.

"We can do something. We need to gather more evidence and expose them. If we don't, more people will suffer," he said, the determination in his voice firming up.

Lucy looked at him, and for the first time in days, she saw the flash of her former partner. The fight in her eyes was contagious, and the resolve to act seemed to reinvigorate the tense atmosphere of the lab.

"Okay, but we have to be strategic." Lucy nodded, her determination now aligned with James's.

As they both prepared to take on BioCore, they knew they weren't just facing a company; they were fighting a corrupt system that threatened not only their lives, but the lives of many others.

As night approached, the tension in the lab became palpable. Lucy and James prepared for their mission, reviewing every document and every plan. They had to be careful. Danger lurked around every corner, and the threat from BioCore was greater than they had imagined.

"James, there's something I haven't told you," Lucy said, her voice tense. "I've been receiving strange messages. I don't know if they're related, but…"

"Messages? From whom?" James interrupted, feeling uneasiness creeping up on him.

I'm not sure. They're just warnings. They tell me to be careful, that BioCore is watching.

James felt a chill run down his spine.

This was all a dream.

That he had woken up from.

Another dream. He muttered.

Chapter 6

The monotonous hum of dental equipment and the low murmur of conversations mingled in the office. It was a day like any other, but for Dr. James, each step he took towards his office felt heavier than the last. The bright white lights of the place seemed to make him feel even more disoriented. Patients were lined up in the waiting room, flipping through old magazines or looking at their phones, completely oblivious to the storm brewing above him.

Lucy, his assistant, was behind the front desk, organizing files. She looked up when she saw him enter.

"Hello, Dr. James," she said in a tone that tried to be optimistic, but that let her concern show.

He walked past her without stopping, his mind caught in somber thoughts. He hadn't slept well the night before, his mind replaying over and over the images of particles under light, the research on Charles Lieber, the relentless skepticism of the American Dental Society.

"Everything okay?" Lucy asked, her voice soft but filled with trepidation.

"Yes," he replied, dry and distant, not pausing to speak further.

He knew Lucy cared about him, but he couldn't explain to her what was going on. She wouldn't understand. No one did. His discovery had pushed him to the edge of something big, but no one was willing to listen.

As he was about to reach his office, Dr. Taylor appeared in the doorway, grinning cockily. He was the kind of person who radiates confidence with every step, always with a joke or sarcastic comment ready on the tip of his tongue.

"What's this I hear about you chasing government conspiracies?" "He laughed, settling into a nearby chair with his arms crossed, as if enjoying every second of James's discomfort.

Dr. James paused, visibly tensing. He had no patience for teasing today.

"It's not a conspiracy, Sam," he replied, his jaw set. "There's something real going on here, and it's bigger than you think."

But Dr. Taylor simply smiled, that smile that had always irritated James. He stood up slowly, patting James' back condescendingly as he passed.

"Sure, sure. Just make sure you don't start treating aliens afterward."

Taylor's words echoed around the room for a moment before he walked out, leaving him alone with his frustration. Lucy looked up at him from her desk, a mix of sympathy and insecurity reflected in her face. She didn't know how to help her boss, but she knew something in him had changed.

"I'm sure you'll figure it out, Dr. James," she said, trying to cheer him up.

James gave her a slight nod, but his expression remained grim. He knew she meant well, but empty words weren't helping. He slipped into his office, closing the door behind him with a soft click.

****

Hours later, when the office was almost empty, James sat at his desk, staring at the sample jar in front of him. The metallic particles shone faintly under the desk light. He knew what he had found was no fluke. It wasn't a mistake or contamination. There was something else, something that connected his patients, those particles, and Lieber's research. But he was alone in this.

Frustration washed over him as he re-examined the scientific papers he had found on Lieber. The details about magnetic nanoparticles and their potential use in biomedicine and weaponry made him increasingly uneasy. What if these advances were already being applied, covertly, without anyone knowing? What if his patients were just the beginning of something bigger?

His phone vibrated in his pocket, momentarily bringing him out of his thoughts. He pulled it out and saw a message from Rachel, his biotech colleague.

"Let's meet tonight at my lab. I need to see what you've found."

James stood up quickly, feeling a mix of relief and nervousness. Rachel was the only person he trusted at the moment, the only one who could help him figure out what was going on. He grabbed the vial of particles and some of his paperwork before walking out of the office, leaving Lucy to watch as her boss walked away, once again, without saying goodbye.

****

Rachel's private lab was in a quiet part of town, away from the bustle of downtown. The small facility didn't look like much from the outside, but James knew that Rachel had worked on some of the most advanced biotechnology projects in the country before opening her own lab. If anyone could help him understand the implications of what he'd discovered, it was her.

As he arrived, Rachel greeted him at the door, her expression serious.

"Come on in quickly," she said, looking around as if expecting to see someone else.

He followed inside, feeling a growing sense of urgency. Once inside, Rachel led him straight to a small research room where she already had a microscope and several tools set up. James set the sample jar on the table and stood back as she began to set everything up for analysis.

"What do you think you found?" Rachel asked without looking at him, focused on her work.

"They're nanoparticles, I'm sure of that," James replied, his voice tense. "I've seen them react to magnetic fields in a way I've never seen before. And after everything I've read about Lieber's work, I can't ignore the similarities."

Rachel nodded slowly as she picked up a small amount of the particles with a tool and placed them under the microscope. The lab was silent as she watched, her face barely visible in the dim light of the microscope.

"And what do you think about Lieber?" she asked, not taking her eyes off the lens.

James hesitated for a moment.

"If he was arrested for his ties to the Chinese government, and all signs point to him working on secret military projects… Then I think what I'm finding in my patients could be part of something much bigger. Maybe they're not just patients, maybe they're test subjects."

Rachel looked up, her face now filled with concern.

"This is more serious than I thought. These particles… they're not just advanced. They seem to have some kind of built-in programming. It's like they're designed to do something specific inside the body."

James' heart raced.

"What does that mean?" he asked, though he feared the answer.

"It means someone could be using advanced nanotechnology to control or modify bodily functions without anyone knowing. If this is what I think it is…" Rachel paused, clearly disturbed by her own thoughts, "…this could be a large-scale experiment. And the patients you've seen could just be the tip of the iceberg."

The silence in the lab was deafening. James knew he was right, but hearing Rachel confirm his fears made it even scarier.

"What do we do now?" he finally asked, his voice low.

Rachel looked at him gravely.

"We have to be very careful who we share this with. If anyone else knows you have these samples, you could be in danger. But first we need more tests. We're going to need access to more advanced equipment, and that means we need to keep this a secret for now."

James nodded, sensing the situation was becoming more and more dangerous. But he couldn't stop. He'd already come too far to back out.

As they both began to plan their next steps, an uneasy feeling settled in James' stomach. He knew he was about to step into dangerous territory, one he might not be able to emerge from unscathed. But the truth was too important to ignore.

Rachel turned off the microscope and turned to him.

"We're going to run more tests tonight, but after that, we have to be very careful." We don't know who else is behind this, or how far they're willing to go.

James nodded again, aware that they had just crossed an invisible line. The stakes were high, and time was not on their side.

Chapter 7

Dr. James closed the door to his office and leaned against it, feeling the weight of the world on his shoulders. He closed his eyes and took a deep breath, trying to calm the storm in his mind. The nanoparticle samples still sat on his desk, becoming more and more urgent. He knew time was running out, and every second counted.

He walked over to the desk, looking at the samples with a mix of determination and anxiety. Everything he had discovered had led him to this point, and he couldn't let the skepticism of others stop him. With a shaking hand, he put the containers away in a drawer. It was time to act.

He picked up his phone and dialed a number, feeling his heartbeat quicken as he waited for a response. The line connected and a familiar voice answered.

"Hello. It's me. Are you busy tonight?"

He nodded, though the person on the other end couldn't see him. The slight smile that appeared on his face was a small respite amidst the pressure. Tonight he would have the chance to share his discoveries with someone who truly understood him.

****

The lights of the bar flickered, a beacon in the darkness of the night. The place had a welcoming air, but also a sense of secrecy, a refuge for those seeking to escape the outside world. James entered, his gaze searching for Emily.

The murmur of conversation and laughter enveloped him as he approached a table in the back where Emily Carter, a woman in her 40s with an exotic aura, was waiting for him. She was relaxed, enjoying her glass of wine, but her expression turned serious at the sight of him.

"Rich, what's going on?" he asked, observing her tense face.

"Emily, I'm telling you, what I've found in these patients... it's nothing like I've seen before. It's not just one patient, but several." "All of them unvaccinated," he explained, his voice low but firm.

Emily took a sip of her wine, taking in the information. Her gaze never wavered from him.

"Rich, you're a dentist, not a physicist. You're seeing something weird, but maybe you're just looking... wanting to find something."

James shook his head, frustrated.

"It's not that. There's a real connection. Lieber was working in nanotechnology, military-grade stuff. Makes sense, right?"

Emily sighed, clearly concerned.

"Look, you've always been passionate about your work, more so than most in your field. But you're connecting dots that may not even exist. Lieber's case has nothing to do with dentistry. So, before you go chasing this, I want you to be sure that it's worth risking your career."

Emily's words were an echo of the doubt James had been feeling. His resolve didn't waver, though.

"For once, can you trust me? You owe me that," he said, his voice a whisper laden with emotion.

Emily shifted uncomfortably in her seat, the memory of their past together bubbling to the surface, bringing with it a shadow of guilt.

"We're not married anymore, Rich. You can't ask for favors like that. And what would you want me to do?"

The tension between them was palpable, a delicate thread that threatened to snap.

"I'm not asking for that… although I should. You walked away with more than half," he said, the spite barely disguised in his tone.

She shrugged, disinterested, but he continued.

"I'm asking because no one else will listen to you. You know I wouldn't come to you unless it was serious. Please, for old times' sake."

Emily took a deep breath, contemplating his request as she studied his body language. There was something in his voice, a sincerity that she couldn't ignore.

"Okay." But before I get involved in ghost chasing, you should talk to Dr. Reinhardt," he finally said.

"Who?" James asked, intrigued.

"He's a biomolecular scientist. If there's anyone who can make sense of what you've discovered… he's your man."

James felt a spark of hope.

"Thanks," he said, his voice lighter.

"(Chuckling) Don't get too excited. I'm not jumping on the conspiracy bandwagon just yet. But I'll put you in touch with Reinhardt. If nothing else, he'll either validate your theory or debunk it. And we'll go from there."

James smiled, a small relief flooding through him.

"Can I buy you another drink? Maybe celebrate our reunion?"

Emily hesitated for a moment, her gaze wavering.

"No, Rich. I think it's best if we keep things separate."

He nodded, understanding. When he took her hand from the table, she noticed the gesture and quickly pulled it back, drinking the rest of her wine in an attempt to deflect the tension.

The conversation became lighter, but James couldn't shake the feeling that they were at a crossroads. The fate of his career, and even his patients, hung in the balance. As his mind continued to spin, a new fear settled in his chest: if Lieber's research was more than a
A simple scientific curiosity could lead to dangerous waters.

****

With every sip of his drink, James tried to shake off the uncertainty. There was a truth there, hidden in the shadows, and he was determined to expose it. But fear followed him too, ever more present. In his mind, the faces of his patients overlapped, each a potential victim of what was to come.

When he finally said goodbye to Emily, a torrent of thoughts accompanied him as he drove away from the bar. The lights of the city shone in the distance, but he felt trapped in the darkness. He knew he had to act quickly.

He sat in his car, engine running, as he looked around. The night was quiet, but there was a tension in the air, as if the world knew something was about to happen. James pulled out his phone and dialed Dr. Reinhardt's number, wishing he was available.

"Hi, it's me." "I need to talk to you," James said as soon as the scientist answered.

"Is it urgent?" Reinhardt asked, his tone professional.

"Yes. I need you to meet me as soon as possible. I found something I think might be important."

There was a pause on the other end of the line.

"Okay, Rich. Where and when?"

"At the café around the corner from my office. Ten."

"Perfect. I'll be there," Reinhardt replied before hanging up.

James exhaled slowly, feeling momentary relief. Every step he took brought him closer to the truth. But as he drove to the café, he couldn't shake the feeling that with every revelation, he was drawing more shadows to himself.

****

The café had a cozy atmosphere, but James' heart was pounding as he waited for Reinhardt. The soft lights and rustic decor contrasted with the storm raging inside. He sat down at a table in the back, with a clear view of the door, and ordered a black coffee to keep his mind alert.

As the clock ticked towards ten, his uneasiness grew. Finally, he saw Reinhardt enter, a serious-looking man with thin-framed glasses. James stood up to greet him, and Reinhardt nodded in acknowledgement.

"Rich," Reinhardt said as he sat down. "What's so urgent?"

James wasted no time and pulled the sample containers out of his bag. He placed them on the table, making sure Reinhardt could see them.

"I've found these particles in several patients. I think they're related to Dr. Lieber's nanotechnology research," he explained, his voice full of fervor.

Reinhardt frowned, taking one of the containers and examining it closely.

"Are you sure this is what you think it is?"

James nodded, his eyes fixed on the scientist.

"I've seen how they react to magnetic fields. And they're not just ordinary particles. There's something else here, something that could be being used without our knowledge."

Reinhardt fell silent, assessing the information as he fiddled with the vial in his hands.

"If what you say is true, this could be a big problem. But we need more proof before we make accusations."

James felt a flash of hope.

"That's what I want. I need you to help me analyze these samples, to see

if there's something else behind them."

Reinhardt leaned forward, his eyes locked on James's.

"Okay, I can help you. But first, I want you to tell me how you came to this. I need to understand your thought process so I can track down any errors."

James began to explain how he had come to discover nanoparticles, mentioning his patients and the connection he had made to Lieber's research. As he spoke, he realized that each detail felt more real, more urgent.

As they argued, a couple of customers at the next table began to look over, their faces showing interest in the conversation. James felt uncomfortable, but Reinhardt didn't seem distracted.

"We need a plan, Rich. This isn't something we can approach lightly," Reinhardt said, his tone grave.

"I know. But if there's a chance this is related to a military use of nanotechnology, we need to act fast."

"Understood. But first, make sure these samples don't fall into the wrong hands. If there's someone behind this, they won't want it to get out."

Reinhardt's warning hit him. The feeling that he was being watched intensified, but he knew he had to press on. The truth was too important.

"Where can we do more testing?" he asked, determined.

"I have a more equipped lab. We can work there, away from prying eyes. But we need to be careful," Reinhardt replied.

James nodded, feeling the burden of responsibility crush him a little more.

We will. I'm willing to take the risk.

Chapter 8

Dr. James sat across from Dr. John Reinhardt in the lab, surrounded by scientific equipment and flickering screens. The atmosphere was tense, the air thick with the gravity of their discoveries. Reinhardt was engrossed in his work, peering through a microscope, muttering under his breath.

"Lieber's work has been under scrutiny for years. The idea of weaponized nanoparticles is not far-fetched, especially with the level of funding and secrecy involved," Reinhardt said, his gravelly voice echoing through the lab.

James watched anxiously, Reinhardt's every word amplifying his fears.

"What have you found?" he asked, his heart pounding.

Reinhardt adjusted the microscope, his gaze focused on the particles.

"They are definitely magnetic nanomaterials." The way they react, clustering together, suggests they're designed to target specific molecular structures. Maybe even biological cells.

James felt a wave of worry wash over him.

"Could they be weapons?"

Reinhardt straightened, removing his gloves and turning to James.

"Yes. And it could be, from the looks of things, a delivery system. The way they interact with water molecules… This is a stretch, but the particles could be programmed to target living cells or even manipulate chemical processes."

"So this could be intentional?" James asked, fear echoing in his voice.

Reinhardt walked over to a whiteboard, drawing diagrams illustrating the molecular structure of nanomaterials and their potential interactions with the human body. James watched in confusion, trying to grasp the magnitude of what they were dealing with.

"It's possible," Reinhardt said. "But the question is: why?" Why do these particles appear in random patients, and how are they exposed to them?

James slowly shook his head, feeling insecurity rising within him.

"Could it be a government cover-up?" he asked, the terrifying thought taking shape.

Reinhardt stepped closer, lowering his voice, his gaze intense.

"Think about it, Richard. Nanotechnology like this… it's not developed in a public lab. This is military-grade material. If these particles are in the public, it's not by accident. Someone is testing it, or worse, deploying it."

"And if the government is involved, they'll do anything to keep it quiet," James murmured, the gravity of the situation beginning to weigh on his shoulders.

Both men shared a heavy silence, each trapped in their own thoughts. James felt the shadow of impending danger loom over them.

"How do we test this?" he finally asked.

"We need to run more tests, find out exactly what these particles are capable of and how they are getting into people's bodies," Reinhardt replied, his tone determined.

"Will you help me, then?" James asked, his voice full of hope.

"Yes, but we need to be careful. Who else knows about this?" Reinhardt said, his expression serious.

"Apart from you and me, only Emily," James lied, feeling the weight of his answer.

He knew he didn't add Lucy and Sarah.

"Keep it that way," Reinhardt said, nodding gravely.

James took a deep breath, feeling relieved to have an ally in this dangerous quest. Determination flared within him, and he knew he must do everything he could to uncover the truth.

"Thank you, and I will," he replied, his voice firm.

****

James walked out of the lab, his mind boiling. The information he had received from Reinhardt had left him stunned. It wasn't just a medical problem; It was a matter of life and death, a riddle that threatened to spill out of his hands.

As he walked to his car, his mind filled with questions. What were the true intentions behind these nanoparticles? And what role did the government play in all of this? He paused for a moment, feeling the weight of his thoughts.

He had to talk to Emily again. He needed her to understand the seriousness of the situation and her role in it. James headed toward his car, determined to make the call.

****

As he started the engine, he dialed Emily's number. He waited anxiously as the ringtone rang through the receiver. Finally, her familiar voice broke the silence.

"Rich? What's wrong?"

"Emily, I need to talk to you. It's urgent," James said, feeling his heart racing.

"What's this about?"

"I can't explain it over the phone. Can you come to my office?"

"Okay." I'll be there in a few minutes," he replied, his tone changing to a more serious one.

James hung up, feeling a knot in his stomach. He didn't know how Emily was going to react to the gravity of the situation, but he knew he had to try to convince her of what they were facing.

****

When Emily arrived, she was greeted at the entrance to the office. Her face was marked with concern.

"Rich, what's going on?" she asked, her gaze scanning his expression.

"I need you to listen carefully," James said, leading her into his office. "What I've discovered is more serious than I thought."

Emily sat, her eyes fixed on him as James began to explain the situation. He talked about the nanoparticles, Lieber's work, and his conversations with Reinhardt. Each word seemed to increase the weight of the reality they were facing.

"So you're saying these particles could be designed to attack people?" Emily asked, her voice tense.

"Yes. And it could be part of a larger experiment. I don't know if this is accidental or intentional, but we can't ignore it," James replied, his gaze intense.

Emily fell silent, absorbing the information.

"This is serious, Rich." If there is truth to what you say, we could be in danger.

"I know. But we need to act. We need more evidence and help, and you are the only person I trust to stay on top of this," James said, his voice pleading.

"What do you want me to do?" Emily asked, her tone changing from concern to resolve.

"I want you to help me investigate this further. I want you to talk to your contacts at the hospital and see if there are any more cases like the ones I mentioned."

Emily nodded slowly, determination showing on her face.

"Okay. I'll do what I can. But this won't be easy, Rich. If anyone finds out we're investigating, we could be targeted," she warned, her gaze serious.

James felt a surge of gratitude towards her.

"I know, and I appreciate it more than you can imagine. I'm not sure what we'll do next, but we need to be prepared."

The conversation became more strategic, coming up with a plan to investigate further. Emily proposed to speak to some of her colleagues at the hospital to see if there were any other cases of patients who had shown strange symptoms. James felt hopeful to see that Emily was willing to help.

****

Later that night, as the office was quiet, James was left alone with his thoughts. The gravity of the situation overwhelmed him. If there really was a conspiracy afoot, they needed to act quickly.

Suddenly, his phone rang. It was Reinhardt.

"Rich, I have some updates," Reinhardt said, his voice gravelly.

"What have you found?" James asked, feeling the adrenaline starting to rush through again.

"I've been looking more thoroughly at the samples. There's something else here. The particles seem to have a unique chemical signature that doesn't match anything I've seen before. This isn't just nanotechnology; there's a biological component involved."

James felt his heart stop for a moment.

"Biological? What do you mean?"

"Whatever they did, these particles are designed to interact with the human body in a way that appears to be intentional. We're talking about something that goes beyond a simple military experiment."

James felt cold.

"So we're talking about some kind of secret biotechnology?"

"It's possible. And if so, there could be devastating consequences if it's released to the public," Reinhardt said, his tone urgent.

"What do we do now?" James asked, feeling more lost than ever.

"We need a more aggressive approach. I want you to come to the lab tomorrow. We need to run some more tests and see how we can get more information without raising suspicion."

"

Understood. I'll do whatever it takes," James replied, feeling determination ignite within him.

Later that night, when the office was quiet, Dr. James was left alone with his thoughts. The gravity of the situation overwhelmed him. If there really was a conspiracy afoot, they needed to act quickly.

As he tried to focus on his research, his mind traveled back to the moments that led him here. There was something about the way the evidence was presented, something about the data that felt off. The combination of nanomaterials and biology wasn't just a scientific curiosity; it was a weapon in the wrong hands.

Suddenly, his phone rang. It was Reinhardt. His colleague's deep voice echoed through the speaker.

"Rich, I have some news," Reinhardt said, his tone immediately catching James' attention.

"What have you found?" he asked, feeling the adrenaline starting to kick in again.

"I've been looking at the samples more thoroughly. There's something else here." The particles seem to have a unique chemical signature that doesn't match anything he's seen before. It's not just nanotechnology; there's a biological component involved.

James felt his heart stop for a moment.

"Biological? What do you mean?"

"Whatever they've done, these particles are designed to interact with the human body in a way that appears to be intentional. We're talking about something that goes beyond a simple military experiment."

Chill ran down his spine.

"So, are we talking about some kind of secret biotechnology?"

"It's possible. And if so, there could be devastating consequences if it's disclosed to the public," Reinhardt said, his tone urgent.

"What do we do now?" James asked, feeling more lost than ever.

"We need a more aggressive approach. I want you to come to the lab tomorrow. We need to run some more tests and see how we can get more information without raising suspicion."

"Understood." "I'll do whatever it takes," James replied, feeling determination flare within him.

****

That night, James couldn't sleep. He realized that every hour that passed was an hour of closer danger. He imagined those "super soldiers" he'd read about in reports about Russia, developed with the very technology they were researching. Those soldiers were a terrifying reality, a product of an unbridled ambition for military power.

In his mind, the images were vivid: elite soldiers, enhanced with nanomaterials, able to withstand bullets and carry out tasks that a normal human couldn't handle. The story had begun to take shape. Everything he'd learned about biotechnology and nanotechnology was weaving into a narrative of horror and manipulation.

That morning, as he arrived at the lab, the atmosphere was different. There was an air of tension, as if the walls themselves were aware of the uncertainty lurking around every corner. Reinhardt was already there, reviewing the data on a screen that displayed a series of graphs and formulas that James could barely understand.

"What do we have?" James asked as he approached.

"I've found unusual patterns in the DNA sequence we've been analyzing," Reinhardt said, his voice low and strained. "These particles aren't just designed to interact with the body; they're altering the DNA. What we've seen in the initial tests is just the beginning."

James frowned.

"Are you saying they could be creating a new species?"

"Not only that," Reinhardt continued. "It could also be a biological weapon. There are rumors that these experiments are taking place in Russia. Intelligence indicates that they're using nanomaterials to develop super soldiers—people who don't feel pain, who are faster, stronger."

James felt a knot in his stomach.

"That's not possible. Who would be behind something like that?"

"Governments, corporations, anyone who wants power," Reinhardt said, staring at the screen as if the answers were there, hidden among the numbers.

At that moment, the door to the lab swung open with a loud bang. Lucy, a young researcher who had always shown an exceptional interest in Dr. James' work, walked in with a worried expression.

"What's going on here?" she asked, her eyes darting from one to the other.

"We're in the middle of something big, Lucy," James replied. "Something that could change the world as we know it."

"I've heard rumors in the scientific community," Lucy said, coming closer. "Some are talking about clandestine experiments. Is that true?"

James and Reinhardt exchanged glances.

"It's worse than you imagine," Reinhardt said finally. "And we need you to stay alert."

Lucy nodded, understanding the gravity of the situation.

"What can I do?"

"We're about to run some tests that will give us more clarity about the particles and their origin," James said.

We need your help.

As they set up for testing, time seemed to stand still. The tension was palpable. They knew that any misstep could cost them not only their careers, but their lives. As they dove deeper into the investigation, each of them wondered if they were truly prepared to face what they would discover.

The hours passed and the lab became a hive of activity. Lucy, James, and Reinhardt worked tirelessly, absorbing information and performing tests, attempting to unravel the mystery of the particles. As the data piled up, the magnitude of the danger they faced became more apparent.

As night fell, an eerie sound echoed through the lab. Lights flickered and a dull echo spread through the space. James froze, his heart pounding. Reinhardt and Lucy exchanged worried glances.

"What was that?" Lucy asked, her voice barely a whisper.

James walked over to the window, trying to see past the shadows. In the distance, he could see figures dressed in hazmat suits, moving with military precision.

"We need to get out of here. Now," James said, adrenaline pumping through his veins.

As they prepared to escape, they realized that time was running out. The conspiracy they had begun to unravel was bigger than they ever imagined. With every step they took, they were getting closer to the truth—and closer to the danger lurking in the shadows.

Outside, the world continued to spin, oblivious to the storm raging in their lab. But for James and his team, the chaos was just beginning.

Chapter 9

Dr. James stepped out of the modern glass building, his footsteps echoing on the concrete floor. With the sun shining on his face, he felt a mix of relief and anxiety. He knew the conversation with Reinhardt had been crucial, but the implications of his findings kept him on edge. He pulled out his phone and dialed a number as he walked to his car.

Emily was immersed in her work, the sound of keys filling the air as her phone rang. Seeing it was Dr. James, she quickly answered the call.

"Rich? How did it go?" she asked, her voice filled with concern.

Dr. James/Emily Intercut

"I'm in. Reinhardt believes me," Dr. James said, his voice tense but hopeful. And he thinks there might be a government cover-up.

Emily fell silent, shocked by the severity of the revelation.

"A government cover-up? Are you sure about this?" Her tone turned serious.

"He's going to help me run more tests. But look, this is bigger than I thought, Em. Much bigger," James explained, fiddling with his keys as he walked over to his car.

"Can you meet me at my house tonight? I want to go over everything with you."

"Okay. I'll be there after 7. Just be careful, okay?" Emily replied, feeling a surge of anxiety.

"I'll see you tonight," James said before hanging up. He pocketed the phone and got into his car.

****

The engine roared to life, and Dr. James pulled out of the parking lot, his mind still swirling around Reinhardt's words. As he turned the corner, he didn't notice that a dark sedan with tinted windows had silently pulled out of its spot and was following at a distance.

****

Later that night, Dr. James was at home, staring out the window, taking in the darkness outside. His mind was busy, reliving every conversation, every piece of data he had collected. He felt anxious, and the silence in the house seemed heavier than usual.

The sound of the doorbell brought him out of his thoughts. He turned and opened the door to find Emily standing there, a worried expression on her face.

"Hey, Rich. Are you okay?" she asked, noticing his anxiety.

"Yeah, just... it's been a long day," she replied, trying to smile.

They entered the house, and James led Emily into his office, where he had gathered notes and samples of what he had found. The atmosphere was tense.

"Look at this," James said, pointing to a chart on the wall. "Reinhardt thinks the nanoparticles are designed to target specific cells. This is no accident."

Emily walked over to the chart, studying it closely.

"That's disturbing. But how do we know it's not just a coincidence?"

James sighed, feeling the weight of doubt weigh on his chest.

"We don't know. But there's more. This could be a government cover-up. Reinhardt thinks if there's something, they're probably testing it on the population without them realizing it."

Emily looked at James, her eyes reflecting fear and worry.

"And what are we going to do about it?"

"We need to get more evidence. Talk to more people, collect data. And we also need to be cautious. If there's any truth to this, we could be targeted."

Emily nodded, her face turning serious.

"Do you have any idea who else might be involved?"

"No. Not yet. But we need to be smart about it. We need to act discreetly," James said, sensing the situation was becoming more complex.

****

Meanwhile, in the dark sedan that had followed James, a hooded figure was watching the house intently. The lights were on, and he could see the shadows of the two inside.

The driver, a man with a cold gaze, was speaking on the phone.

"Yes, they're in the house. They don't seem to notice that we're watching them."

The voice on the other end of the line was serious.

"Make sure they don't get away. We need them to keep their mouths shut."

Inside, James and Emily continued their argument, the atmosphere fraught with tension. James felt like every moment they spent together increased the risk, but the urgency of the situation kept them together.

"I'll talk to Reinhardt again tomorrow," James said, his gaze fixed on the computer screen. "We need more information, and perhaps he can provide us with some backup."

"Yes, and I'll try to talk to some of my colleagues at the hospital. If there are other patients affected, we need to find out," Emily replied, feeling
His heart was beating faster.

James felt a pang of worry as he thought about the implications of what they were finding out. It wasn't just his career at stake, but the lives of many people.

****

"What if there's someone else involved?" Emily asked, her voice shaking slightly.

"That's what worries me the most. We can't trust anyone but ourselves right now," James said, his look of determination.

"But how can we make sure no one hears us?" Emily asked, feeling paranoia starting to take its toll on her.

James looked out the window, taking in the darkness surrounding them.

"I don't know. But we need to be sneaky. We need a plan that will allow us to act without alerting anyone.

The man in the sedan continued to watch, his mind working on a plan. He knew they couldn't let James and Emily dig into the matter any further. The stakes were too high, and it was time to act.

****

As the hours passed, James and Emily discussed strategies and plans, each fueling the fire of their determination. They felt closer than ever, facing an invisible enemy that threatened to destroy everything they had built.

"Rich, I promise I won't let this end badly," Emily said, her voice full of fervor.

"I know, Em. And I'll do everything I can to protect you," James replied, feeling a surge of gratitude towards her.

Meanwhile, the man in the dark sedan made a final call.

"We need to act now. We can't let them dig any further. It's best to end this once and for all."

'Wait up, don't yet another voice called.

Chapter 10

Dr. James stood by the window, looking out onto the dark street. The dim light from the lamps illuminated the modestly furnished space, creating an almost cozy atmosphere, but his mind was far from calm.

In the living room, memories of his conversation with Emily and Reinhardt plagued him. There were too many unanswered questions, and the shadow of an impending threat weighed on him. He poured himself a glass of whiskey, feeling the warmth of the liquor as he brought it to his lips.

Outside, darkness enveloped the house. The only light came from the street lamps, casting shadows that danced on the sidewalk. The bark of a dog echoed in the distance, breaking the eerie silence of the night.

James squinted as he noticed something odd on the street. His dentist instincts had trained him to notice subtle details, and now, that attention to his surroundings seemed to come to life.

A car, barely visible, was parked at the end of the street. At first, it seemed like just another part of the night, but then he noticed a second car that stopped silently further down the street.

Shadowy figures moved near the second car, just out of reach of the light. Their silhouettes were blurry, but their postures were tense, as if they were in the middle of a furtive conversation, or perhaps watching the house.

Tension rose in Dr. James' chest. He moved closer to the window, leaning against the frame, his heart pounding.

"Who are they?" he muttered to himself, sensing something wasn't right.

The whiskey in his hand felt heavier and heavier. Still watching, he tried to remember if he had noticed those cars before. Was there someone following his steps? He couldn't risk Emily being in danger.

The figures continued talking, their gestures becoming more agitated. One of them, taller than the others, approached the car and leaned in to look inside. James felt like a spectator in a thriller, his mind racing.

Determined not to sit idly by, he set his glass down on the coffee table and headed into the kitchen. He needed a way to protect himself and Emily.

"I must have something at home," he muttered, searching through the drawers. His heart was pounding as he searched for a knife or something he could use as a weapon.

Meanwhile, the conversation outside had become more intense. Figures began to move, and James felt time stop.

One of the figures looked towards the house, and James felt the air escape him. It was a brief moment, but enough for him to feel like he had been detected. Without thinking, he hid behind the wall that separated the living room from the kitchen.

With the knife in his hand, James took a deep breath, trying to calm himself down. Adrenaline was coursing through his body as he heard footsteps approaching. He had to act fast.

The sound of a knock echoed at the front door. James felt his heart stop.

"Rich!" Emily's voice, though tense, sounded familiar and comforting.

James rushed to the door, feeling a mix of relief and dread. What was Emily doing here at this hour?

He opened the door quickly.

"Um? What are you doing here?" he asked, unable to hide his concern.

Emily was breathing heavily, her pale face illuminated by the light inside.

"Rich, there's something strange. I felt watched on my way here," she said, her eyes nervously glancing back. "I saw a car following me."

James tensed. It couldn't be a coincidence.

"Did you see it?" he asked, leading her inside and carefully closing the door.

"No, but I'm sure I wasn't alone. I feel like we're being watched," Emily replied, her voice shaky.

James looked out the window again, but the figures were gone. Yet the feeling that something was wrong persisted.

"We can't stay here," James said, his voice firm. "We need to get out of here."

Emily nodded, feeling the weight of the situation.

"Where are we going?" she asked.

"To Reinhardt's. It's the only place we'll be safe," she replied, feeling it was the only viable option.

James grabbed his phone and checked it. No signal. Anguish washed over him.

"Shit!" he exclaimed, slamming his fist on the table.

"Calm down, Rich," Emily said. "We need to think clearly. What do we do?"

James knew they couldn't stay in his house.

"I'm going."

"I'm going to get the car keys. You stay here and make sure there's no one outside," he said, feeling time running out.

As James moved quickly towards the kitchen, he thought about what they might have found. Reinhardt had mentioned the importance of acting stealthily, and now it seemed like everything was falling apart.

He took the keys from the hook on the wall and turned to Emily, who was looking at him with concern.

"Ready?" she asked nervously.

"Yes, but we have to be quick," he replied, sensing the urgency of their situation.

James opened the front door, and a chill ran down his spine. The air was cold and silent.

"Come on," he said, moving towards the car.

Emily followed him, looking around, feeling invisible eyes watching them.

Once inside, James started the engine and pulled out of the driveway. As he drove, his mind was focused on Reinhardt's words. He knew they needed to act quickly.

"Are you okay?" Emily asked, seeing the tension on his face.

"No, but I will be when we get to Reinhardt's house," she replied, feeling like every second counted.

As they drove towards Reinhardt's lab, James couldn't shake the feeling that they were being followed. Paranoia enveloped him, every car that passed seemed like a potential danger

Driving through the darkness, the road was deserted. The moonlight illuminated the road, but its clarity did nothing to ease the anxiety they both felt.

"Rich, I think we should call the police," Emily suggested, her voice shaking.

"No. If there's a cover-up, we can't risk them getting involved. We need to keep this a secret," James said, gripping the steering wheel tightly.

Emily felt uncomfortable with the idea, but she trusted him. However, the thought of facing a possible government cover-up filled her with terror.

"What if we show up and Reinhardt doesn't believe us?" she asked.

"I don't know. But we need answers, Em. And if he won't help us, we'll find someone who will," James replied, feeling the pressure mounting.

Arriving at Reinhardt's house, James quickly parked, looking around cautiously. Everything seemed calm, but the feeling that something was wrong remained.

"Come on," he said, getting out of the car with Emily at his side. They approached the door and James knocked, his heart pounding in his chest.

Time seemed to stretch out as they waited.

Finally, the door opened and Dr. Reinhardt appeared, a look of surprise on his face.

"Rich? What are you doing here at this hour?" he asked, his voice filled with concern.

"We need to talk. It's urgent," James said, sensing that danger was closer than he thought.

Reinhardt ushered them in quickly, closing the door behind them.

"What's going on?" he asked, looking at both of them with a mix of curiosity and fear.

"We think we're being watched. And something bigger is at play," James replied, feeling the pieces of the puzzle starting to fit together.

Outside, The same dark Sedan pulled up at a safe distance, its lights off. The hooded figure inside watched, a glint of interest in his eyes.

****

James, Emily, and Reinhardt sat at the kitchen table, the atmosphere tense and filled with uncertainty. Each knew they were about to unravel a mystery that could change their lives forever. The night was just beginning, and dangers lurked in the shadows.

The conversation turned to James' discoveries and the implications of nanoparticles. As they talked, the sense of urgency grew, knowing that time was running out.

"We must act quickly," Reinhardt said, his voice firm. "If there is a cover-up, we need proof."

"Yes, but we must be careful," James said, feeling the pressure of the situation. We can't let them find out about our movements.

Chapter 11

Dr. James walked out of the patient's room, the conversation with Dr. Taylor still echoing in his head. Even though he had tried to act normal, the weight of the patients' complaints and his colleague's concerns were crushing him. He knew something wasn't right, but he didn't want to discuss it. He didn't want anyone to know that he felt out of control.

He made his way to his office, each step echoing in the silence of the office. The usual decor—the diplomas on the wall, the photos of his family—felt foreign to him now. When was the last time I felt good here?

As he entered, he paused, looking at the pile of undone work on his desk. In that instant, his mind wandered, remembering Emily, her voice full of concern, the way her gaze darkened when he told her of his concerns. I can't go on like this. I need answers.

With a sigh, he sat down and began to go through his notes. He had been researching the strange behavior of some of his patients, but there was nothing conclusive. He wondered if, in his eagerness to find answers, he was losing his mind. But that couldn't be true. There had to be something else.

His phone vibrated, bringing him out of his reverie. It was a text from Emily: Still at work? I need to talk to you.

Dr. James frowned. The urgency in her message made him shiver. What has she found this time?

When he met Emily, the atmosphere of the cafe was warm, but he only felt cold. She was sitting at a table in the corner, her laptop open, the screen illuminating her worried face.

"Richard," she began, "I don't know how to tell you, but I found something disturbing."

He sat down, leaning towards her. "What is it?"

"It's about the project I talked about earlier. There's more information than I imagined. This is much bigger than we thought." Her voice shook as she spoke. "Dr. Reinhardt is involved. Not only is he experimenting with the nanoparticles, but there are also reports of patients who have had extreme reactions after the treatments."

Dr. James felt his heart race. "Extreme reactions? What kind?"

Emily slid her laptop towards him, displaying a series of documents. "These are patient reports. Some people have had hallucinations, erratic behavior. And some have even disappeared."

"Missing?" Dr. James repeated, feeling the air escape from her. "How many people?"

"At least five in the last few weeks," Emily said, her eyes filled with concern. "They'd all been under treatment at the same place. They're linked to Reinhardt's lab."

Dr. James ran her hand over her face, trying to take in the information. "This is… this is serious. We need to do something."

"But what?" Emily asked, almost pleading. "We can't go to the police. Not without proof."

"No, we can't," he conceded, his mind racing. "But maybe we can talk to Reinhardt. He has to know something. It could be our only chance to understand what's going on."

They both walked out of the café, the cold air whipping at their faces. Dr. James looked around, sensing someone watching them. "We need to be discreet. I don't want anyone to know what we're doing," he said.

Emily nodded, but couldn't hide the worry in her eyes. "And if Reinhardt is involved, we could be in danger."

"If that's the case, we need to act fast," he replied, quickening his pace.

Upon arriving at Reinhardt's office, the atmosphere was thick and tense. Dr. James knocked on the door, feeling a mix of anticipation and fear. When Reinhardt opened it, his face showed surprise.

"James, what brings you here?" he asked, his casual tone contrasting with the seriousness of the moment.

"We need to talk," Dr. James said, entering without waiting for a response. Emily followed, closing the door behind them.

Reinhardt frowned, looking at them closely. "This doesn't seem like a regular appointment. What's going on?"

Dr. James stood in front of him, his nervousness barely contained. "I've been researching nanoparticles and their effects on some patients. There are reports of very serious reactions. What's going on, Reinhardt?"

The doctor hesitated, his expression changing subtly. "I don't know what you're talking about. Trials are ongoing, and the results have been positive."

"Positive?" Emily exclaimed, her voice raised. "Do you think it's a good thing that people are disappearing? That's not normal!"

Reinhardt tensed, but managed to remain calm. "The tests are delicate. We have to make sure everything works. Sometimes there are side effects."

"Side effects that are causing people to lose their sanity," Dr. James interrupted, sensing the urgency to "This isn't just a matter of lab results. We're talking about human lives."

"I understand, but I can't provide information about the trials right now," Reinhardt said, trying to steer the conversation away.

"You can't or won't," Dr. James challenged, taking a step closer. "We need you. We need to do something before this gets out of hand."

Reinhardt fell silent, contemplating the situation. Finally, he relented. "Okay. There's something else you should know."

The three of them headed to the lab, where Reinhardt opened the door with a shaking hand. Inside, there were sample vials, humming machines, and a tense atmosphere.

"What is this?" Emily asked, her eyes scanning the room.

"This is the place where we're conducting the trials. But the results have been... unexpected," Reinhardt admitted, his voice now gravelly.

"Unexpected how?" Dr. James probed, feeling the pressure mounting.

"Some patients have shown abilities we never imagined. Abilities that shouldn't exist," Reinhardt said, looking down at the floor. "But they've also had bouts of madness. I'm not sure what we've unleashed here."

"This is much bigger than we thought," Emily murmured, stunned. "We must stop this before it becomes irreversible."

Dr. James felt at a crossroads. He had to act. "Reinhardt, we need to stop the trials. We need to thoroughly investigate what's going on."

"If we do that, it will be the end of my career," Reinhardt said, his voice filled with desperation. "And not only that. There will be repercussions far greater than you can imagine."

"We can't let that stop you. "The lives of those patients are at stake," Dr. James insisted, his resolve reborn.

"If you want to stop him, you'll need more than just words. You'll need proof and allies," Reinhardt said, his gaze finally giving in to the gravity of the situation. "But I can help you. I must."

As they left the lab, darkness enveloped the night. Dr. James felt a mix of relief and fear. They had made a small progress, but they knew the worst was yet to come.

"This is just the beginning," Emily said, her voice serious. "We can't let our guard down. There are too many risks."

"I know," Dr. James replied, looking around. "We must be careful."

Suddenly, a scream cut through the night, coming from the direction of the lab. Their hearts stopped.

"What was that?" Emily asked, her eyes widening in terror.

Dr. James turned back to the lab, her mind racing. "I don't know, but we have to find out."

They ran back to the lab, each step thundering in their chest. What had started as a simple consultation had now turned into a desperate fight for the truth.

When they entered the lab, they were met with chaos. Lights flickered, and one of the machines beeped alarmingly. Reinhardt stood in the center of the room, his face pale.

"Quick! Help me!" he screamed, struggling to maintain control of the situation.

"What's going on?" Dr. James asked, feeling panic set in.

"One of the subjects … can't control it. He's… he's out of it," Reinhardt stammered, his hands shaking.

Dr. James exchanged a glance with Emily, both understanding the gravity of the situation. "Where's the subject?"

"In the containment room. But we can't open the door," Reinhardt said, his voice filled with desperation. "If we do, it could cause a disaster."

"Then we need a plan," Dr. James said, his mind working rapidly. "What do we know about him?"

"His name was Tomas. He was a good boy before… all this. But now… I don't know what's inside him," Reinhardt replied, his voice shaking.

"We must try to calm him down. We can't let this end in tragedy," Emily said, stepping forward.

"How?" Reinhardt asked, his eyes filled with fear.

Dr. James felt the pressure intensify. "We must go. I'll talk to him. Emily, you try to find something we can use to contain him if we need to."

Emily nodded, moving quickly to the work tables, searching for anything that might help.

Dr. James headed toward the containment room, uncertainty crushing her chest. As she opened the door, a shriek echoed through the room. Tomas was there, crouched, his body shaking. His gaze was wild, as if he was fighting something that possessed him.

"Tomas," Dr. James said, trying to sound calm. "I'm Dr. James. I'm here to help you."

Tomas turned his head toward him, his breathing erratic. "I can't... I can't control it!" he cried, his voice filled with anguish. "It's consuming me!"

"Quick! Help me!" he shouted, as he struggled to maintain control of a machine that seemed to have taken on a life of its own.

"What's going on?" James asked, feeling panic beginning to take hold.

"One of the subjects... can't control it. He... he's out of his mind," Reinhardt stammered, his hands shaking.

James looked at Emily, who followed closely behind him. They both understood that they were in the midst of a crisis.

"Where's the subject?" James asked, his voice steady despite the pressure.

"In the containment room." But we can't open the door," Reinhardt replied, desperation in his eyes. "If we do, it could cause a disaster."

"Then we need a plan," James said, trying to calm down. "What do we know about him?"

"His name is Tomas. He was a good boy before... all this. But now... I don't know what's inside him," Reinhardt replied, his voice filled with terror.

"We must try to calm him down. We can't let this end in tragedy," Emily said, taking a step forward.

"How?" Reinhardt asked, his voice shaking.

James' mind was working a mile a minute. The situation was critical, and they couldn't afford to waste any more time.

"We must go. I'll talk to him. Emily, find something we can use to contain him if necessary," he ordered.

Emily nodded and headed toward the work tables, moving jars and equipment in search of a solution. James, for his part, approached the door to the containment room, feeling uncertainty grip his chest.

As he opened the door, a heart-wrenching scream echoed through the room. Tomas stood there, hunched over, his body shaking violently. His gaze was wild, as if he were fighting an invisible force that possessed him.

"Tomas," James said, trying to sound as calm as possible. "I'm Dr. James. I'm here to help you."

Tomas raised his head, his breathing erratic.

"I can't… I can't control it!" he screamed, anguished. "It's consuming me!"

Panic filled the room as James tried to connect with the young man. But before he could say anything else, a deafening scream tore from Tomas' throat.

Suddenly, his body began to twist unnaturally. James felt fear take hold of him, unable to look away from the transformation unfolding before his eyes. Tomas rose, his muscles enlarging and dark, rough skin sprouting from his body. The young man's eyes, once filled with anguish, became inhuman, a mix of madness and rage.

"No! Tomas!" James screamed, taking a step back.

Tomas, now a monstrous mutant, shattered the containment room with a terrifying scream. With one brutal movement, he knocked over the equipment around him, causing the machines to screech and creak. Fury and desperation drove him into a state of uncontrollable frenzy.

"Let's get out of here!" Reinhardt shouted, as Emily backed away, terrified.

Without thinking, Tomas lunged at them, his sharp claws glinting in the flickering light of the lab. James didn't have time to think, he ran for the exit, his survival instincts taking over.

The group escaped the lab just before Tomas could reach them. They ran into the nearby woods, the sound of Tomas' screams echoing behind them like a terrifying echo. James felt his heart pound as they crossed the threshold of the trees.

"What do we do now?" Emily asked, her voice shaking.

"We must find a safe place," Reinhardt replied, breathing heavily. "We can't stay here."

As they made their way deeper into the forest, the sky darkened. The cold evening breeze made James shiver. They paused for a moment to catch their breath, but soon heard a rustling in the underbrush behind them.

"It's close," Emily whispered, looking back with fear in her eyes.

James could barely hold his breath. There was no doubt that Tomas was following them, guided by a dark force that had transformed him into something unrecognizable.

"What's going on?" Reinhardt asked, looking at the scene in shock.

'Lets keep this a secret. Emily advised.

Chapter 12

The next day Dr. James leaves the office the parking lot is nearly empty, lit by a dim yellow light. The moon reflects off the parked cars, creating long shadows that seem to move with him. His mind is a whirlwind of thoughts: patient complaints, his growing paranoia, and the feeling that something dark is looming over him.

As he walks, he carries a box full of personal items in his hands. He pauses for a moment, feeling the weight of his decision. A pen slips out of the box and falls to the ground. He bends down to pick it up, his gaze fixed on the asphalt, trying to avoid thinking about what he's left behind.

Suddenly, the sound of an engine grows louder. He looks up just as a white van pulls into the parking lot. The van comes to an abrupt stop beside him. His heart races.

"What the hell?" he mutters, feeling a chill run down his spine.

Before he can react, the side door of the van swings open and two masked men jump at him.

"Get in the van!" Masked Man 1 shouts, gripping him tightly.

Dr. James staggers back, dropping the box. His personal items scatter across the asphalt: pens, files, photos of his family. Everything that represents his life is falling apart before his eyes.

"Let me go!" he screams, struggling with all his might.

The men grab him tighter, but he resists, kicking and pushing. He manages to trip one of them, who falls against the van, while the other advances, determined to catch him. In a moment of pure adrenaline, Dr. James launches himself towards the main street.

"Get him!" —Masked Man 2 orders, giving chase.

Dr. James runs, his feet pounding the pavement, the cold night air cutting into his skin. The sound of the men's footsteps behind him resonates like a terrifying echo. He doesn't look back; he knows that if he does, he'll lose the advantage. His mind works fast, searching for a way out, a shelter.

The streets are deserted at this hour. There's not a soul in sight, only the shadow of the trees that seem to lengthen, as if trying to trap him. Dr. James feels like his heart is going to burst. Every step feels heavy, every breath a reminder of his mortality.

Suddenly, to his left, he sees a bright light. A gas station. Hope surges in his chest as he heads toward it.

As he enters, the sound of the little bell on the door makes him feel a little safer. He approaches the counter, his face pale and sweaty. The employee behind the counter looks at him, visibly shocked.

"Are you okay?" the employee asks, noticing the distress on Dr. James' face.

"I need help… two men are following me," he says, his voice shaking.

"Men?" the employee asks, but before Dr. James can answer, he sees the masked men peering through the window. Adrenaline is pumping through his veins again.

"Lock the door!" Dr. James shouts, looking at the employee.

The man quickly does as he is asked, but Dr. James knows he won't last long. He looks around, looking for something he can use as a weapon or to block the door. He sees a rack of soda cans and a fire extinguisher.

"Do you have a phone?" he asks urgently.

The employee nods, pointing to an old phone in the corner. Dr. James runs towards him, but not before the masked men start banging on the door.

"Open up!" Masked Man 1 shouts from outside.

Dr. James picks up the phone, shaking.

"Call the police!" he orders the clerk.

The man quickly dials the emergency number as Dr. James rushes to find something to protect himself.

"Quickly…" he whispers, feeling cold sweat trickle down his forehead.

The masked men begin to force open the door. Dr. James can hear the wood creaking under the pressure.

"What are you doing?!" Masked Man 2 shouts, frustrated.

"I can't open the door, it's locked!" the first one replies.

Dr. James spots the fire extinguisher and grabs it with both hands. His mind is in chaos, but he knows he can't let them catch him.

"That's it!" the employee shouts, ending the call. "The police are coming."

"Quick!" Dr. James shouts, as he hears a loud knock on the door.

In an instant, the door begins to slowly open. Dr. James, fire extinguisher at the ready, prepares to attack.

When the door finally opens, the masked men pour in, but Dr. James doesn't wait. With a cry of despair, he hits Masked Man 1 in the head with the fire extinguisher.
tor.

"Take that!" he shouts, feeling a flicker of hope as he watches him fall.

Masked Man 2 lunges at him, but Dr. James isn't about to give up.

Outside, the patrol car's lights approach, illuminating the scene in a blue and red flash. The sound of sirens echoes in the distance. Dr. James feels the air fill with relief, but he knows he can't stop fighting.

As he struggles with the second masked man, he hears the voices of arriving officers.

"Police! Hands up!" the officers shout, as they enter the gas station.

Dr. James, his heart pounding, continues to struggle.

"No! Help!" the clerk shouts, but the chaos of the fight deafens his words.

Finally, one of the officers lunges at Masked Man 2, disarming him.

"Get down!" the officer orders, as Dr. James falls to the ground, exhausted, but relieved.

The masked men are quickly subdued, and the tension in the air begins to dissipate.

"Are you okay?" one of the officers asks Dr. James, who struggles to regain his composure.

"I don't know... I don't know what's going on..." he answers, voice shaking.

The officers surround him, making sure he's safe.

The lights of the patrol car illuminate the place, as other officers arrive to take the masked men away. Dr. James watches, still feeling like he's in a nightmare.

"Are you hurt?" an officer asks, checking on him.

"Just... a little dazed," he replies, trying to calm himself down.

As the chaos calms down, Dr. James realizes that it's been a dangerous step, but it's a step toward the truth. And he's determined to find out what's going on.

Dr. James sits on a bench, watching as the masked men are led into a patrol car. The adrenaline begins to wear off, leaving an emptiness in his stomach.

"Thanks," he says to the officer who helped him.

"He's just doing his job," the officer replies, before turning to speak to another officer.

Dr. James looks out at the outside of the gas station, the night now quiet, but his mind still racing.

****

The atmosphere at the station is chaotic, but Dr. James feels like he's trapped in a bubble of anxiety. All around him, police officers move with purpose, oblivious to his distress. He stands at the reception desk, talking to Officer Bradley, a thirty-something man who seems more interested in his computer than the distraught man in front of him.

"I'm telling you! They tried to grab me right outside my office. Two guys in masks, in a van," Dr. James insists, his voice full of urgency.

Officer Bradley, unimpressed, continues typing, keeping his gaze fixed on the screen.

"Yeah, right. Did you get a badge number?" he asks, as if the matter is trivial.

"No, I didn't get the badge. I was busy trying not to get kidnapped," Dr. James replies, frustrated.

"And you said it was a white van? What kind of van?" Bradley asks, still writing.

Dr. James ducks his head, remembering the terrifying scene.

"I don't know. I just know it was a van with dark windows. That's all I saw," he replies, feeling desperation rising inside him.

"But don't you know anything else?" the Officer asks, his tone seeming mocking.

"No!" Dr. James exclaims, feeling his patience wearing thin.

Officer Bradley sighs and finally looks up. His expression is one of utter indifference.

"Maybe someone you had an argument with at work? An angry patient. It just seems pretty random that they'd try to take a dentist away," he says, shrugging.

"Look, this isn't a coincidence!" Dr. James shouts, leaning forward. "Something's going on... there are people following me." They're trying to keep me quiet.

Whispers of conspiracy echo in his mind, and he feels he has to share their fear.

"There's a conspiracy at play here," he adds, voice shaking.

Bradley raises an eyebrow, still skeptical, but also sensing the doctor's desperation.

"A conspiracy, huh? Tell me more. If that's the case, then we can put you in touch with the government agencies, who-"

"No! That's not necessary," Dr. James interrupts, feeling the situation slipping out of his hands.

The Officer leans back in his chair, clearly underestimating the seriousness of the matter.

"Sir, if you don't have any names, a clear description of the boys, or more information about the van, there's not much we can do," he says.

"I know what I saw. I'm telling you, they're after me for something I've discovered. This is bigger than me... bigger than you." "So please file the report," Dr. James exclaims, his voice raised.

Officer Bradley looks at him, measuring his disbelief with a hint of thoughtfulness.

"Okay, okay. I'll file the report. But without more information, I doubt it will do much good. It could have been anything… a prank, wrong place at the wrong time," he says, trying to dismiss the seriousness of the matter.

Dr. James slams his hands on the desk, his anger and helplessness surging. The other police officers in the room begin to turn their attention to him, interest dawning on their faces.

"This is not a joke. People's lives are in danger. Please take this seriously," he says, taking a deep breath and trying to calm himself.

Officer Bradley nods, a glint of recognition in his gaze.

"Okay, doctor. I'll make sure it's on the record. But just so you know, without more evidence, not much can be done."

"As long as it's on the record," Dr. James replies, feeling a small surge of relief.

He pushes away from the counter, trying to compose himself. His mind is still spinning, trying to make sense of what just happened.

"Something's going on. And everyone will see it soon enough," he mutters to himself, the echo of his words ringing in his mind.

Dr. James walked out of the police station, his heart pounding in his chest. Frustration and fear intertwined in his mind as he paused on the steps, breathing deeply. His eyes scanned the empty street, a palpable paranoia in every fiber of his being. .

Chapter 13

Dr. James returns to his office, the bright light of day hurting his eyes. The place is silent, with the echo of dental tools ringing through the room. He sits at his desk, the box of his belongings still open beside him. Photos of his family stare at him, and he feels a knot in his stomach as he remembers the anguish of the night before.

As he organizes the papers, his mind wanders to the conversation he had at the police station. He can't shake the feeling that someone is watching him. The phone rings, breaking his concentration. He rushes to answer.

"Dr. James?" Dr. Taylor's voice comes on the other end.

"Yes, it's me. What's wrong?" he answers, feeling a mix of anxiety and need for answers.

"I need to see you. It's urgent. Can we meet?" Dr. Taylor says, his tone grave.

"Sure. Where?" Dr. James asks, feeling his heartbeat quicken.
lera.

"At the café on the corner. I need to talk to you about something I found out. It's about the patients who complained," Dr. Taylor replies.

Dr. James nods, though he can't see his colleague.

"Okay, I'll be there in a moment," he says, feeling like this meeting might bring him one step closer to the truth.

****

The café is packed with people, but Dr. James feels isolated in the crowd. He sits at a table in the corner, looking around nervously. The place smells of fresh coffee and pastries, but his stomach is in knots.

Finally, Dr. Taylor arrives, looking serious. He sits across from Dr. James, looking around before speaking.

"Thank you for coming," Dr. Taylor says, lowering his voice. "I've been looking into patient complaints, and there's something I don't like."

Dr. James leans forward, feeling like there is finally some hope.

"What did you find out?" he asks anxiously.

"Some of the patients who complained had something in common. They were related in some way. Beyond that, several of them have been getting strange calls before their appointments. Calls they can't trace," Dr. Taylor says, frowning.

"That can't be a coincidence. Do you think there's something more behind all of this?" Dr. James asks, feeling paranoia beginning to seep into his thoughts.

"Definitely. I've been wondering if there's something someone wants to hide, something to do with the dental practice. And I think we need to be careful," Dr. Taylor replies.

Dr. James feels a chill run down his spine.

"What if someone is trying to keep us quiet?" he asks, worry clouding his judgment.

"I don't know, but I think we need to investigate further." We should talk to some of the patients again and see if we can get more information," Dr. Taylor suggests, his tone serious.

Dr. James nods, sensing the truth coming closer.

"Okay. But we need to be careful. I don't know who these guys are, but they're definitely willing to do whatever it takes to keep us quiet."

Both men look at each other, a silent understanding between them. The reality of the situation hangs over them like a dark cloud.

****

Later, Dr. James returns to his office, mind working at full speed. Who else could his work have hurt? Who were those patients who complained, and what could they know? He feels more and more trapped in a maze of doubts and fears.

As he looks through the patient records, the phone rings again. This time, it's an unknown caller. His heart races, and he hesitates a moment before answering.

"Hello?" he asks, voice shaking.

A deep, ominous laugh answers on the other end.

'Hello, Dr. James. I thought we could talk.
'Who is it? he asks, his voice steady despite the growing anxiety.

'It doesn't matter who I am, what matters is that you need to stop digging into what doesn't concern you. Otherwise, you'll regret it, —the voice says

, and the phone abruptly cuts off.

Dr. James freezes, the phone still in his hand. A cold sweat runs down his back. The threat is clear: he is not safe.

He looks out the window, watching the traffic passing by. Life seems to continue outside his bubble of terror, but he knows he's caught up in something much bigger. The truth is calling to him, and he can't ignore it.

Dr. James dropped the phone on his desk, feeling cold sweat running down his forehead. The words echoed in his mind like a haunting echo: "Stop digging into what doesn't concern you." Who could be watching him so closely? The threat had been clear, but what unsettled him most was the voice. He didn't recognize it, but something about it, that dark, dangerous tone, gave him a sense of familiarity.

He stood up from his chair abruptly, pacing back and forth in his small office. He knew he was delving too deeply into issues others wanted to keep hidden, but he couldn't stop himself. Not now, when the truth was so close. As he looked through his patients' files, each name became heavier on his conscience. Who among them was involved? Who had been manipulated or, worse, used as a tool in this whole power game?

"Emily... Reinhardt..." he muttered to himself, rubbing his temples with both hands. How had he gotten to this point? Those who used to be his allies were now pieces of a much larger, much more dangerous puzzle.

As he continued to fret, the phone rang again. His heart skipped a beat. This time, the screen didn't show an unknown number; it simply said "private." He hesitated, but picked up the phone again. He knew he couldn't ignore it.

"Hello?" he asked with a mix of fear and determination.

On the other end of the line, a laugh echoed. It was the same, deep and sinister, but something had changed. The tone was more mocking, as if the person behind the call enjoyed his bewilderment.

"James, James... you shouldn't have gotten so involved." The voice seemed more familiar this time, but he still couldn't place it. "You were always a smart man. Why put yourself in danger for something you can't change?"

James pressed the phone to his ear, feeling his anger mix with fear.

"Who are you? What do you want?"

A deep sigh preceded the answer.

"That doesn't matter now. What matters is that you understand the rules of the game. And the rules say that if you keep digging, if you keep sticking your nose where it doesn't belong, you will end up dead." The voice paused, as if wanting James to reflect on those words. "This isn't a warning, doctor. It's a promise."

Dr. James took a deep breath, trying not to be intimidated.

"If you think you can scare me, you're wrong," he replied with a firmness he didn't feel inside. "I'm not going to stop. Not until I know the truth."

A laugh echoed on the other end of the line, louder than before.

"Oh, doctor, you have no idea what you're saying," the voice replied, its tone turning somber. "But that's okay." You may not care what happens to you. But what about the people you care about? What if Emily, or Reinhardt, or even your patients… paid the price for your actions?

James's heart skipped a beat. The threat wasn't just against him. He knew what that meant. He stumbled back to his chair and slumped down, feeling the weight of the world crushing him.

"You have no right to involve others in this," he replied, voice shaking a little.

"I don't make the rules," the voice said, with cold indifference. "But I assure you that I know how to follow them. You have been warned, James. There will be no other chance."

The call was abruptly cut off.

James stood still for a moment, the phone still in his hand. A feeling of helplessness washed over him. He knew that, from that moment on, everything he did would be under a microscope. Every move, every decision, could put not only his life at risk, but the lives of everyone around him.

He set the phone down and stared at the papers on his desk. Among them were the patient records, Reinhardt's notes, and the preliminary report on the BioCore project. Something about it all didn't add up, and he needed to figure it out before it was too late.

****

As Dr. James tried to gather his thoughts, across town, in a dark, cluttered apartment, two men stared at a screen. One of them, a stocky man with scars on his face, leaned toward the table, turning off the call.

"Do you think he'll fall for it?" the younger man beside him asked, a thin guy with dark, slicked-back hair.

The stocky man, known as Antonio, chuckled.

"James is smart, but not that smart. We'll have him in our hands before he knows it."

The youngest, JJ, nodded as he lit a cigarette, exhaling the smoke slowly.

"I don't know, Antonio. The guy seems more resilient than we thought."

Antonio looked at him with disdain.

"Don't worry. What matters is that we have Emily and Reinhardt on our radar. James will come to us, because he won't have any other choice. He's trapped."

He shrugged, flicking the ash from his cigarette into an old tin can on the table.

"And what will we do with them when they arrive?"

Antonio stood up from his chair and walked over to a window, looking out at the city lights that stretched out like an ocean of chaos. He smiled with a coldness that would chill anyone's blood.

"What we always do. We'll use them. BioCore isn't going to survive if we rely on empty threats alone. We need results. And if that means forcing their hands, then that's what we'll do."

JJ set the cigarette aside and looked at him curiously.

"And what if Reinhardt doesn't cooperate?"

Antonio turned around, his eyes shining with latent danger.

"Then he'll be more useful as an example than as a scientist."

****

Back in his office, Dr. James sat, looking over and over at the records in front of him. He knew that every minute counted, but the words of that unfamiliar voice echoed in his mind. "This isn't a warning… it's a promise." The implications of that were too great to ignore. But he also knew that he couldn't stop.

He made a decision. If Emily and Reinhardt were in danger, he wasn't going to let them fall into the wrong hands He stood up, grabbing his coat and walking out of the office without a second thought. As he walked to his car, his mind filled with questions. Who were these people? What did they want with BioCore, and more importantly, how far were they willing to go to get it?

As he walked, he couldn't help but feel a sense of urgency growing inside him. He knew that time was running out, and that he had to find Emily and Reinhardt before it was too late.

With renewed determination, Dr. James leaves the office. He walks through the city streets, each step taking him closer to the truth. The menacing voice echoes in his mind, but he is determined not to let fear paralyze him.

"I'm not going to let this end like this," he mutters, clenching his fists.

He forced himself forward into the parking lot, each step heavy with the feeling that someone was watching him. He looked around, head down, as if the earth might open up and swallow him. In his mind, he repeated the mantra: **No one is here. There is no one here**. But the echo of his own voice wasn't enough to calm him.

As he approached his car, he noticed that the silence of the street was eerie. His mind replayed the conversation with Officer Bradley. Even though he had taken his report, James knew that the police would not take his warning seriously without more evidence. Bradley's disbelief had left him feeling helpless.

"Damn!" he muttered, opening the door of his car with a jerk. He sat down, but did not start the engine immediately. Instead, he let his head fall back against the steering wheel, feeling the exhaustion take over.

The sound of a door closing made him look up. He saw a tall man walk out of the police station, dressed in a leather jacket. The man stopped at the curb, staring in the direction where James stood. A wave of unease ran through his body. Who is it? He couldn't help but think that it could be one of them, one of the ones who had tried to capture him.

Stomach churning, he started the engine. The police van was parked off to the side, and the man continued to stare. Without thinking, James turned the wheel and pulled out of the parking lot.

As he drove, he tried to focus on the road, but his mind kept wandering. Why were they chasing him? What had he discovered that was so dangerous? Images of his discoveries flashed before his eyes. Reinhardt's reports on nanomaterials, the possible military application. He felt like he had opened a Pandora's box.

His phone vibrated on the passenger seat. He picked it up and saw that it was a text from Emily. "Are you okay? I've been trying to call you." He felt momentary relief at seeing her name, but he also knew he couldn't share all the details. Right now, he had to protect her.

"I'm handling it. I need to talk to you," he typed quickly, keeping his eyes on the road. As he sent the text, he remembered his conversation with her about what he had discovered. He needed her to be safe, but he also knew that she was committed to the truth as much as he was.

The traffic was light, and soon he found himself on a deserted road that led into the countryside. As he drove on, the feeling of being watched crept up on him again. He decided he needed a safe place. Maybe a cafe where he could reflect and plan his next move.

When he reached a small roadside cafe, he parked and went inside. The smell of fresh coffee and pastries greeted him, but he couldn't enjoy it. He sat in a corner, as far away from the door as possible.

While he waited for his coffee, James observed the few customers there. A couple on the corner seemed very interested in each other, and an older man read the newspaper, but no one seemed to pay attention to him. It felt like the world was going on while he was trapped in his nightmare.

The coffee arrived, and James took a sip. The warm liquid comforted him, but not enough. Just then, his phone vibrated again. It was a text from Emily. "Where are you? I'm worried."

"I'm sorry, I'm fine." I'm in a café. He paused for a moment before typing the next message. Please don't go out. Stay home.

As he sent it, he felt a pang of guilt. He knew he should have included her in this, but in his mind, her protection was the most important thing. At that moment, the outside world was fading away and there was only him and the uncertainty of what was to come.

He finished his coffee and decided he had to act. He couldn't just stand there doing nothing. He pulled out his laptop and began to go through some files, looking for clues that would lead him to the truth. As he read, a name jumped out at him: *Reinhardt.* He had to talk to him again. He needed more information, something that could give his case more weight in front of the police.

He quickly stood up, leaving some bills on the table and leaving the café with determination. The conversation with Reinhardt was vital, but the fear of his enemies following him weighed on his mind.

As he got back into his car, he looked over his shoulder. No one seemed to be following him, but that feeling of being targeted consumed him.
He started the engine and headed in the direction of Reinhardt's house.

****

The road took him through a landscape that was slowly becoming more familiar. He wondered if Reinhardt would help him or if he would also be a risk. When he finally reached his colleague's house, he stopped in front of the entrance, breathing deeply.

The doorbell rang and a noise could be heard inside. Reinhardt opened the door, his surprised expression turning to concern.

"James, what's going on?" Reinhardt asked, looking him up and down.

"I need to talk to you. It's urgent," Dr. James replied, feeling that each word was loaded with meaning.

Reinhardt nodded and let him in. Once inside, Dr. James couldn't help but look out the window, looking for any sign of danger. Reinhardt noticed his uneasiness.

"Are you okay? You look paler than usual," Reinhardt said, closing the door behind him.

"I'm not okay. There's something big at stake, and I think they're trying to shut me up."

Reinhardt frowned, his voice deepening. "What have you discovered?"

James sat down in one of the kitchen chairs, feeling the tension building. "What you told me about nanomaterials, about their use as a weapon... I think they're onto something else. I've been doing some research, and I found connections that suggest there's a conspiracy to use them in a secret military program."

Reinhardt fell silent, processing the information. "Do you have proof?"

"No, not yet. But I know there are people after me. They tried to kidnap me this afternoon." The words flowed like a torrent, letting the gravity of the situation drop.

"Are you sure?" Reinhardt asked, now with a mix of disbelief and concern.

James leaned back in his chair, feeling vulnerable but determined. "I know what I saw. I'm not crazy. I need you to help me out of this."

Reinhardt walked over, sitting down across from him. "Okay, but we have to be cautious. If there really is something you're talking about, we can't leave a trace."

As they argued, James's concern deepened. He knew he wasn't just fighting for his life, but for the truth that could change everything. The pressure was mounting, and with each passing minute he felt like time was slipping through his fingers.

"We have to find a way to gather more information, and do it safely," Reinhardt said, laying out a plan.

James felt adrenaline rush through his veins. The fight had just begun, and he was determined to see it through to the end, no matter the cost.

Chapter 14

Night was falling over Dr. Reinhardt's lab, a haven lit by the dim light of monitors and the constant hum of machines. The atmosphere was tense, almost oppressive. Dr. James fidgeted near a computer screen displaying sample data. He had arrived there with the urgency of a cornered man, and the anxiety of his situation tightened his chest.

"Let's take another look at the molecular structure," Dr. Reinhardt said, not taking his eyes off the microscope, where he was meticulously adjusting the settings.

James moved a little closer, his gaze fixed on the screen. He knew that what they were about to discover could change everything, not just for them, but for the entire world.

"What are you looking at?" he asked, trying to remain calm.

Reinhardt pressed a button, and the microscope image enlarged, revealing nanoparticles that seemed to pulse, coming to life and manipulating hydrogen molecules in complex patterns. James felt a chill run down his spine.

"This is… hydrogen," he said, confused, as he stared at the screen.

"Hydrogen bonds," Reinhardt replied, his voice strained. "And it seems these particles have been designed to manipulate them."

"What would be the point?" James asked, his mind working rapidly.

"Hydrogen is one of the key components of water. If you break hydrogen bonds, you're altering the structure of water itself," Reinhardt explained, staring intently at the microscope.

The puzzle pieces began to fit together in James' mind. He moved closer to the screen, horror spreading across his face.

"If these nanomaterials can manipulate hydrogen bonds, they could affect water molecules by breaking them," he said slowly, the words coming out almost as a whisper.

"And if water molecules start breaking down on a large scale…" Reinhardt continued, his voice also filled with disbelief.

"Mass evaporation, droughts, ecological warfare…" James finished, his mind racing a mile a minute.

A heavy silence fell over the room as James picked up a map of the nearby world and pointed out areas with precarious water levels: deserts, coastlines, and densely populated cities. He studied each region for several seconds, his mind spinning with an idea.

"If someone were to use this as a weapon, they could create specific droughts, right?" he asked, his voice heavy with urgency.

Reinhardt nodded, his attention focused on the map. James began pacing back and forth, his mind racing with intensity.

"They could control water supplies, starving some nations. Water shortages would lead to wars, economic collapse." Stopping, he looked at Reinhardt with a grave expression. "It would be total chaos."

"And we're not just talking about small-scale disasters. This kind of technology, if deployed in the atmosphere, could easily affect millions of people… if not billions," Reinhardt admitted, his voice gravelly.

James felt his stomach drop. His mind drifted back to his last conversation with Lieber.

"This is what Lieber was working on… this is what he was hiding." His voice trailed off as he turned his attention to the computer screen, where nanoparticles continued to clump together, manipulating hydrogen atoms. Horror washed over him.

"This isn't just a few patients. What we have here is technology that can destabilize the global water supply. And if they can control water, they control everything," he said, his voice shaking.

Reinhardt ran a hand through his hair, clearly worried. "If this technology falls into the wrong hands... we have to alert someone."

James' mind filled with fear and determination. He stood up, his mind racing.

"But who do we trust? And is it too late?" he asked, his voice a murmur filled with tension.

"Maybe we should go to the authorities. We need proof," Reinhardt suggested, his eyes staring at the screen.

"The authorities. What if they're involved?" James stopped short, distrust washing over him.

"Not everyone can be involved," Reinhardt said, but his voice wasn't as certain.

James felt more and more cornered. Every decision he made brought him closer to an abyss. "What if we end up like Lieber?" he asked, his eyes wide with fear.

"No, we're not going to let that happen," Reinhardt said firmly, though his voice held a hint of doubt.

"What do we do then?" James asked, panic beginning to bubble up inside him.

"First, we need to gather more data." We need to find a way to test what we've discovered without attracting attention," Reinhardt suggested, beginning to type on his computer.

James walked over and looked over Reinhardt's shoulder. The images on the screen showed increasingly complex patterns of the nanomaterials.
"We need to get access to Lieber's files. There might be more information on these nanomaterials there."

Reinhardt nodded, his gaze fixed on the screen. "That might work, but it will be risky. If someone notices that we are digging, we could be in danger."

"We are already in danger," James replied, his eyes fixed on the data. "If we do nothing, this will get out of hand."

"I understand," Reinhardt said, though his expression showed that the idea made him uneasy. "Okay, let's find out how to access his files."

James felt the adrenaline begin to flow through his system. He had to act, and fast. "There might be a way in."

The night was progressing, and the tension in the lab was palpable. Both scientists were immersed in their work.

Reinhardt was checking the security systems of the building where Lieber's files were stored, while James was going over every detail about the nanomaterials. His mind was clouded with possibilities.

"Here, look at this," Reinhardt said, pointing at the screen. "It looks like Lieber's files are protected by a pretty robust encryption system."

"If we can get access to his network, maybe we can find some weakness," James suggested, trying to remain calm.

"That might take time." Reinhardt frowned as he examined the codes. "I'll need a few minutes."

"Do it. I've got your back," James replied, his mind continuing to jump from one idea to another. Every second that passed felt like another step closer to the edge of the abyss. They couldn't afford to fail.

As Reinhardt worked, James felt increasingly uneasy. The thought of them being watched haunted him, and the echo of the white van seemed to reverberate in his mind.

"Do you think we're being watched?" he asked, trying to put his growing anxiety into words.

Reinhardt glanced at him from the corner of his eye. "It's possible. We need to be careful."

Just then, the sound of the lab door rang out. Both men fell silent, their hearts pounding.

"Did you hear that?" James asked, his voice a whisper.

Reinhardt nodded, his expression grave. "Stay here. I'll investigate."

James nodded, his heart in his throat as Reinhardt moved silently toward the door. Every second felt like an eternity.

Reinhardt slowly opened the door and looked out. The hallway was dark and empty. He stepped back inside, relieved but still tense.

"There's nothing… for now." His voice was a murmur, but the worry on his face couldn't be hidden.

James felt the tension in the air become almost palpable. They had to hurry.

"How close are you to accessing the files?" he asked, trying to change the subject and focus attention.

"Almost. I just need a little more time," Reinhardt said, his gaze fixed on the screen as he typed rapidly.

The minutes passed like hours. James fidgeted, increasingly aware that time was not on his side.

"Reinhardt, please hurry up. I can't shake this feeling that someone is behind us."

Reinhardt paused for a moment, looking up.

"I know. Just a couple more minutes."

Suddenly, the monitor flickered, and the light on the screen changed. James felt a chill run down his spine.

"What was that?" he asked, looking at Reinhardt.

"I'm not sure…" Reinhardt said, concern evident in his voice. "It seems like something is not right with the system."

"Has someone accessed the network?" "James asked, panic beginning to creep into his voice.

Reinhardt went back to typing, his face focused. "I can track the intrusion, but I need a little more time."

James felt the pressure building. Adrenaline was coursing through his veins, and the feeling of being watched came back stronger.

"Speed up. If anyone notices we're here, we won't have time to escape."

"I know. I almost got access!" Reinhardt shouted as his fingers flew over the keyboard.

The seconds dragged on forever, and the silence in the lab turned into a palpable tension. James moved toward the door, unable to stay still. Uncertainty consumed him.

"Come on, come on!" he muttered, staring at the door. Every sound outside seemed to amplify, and anxiety kept him on his toes.

Finally, Reinhardt exclaimed, "Ready!"

James turned back to the screen. The image of Lieber's files appeared in front of them. Reinhardt began browsing through the information, his eyes scanning the documents eagerly.

"Here… look at this!" Reinhardt said, stopping at a file that seemed to contain crucial information.

James walked over, his heart pounding as he read. It was a report on nanomaterials, their applications, and the dangers they posed.

The lab was a whirlwind of activity,. Dr. Reinhardt and Dr. James moved quickly between test tubes and screens, their focus unwavering as they frantically performed more tests. The rhythmic sound of clashing glass mixed with the soft hum of machinery, creating a chaotic symphony of science in action.

Test tubes lined the counter, each filled with water that bubbled ominously as the nanomaterials were introduced. The rapid evaporation sent wisps of vapor into the air, a physical manifestation of the urgency that kept them both on edge.

"Look at this," Dr. James exclaimed, eyes wide as he examined the readings on his monitor. The screen flickered with data, simulations of global water patterns changing drastically in response to their experiments. "This is how they're going to do it."

Dr. Reinhardt, deep in thought, walked behind him, his mind racing to connect the dots. "We're not just talking about water here, Rich. There's also food production, agricultural devastation… Hell, even political warfare."

James stood up, a smile spreading across his face as understanding flooded over him. "Politics? Of course… that's what it's about."

"Explain," Reinhardt urged, sensing the change in James' tone.

"Weapon militarization," James said, his voice dropping to a whisper. "They can control resources on a global scale."

147

"But who?" Reinhardt pressed, skepticism coloring his words.

James hesitated for a moment, weighing the implications. "One has to assume it's China, simply based on the connection to Lieber."

Reinhardt's brow furrowed. "Perhaps."

"You think differently?" James challenged, crossing his arms.

"Never be afraid to look right under your nose, Richard, especially when it comes to government and money."

A weight settled between them as the reality of their situation grew larger. James' resolve hardened. "Then we have to stop him. We have to expose them, get this out into the open before it's too late."

Reinhardt nodded, but the seriousness in his expression maintained the wariness. "Be careful, Richard. Once we make this public, the target will be on both of us."

James fixed his gaze on Reinhardt, a shared understanding passing between them. "I'm afraid it's over."

****

The lab in China was about to make history. A team of scientists, led by Dr. Li Wang, watched the test subjects intently through a thick glass barrier. Monitors around the room displayed the vital signs of the volunteers: five men and women carefully chosen for this experiment. All were young, healthy, and now carriers of nanomaterials inserted into their bodies.

Dr. Li Wang, his brow furrowed, watched the monitors with growing unease. The nanomaterials were not reacting as they should. Instead of a controlled, gradual integration with the subjects' biological systems, something seemed to be out of control.

"What's wrong?" one of the attendants asked, pointing to a graph showing an abnormal increase in cellular activity.

"I don't know," Li Wang admitted, his eyes fixed on the flashing numbers. "The energy levels are too high. This wasn't in the simulations."

A high-pitched beeping sound filled the room. One of the monitors showed that subject number two was beginning to convulse. The pulse skyrocketed.

"Quick! Reduce the dosage of nanomaterials in subject two's body," Li Wang ordered, his voice now tinged with urgency.

But before they could act, subject two's screen went black. Then, another monitor began to beep. Subject four was also experiencing the same symptoms.

"Oh my God!" one of the technicians exclaimed, as the graphs on the screens showed an alarming increase in intracellular pressure. "It's spreading!"

Dr. Li Wang watched, horrified, as convulsions began to affect the other subjects. What should have been a simple test to integrate nanotechnology with the human body was going horribly wrong. The subjects' bodies began to shake uncontrollably, their faces distorted in pain.

"Stop him!" one of the technicians shouted. Shut down the system!

But it was too late. A deafening boom echoed throughout the lab as an explosion of energy ripped through the facility. Window panes shattered and the bodies of the test subjects fell to the floor, limp.

Dr. Li Wang staggered back, his breathing ragged as he tried to process what had just happened. The room was filled with smoke, and the smell of burning permeated the air.

"This… this is a disaster," he muttered, his hands shaking as he tried to assess the damage.

One of the technicians, coughing, approached Dr. Li Wang.

"What do we do now?" he asked, his voice cracking.

Li Wang stared at the limp bodies on the other side of the glass barrier. This wasn't just a scientific failure, it was an ethical and humanitarian disaster. Nanotechnology had spiraled out of control, and now, the effects could be devastating far beyond this lab.

"Destroy all evidence," he finally said, his voice cold. "No one must know that this happened here. The country's safety depends on it."

As Li Wang walked toward the exit, aware of the dire repercussions of his work, a sense of doom washed over him. They had toyed with forces they did not fully understand, and now they would pay the price. But the main question remained: if this had happened in a controlled laboratory, what would happen if these nanomachines were released into the global environment?

Meanwhile in a dark, secret room in Beijing, a man in a dark suit, his hair carefully combed back, looked at the footage of the incident in the laboratory. His expression showed no emotion.

"Has the situation been contained?" he asked calmly.

A subordinate at his side nodded.

"Dr. Li Wang has eliminated all evidence. The bodies have been incinerated and the records erased."

The man in the suit nodded slowly, his gaze fixed on the screen.

"Good." This should never have come to light. Nanotechnology is the key to our country's future, but we're not ready for the next step yet. Make sure there are no more mistakes.

The subordinate bowed his head respectfully and left the room. The man in the suit turned off the screen, standing in the dark, deep in thought. He knew nanotechnology had incredible potential, but also a danger they were only just beginning to understand.

However, they would not stop.

****

The night wore on, and the frantic pace was beginning to slow. Exhaustion hung heavy in the air as Dr. James sat in front of the computer, rubbing his tired eyes. The feeling of impending doom hung over him, thick and suffocating.

"Have you thought about the consequences?" he asked, his voice low. "What if we're wrong?"

Reinhardt stopped pacing, considering the implications. "If we're wrong, we face ridicule. If we're right…we could save lives."

James leaned back in his chair, the weight of his discovery pressing down on him. "What if someone wants to silence us?"

Reinhardt sighed, his expression darkening. "Then we need a plan. We can't let fear dictate our actions."

"Okay," James replied, determination surging in his voice. "We need to gather more evidence, contact journalists who can help us shed light on this."

As they planned, the air would thicken with tension. Time slipped by, and every minute brought them closer to a showdown they couldn't ignore.

The first light of dawn filtered through the windows, casting a pale glow over the lab. Exhausted but determined, the three gathered around the table, reviewing their research.

"Once we collect everything, we need to create a secure way to leak it," James said, the urgency clear in his voice.

Reinhardt nodded. "Encrypted emails. We'll be contacting several journalists in the media."

Lisa leaned forward, her sharp eyes filled with determination. "We have to make this count. If we're going to expose them, we need irrefutable evidence."

Tension crackled in the air as they worked, the clock ticking down to a moment that could change everything. Each piece of data they gathered felt like a tight thread around them, a noose that could lead to liberation or destruction.

The three of them worked in silence, the weight of the world resting on their shoulders.

"Remember," Reinhardt said quietly, "we have to protect ourselves. This is bigger than us."

****

The night wore on and the frantic pace began to slow. Exhaustion hung in the air as Dr. James sat at the computer, rubbing his tired eyes. The feeling of impending doom hung over him, thick and suffocating.

"Have you thought about the consequences?" he asked quietly. "What if we're wrong?"

Reinhardt stopped pacing, considering the implications.

"If we're wrong, we'll face ridicule. If we're right…we could save lives."

James leaned back in his chair, the weight of his discovery pressing down on him.

"What if someone wants to silence us?"

Reinhardt sighed, his expression darkening.

"Then we need a plan. We can't let fear dictate our actions."

"Okay," James replied, determination surging in his voice. "We need to gather more evidence, contact journalists who can help us shed light on this."

As they planned, the air would thicken with tension. Time ticked by, each minute bringing them closer to a showdown they couldn't ignore.

The first light of dawn filtered through the windows, casting a pale glow over the lab. Exhausted but determined, the three gathered around the table, reviewing their research.

"Once we gather everything, we need to create a secure way to leak it," James said, urgency clear in his voice.

Reinhardt nodded.

"Encrypted emails. We'll be contacting several journalists from the media."

Lisa leaned forward, her piercing eyes filled with determination.

"We have to make this count. If we're going to expose them, we need irrefutable proof."

Tension crackled in the air as they worked, the clock ticking toward a moment that could change everything. Each piece of information they gathered felt like a thread tightening around them, a noose that could lead to liberation or destruction.

The three of them worked in silence, the weight of the world resting on their shoulders.

"Remember," Reinhardt said quietly, "we have to protect ourselves. This is bigger than us."

With the first light of day, they decided to dig deeper into the emails they had found. Each one revealed a web of lies, something beyond what they had imagined. The particles they were experimenting with weren't just nanomaterials; they were linked to a secret program to develop super soldiers. The news was so shocking that even the thought of bringing it to light seemed surreal.

"Are you ready for this?" Lisa asked as they sat around the computer.

"I've always been ready," James replied, his voice firm but with a hint of doubt.

The three of them focused on the screen. James began to decipher some of the emails, but the information was so encrypted that it was difficult to follow the thread.

"Look at this," Reinhardt said, pointing to a snippet in one of the emails. "They talk about a project in Russia that uses these nanomaterials to create enhanced soldiers."

"Wait, what?" James exclaimed. "Enhanced soldiers?"

"Yes," Reinhardt said, frowning. "It refers to a military program, something they are developing on a large scale."

"So this isn't just an experiment; it's biotechnology warfare," Lisa added, her voice filled with disbelief.

Suddenly, the computer beeped, and the screen froze.

"No!" Reinhardt shouted, trying to reboot the computer. "It can't be!"

James felt panic set in. He looked out the window, as if searching for answers in the cloudy sky.

"I knew it," he muttered. "They're blocking our attempts to leak the information."

"What do we do now?" Lisa asked, looking between them both, desperate.

"We need to be smarter. If we can't send emails, then we'll do it another way," James said, his mind racing. "Maybe we can use external storage devices and let someone else send the information."

The idea seemed risky, but it was the only option they had. As they planned, uncertainty gathered in the air, like a storm ready to break.

****

As the day progressed, they decided to split up. James and Reinhardt would take charge of preparing the data on a USB drive, while Lisa would do a contact search on the journalist network.

"Be careful, Lisa," James said as he said goodbye. "We don't know how far this will go."

"I know," she replied. "But I can't just sit back."

As they walked away, James felt a pang of worry. The pressure of the truth seemed closer than ever, but there was also a dark shadow lurking.

Later that afternoon, as James and Reinhardt worked in the lab, the tension was palpable. The lights dimmed.

They were writing again, and a chill ran down James' spine.

"This doesn't feel right," Reinhardt said, stopping. "Are you sure we should keep going?"

"We have no choice. If we don't, we'll lose everything," James replied, his voice shaking.

"That's exactly what they want. They want us to stop," Reinhardt said, looking at him with concern.

James nodded, knowing they were at a critical point. They needed to act, and fast.

"We're going to finish this. We need to do this for Lisa and for everyone who might be in danger," he said, his voice echoing in the room.

As they continued, a noise at the door caught their attention. Reinhardt peeked in to look, his face paling.

"James, we've got company."

James turned around just as the door swung open. A group of men in dark suits and dark glasses entered, a determination in their eyes that sent shivers down James' spine.

"What are you doing here?" one of them asked, his voice deep and authoritative.

"This is a private lab. Get out of here!" Reinhardt replied, his voice firm.

James felt his heart pound. He knew this couldn't be good.

"We've come to check on your work," the man said, moving closer. "You better not get in the way."

"We're not going to let you take our research," James shouted, feeling adrenaline coursing through his veins.

The men exchanged glances, and in an instant, all hell broke loose. A few seconds later, the lab was in chaos. James and Reinhardt tried to hold back the intruders, but there were too many of them. In the confusion, one of the men punched Reinhardt, knocking him to the ground.

"No!" "James screamed, as panic set in.

With renewed determination, James grabbed a heavy object from the desk and lunged at the nearest man, hitting him in the head. The intruder fell, but James knew it was only a matter of time before the others noticed.

"We have to get out of here!" James shouted, as he pushed Reinhardt towards the emergency door.

They both rushed out, feeling like every second counted. Just as they were about to leave, a scream echoed behind them.

"Don't let them get away!" the leader of the intruders roared.

As they ran into the woods, James felt the weight of truth chasing them. He knew the revelation was near, but the shadow of the threat was darker than ever.

Chapter 15

The silence of the night enveloped Dr. James' house, like a heavy blanket. From the bathroom, the sound of running water stopped abruptly. All was calm, except for a small disturbance that went unnoticed in the dim light of the bedroom.

The bathroom door remained closed while, from the darkness of the room, soft footsteps crept towards the bed. Black shoes barely brushed the floor, avoiding making noise as gloved hands moved with precision. Shadows embraced the figures in the room, while the light filtered from the bathroom barely illuminated the edge of the bed.

The laptop rested among a pile of messy papers. Gloved fingers gently opened it, revealing the flickering screen filled with scientific data. A USB suddenly appeared in one of those hands, inserting itself into the side port of the computer. The screen displayed a simple message: "Installing malware." Without hesitation, a finger pressed the Enter key.

The progress of the installation was advancing rapidly, reflected in a graph. The room remained silent, only broken by the soft sound of the keyboard. Everything seemed peaceful, until the water in the bathroom suddenly stopped running, cutting through the silence with a subtle echo.

The screen now read "80% complete." The gloved hands remained still, waiting. Just a few seconds later, the process was complete. The USB was removed with the same precision with which it was inserted, and the computer was left in the same position as they found it.

The black shoes were removed, sliding out of the room without a sound. Just then, the bathroom door opened, and Dr. James appeared with a relaxed expression, as if he suspected absolutely nothing. Dressed in his nightclothes, he seemed to be ready for bed.

He walked over to the bed, picked up the computer, and placed it on his lap. As the screen lit up in front of him, his eyes scanned the open document intently, losing themselves in the data he had to review. His fingers began to move quickly over the keyboard, continuing his nightly work.

A loud sound from outside made him pause. A screeching of tires, followed by an engine revving. Dr. James looked up, frowning in concern as his fingers remained motionless over the keyboard.

He got out of bed, walked over to the window, and pulled the curtain back slightly. From there, he could see the taillights of a car driving away quickly, disappearing around the corner of the street.

"Who could it be at this hour?" he muttered to himself, watching the lights of the neighboring houses.

The silence of the neighborhood was eerie. No one seemed to have noticed the car that had passed. Dr. James stood for a moment, thoughtful, before returning to his bed. He sat back up, adjusting himself against the headboard, but the discomfort wouldn't leave his mind.

He closed the file on his computer, his mind too distracted now to continue working. Something wasn't right.

***

Hours later, well into the early morning, Dr. James jolted awake. His computer, still on beside the bed, illuminated the room with a soft glow. He glanced at the clock: 3:12 AM. He rubbed his eyes, his mind still clouded by the interrupted sleep.

Suddenly, the sound of a vibrating phone echoed on the nightstand. Glancing at the screen, he saw it was an unfamiliar number.

"Who the hell is calling at this hour?" he asked, irritated, before answering.

"Dr. James?" A male voice, deep and sharp, rang out in the receiver.

"Who is it?" he replied, confused.

"It doesn't matter who I am. Just listen." You have something on your computer that shouldn't be there.

Dr. James fell silent, his breathing becoming heavier.

"What are you talking about?"

"Look at your system, doctor. It's been compromised."

Dr. James' heart began to beat rapidly. Without another word, he hung up the phone and turned to his computer. The screen was still the same, but his instincts told him something was terribly wrong. Immediately, he began to go through his files, looking for anything out of place.

As he browsed through his documents, his hands shook slightly. Everything seemed to be in order, but there was a growing unease in his chest. He opened several programs, checking each one. Yet everything seemed in place.

But the call... that call hadn't been a coincidence.

****

As he pored through, his fingers paused when he noticed a file he didn't remember seeing before. "System_Update.exe" was flashing in a hidden folder. His stomach sank at the sight of the file name. I had never installed that before.

The file was not there before.

Carefully, he clicked on it. Instantly, a message appeared on the screen: "Error opening
"laughter. Access denied."

Dr. James felt sweat begin to form on his forehead. He didn't know much about technology outside of his research, but this… this was unusual. He tried to delete the file, but the system wouldn't allow it.

It was then that he heard a sound outside, a subtle creaking coming from downstairs. His muscles tensed.

"Is anyone there?" he muttered to himself, slowly rising from the bed.

He crept toward the door, fear mounting. The shadows in the hallway seemed to move with a life of their own as he moved forward, listening intently for any sound.

Each step he took felt heavier than the last, as if something was telling him not to go any further. But he had to know.

Just as he reached the bottom of the stairs, the creaking sound repeated itself. From the darkness, a quick flash briefly illuminated the hallway.

The night wore on and the frantic pace began to slow. Exhaustion hung in the air as Dr. James sat at the computer, rubbing his tired eyes. The feeling of impending doom hung over him, thick and suffocating.

"Have you thought about the consequences?" he asked quietly. "What if we're wrong?"

Reinhardt stopped pacing, considering the implications. "If we're wrong, we'll face ridicule. If we're right...we could save lives."

James leaned back in his chair, the weight of his discovery pressing down on him. "What if someone wants to silence us?"

Reinhardt sighed, his expression darkening. "Then we need a plan. We can't let fear dictate our actions."

"Okay," James replied, determination surging in his voice. "We need to gather more evidence, contact journalists who can help us shed light on this."

As they planned, the air would thicken with tension. Time ticked by, each minute bringing them closer to a showdown they couldn't ignore. The first light of dawn filtered through the windows, casting a pale glow over the lab. Exhausted but determined, the three gathered around the table, reviewing their research.

"Once we gather everything, we need to create a secure way to leak it," James said, urgency clear in his voice.

Reinhardt nodded. "Encrypted emails. We'll be contacting several journalists from the media."

Lisa leaned forward, her piercing eyes filled with determination. "We have to make this count. If we're going to expose them, we need irrefutable proof."

Tension crackled in the air as they worked, the clock ticking toward a moment that could change everything. Each piece of information they gathered felt like a thread tightening around them, a noose that could lead to liberation or destruction.

The three of them worked in silence, the weight of the world resting on their shoulders.

"Remember," Reinhardt said quietly, "we have to protect ourselves. This is bigger than us."

****

Hours later, well into the early morning, Dr. James jolted awake. His computer, still on beside the bed, illuminated the room in a soft glow. He glanced at the clock: 3:12 a.m. He rubbed his eyes, his mind still foggy from the interrupted sleep.

Suddenly, the sound of a vibrating phone echoed on the nightstand. Glancing at the screen, he saw it was an unfamiliar number.

"Who the hell is calling at this hour?" he asked irritably before answering.

"Dr. James?" A male voice, deep and high-pitched, rang out on the receiver.

"Who is it?" he replied, confused.

"It doesn't matter who I am. Just listen. You have something on your computer that shouldn't be there."

Dr. James fell silent, his breathing becoming heavier.

"What are you talking about?"

"Look at your system, doctor. It's been compromised."

Dr. James' heart began to beat rapidly. Without another word, he hung up the phone and turned back to his computer. The screen was still the same, but his instincts told him something was terribly wrong. Immediately, he began to go through his files, looking for anything out of place.

As he looked through his documents, his hands shook slightly. Everything seemed to be in order, but there was a growing unease in his chest. He opened several programs, checking each one. Yet everything seemed to be in place.

But the call… that call hadn't been a coincidence.

The unease in his chest turned to panic as he realized that, in the back of his mind, he knew he had crossed a line. Suddenly, a pop-up notification appeared on the screen. Clicking on it, a video began to play automatically.

The screen lit up with shocking images. It was a raw and terrifying video showing a remote location in Venezuela. Men in protective suits were seen, carrying assault rifles. Shadows moved quickly as the camera captured the brutality of what was happening.

"Look!" James shouted, panic in his voice. He was seeing something he wasn't supposed to see.

The footage showed terrified people, fleeing in fear as the men in suits opened fire. The sound of gunshots echoed through the empty room, an echo of what looked like a mass execution. The scenes were chaotic, with screams of anguish filling the air, but the camera never stopped recording.

James felt his stomach turn. Was this what he had unleashed? Was it the result of his discoveries? He realized he was at the center of a conspiracy far wider and darker than he had imagined.

When the video ended, the screen abruptly blacked out, leaving him in darkness. Silence enveloped him and, suddenly, he realized that time was running out. He had to act, and fast.

Desperate, he searched for Reinhardt and Lisa. He got out of bed, shaking as he ran to the control room, where a flickering glimmer of light still remained. The door creaked open, revealing Reinhardt, who looked up, visibly worried.

"What happened?" Reinhardt asked, noticing the paleness on James' face.

"Venezuelans… are being killed," he said, still out of breath. "There's something bigger here, something terrible."

Lisa quickly approached, her face full of concern. "What are you saying? What did you see?"

James rushed to the computer, his heart pounding. "I saw a video. People… innocent people. Someone is behind this. We need to inform the authorities, and fast."

"But how?" Reinhardt said, frowning. "We're in danger." If we try to expose this, we could be the next target.

"We can't just sit back. If this gets out, it could mean a tragedy on a larger scale," Lisa argued.

The determination in the room intensified, but the sense of terror grew as well. James knew there was no turning back. They couldn't let fear stop them. They had to find irrefutable evidence and make sure someone in the world knew the truth.

"We're going to leak it," James said, his voice firm. "No matter the risk. This has to come out."

The three of them gathered around the computer, each with their eyes fixed on the target. It was time to act. The darkness of the conspiracy loomed over them, but there was also a spark of hope.

James took a deep breath, ready to face what was coming. He knew his life was at stake, but he was also convinced that what they were about to do could change the fate of many people.

"Let's make sure it's not just us who see it." James' voice echoed with determination as they began to write their message, ready to defy the darkness that surrounded them.

Chapter 16

The coffee had a faint bitter aroma in the air, a contrast to the palpable sense of tension at the small table in the corner of the shop. Emily held her cup in both hands, her fingers fidgeting nervously as she looked at Dr. James, who ate in silence. His thoughts were obviously elsewhere, absent yet present in the moment.

Emily watched him with a mix of concern and frustration, waiting for him to speak. Finally, Dr. James wiped his mouth with a napkin and took a sip of his drink. He seemed to gather his strength before throwing out the question that hung in the air.

"So, what do you think?" he asked, his eyes searching for a sign of approval, some indication that there was a way out.

Emily set her cup down on the table and leaned towards him. Their eyes met, and though her tone was soft, the intensity behind her gaze said it all.

"I think going to the government is a terrible idea," he began, his voice barely a whisper. "But you don't have many options left, do you?"

Dr. James exhaled in frustration, leaning back in his chair. He knew Emily was right, but that didn't make his decision any easier. He looked around, the bustle of the café contrasting with the mental chaos he was experiencing.

"But our hands are tied," he said in a defeated tone. "The burden of preventing a total disaster falls on us, right? If we don't, no one will."

Emily shrugged, as if the situation was less complex than he made it out to be.

"Maybe," she replied coldly.

Dr. James frowned, surprised by her indifference. He knew Emily was pragmatic, but this... this was beyond what he expected.

"What do you mean?" he urged.

Emily tilted her head, lowering her voice even further.

"Listen to me, Rich. You're getting yourself into a mess. We both know it, so you can always just let it go and—"

"So what?" he interrupted. "Allow this weapon to be used to wipe out a large portion of the world's water supply? No, thank you."

Emily sighed. She knew he would react like that, but she had to try.

"But if—"

"No!" he shouted, cutting off the conversation with a firm slam on the table that made several in the café turn their heads. "And I can't believe you're suggesting I walk away from this. It's not an option."

She leaned back in her chair, crossing her arms, clearly knowing this discussion wasn't going anywhere.

"You can always let Reinhardt take the lead," Emily said in a softer tone of voice, trying to offer an alternative.

Dr. James didn't respond immediately, just staring out the window, lost in thought. Reinhardt's name echoed in his mind, filling him with doubt. He knew the man had resources, contacts, but he also knew he had his own interests and trusting him would be like handing over the keys to a predator.

Emily watched him silently. She knew her comment had disturbed him, but she also knew she needed to snap him out of his confused state.

"Okay," she finally said, breaking the awkward silence. "I can see I'm getting nowhere with this, so what's next?"

Dr. James shook his head, as if trying to clear it. He looked at Emily, but he had no answers. Everything she had said was true. He didn't know where to go, or who to trust.

Meanwhile, on the street, the black sedan was still parked, its tinted windows hiding whoever was inside. Among several other cars, it looked harmless, but those keeping watch knew it wasn't a coincidence.

****

Minutes later, Emily and Dr. James left the cafe in silence, neither of them saying a word. The cool morning air made them both tense, and though they tried to continue the conversation, they couldn't ignore the feeling of being watched.

Dr. James cast a quick glance around before opening Emily's car door.

"I don't like this," he muttered, glancing sideways at the black sedan that was still there, motionless.

"What thing?" Emily asked as she buckled up.

"That car... it's been there since we got here."

Emily frowned and looked where he was pointing. The black sedan looked like just another car, but in the situation they were in, everything seemed suspicious.

"Do you think it's something?" she asked, starting the engine.

"I don't know... but something doesn't add up."

As Emily turned the wheel and they drove away from the cafe, the black sedan turned on its lights and began following them at a safe distance. Dr. James noticed immediately.

"They're following us," he said quietly, his gaze fixed on the side mirror.

Emily glanced at him sideways, her hands tightening on the wheel.

"Are you sure?" she asked, though she already knew the answer.

Dr. James nodded, his gaze cold and calculating.

"Go faster," he ordered.

Emily accelerated without another word. The car behind them kept its

distance, but he didn't lose sight of them. They both knew something was wrong, but they couldn't stop. Not now.

****

The speed increased. The streets they passed were increasingly deserted as they moved away from the center.

Emily pressed the accelerator harder, her jaw clenched as her eyes constantly checked the mirrors. She knew the black car wasn't going away.

"What do we do if they catch up to us?" she asked, her voice higher than usual.

Dr. James didn't answer right away. His eyes moved between the road and the mirror, calculating every second, every possibility. There was no time for mistakes.

"Keep driving," he finally said. "If they get too close, we turn west. There's a tunnel up ahead."

Emily nodded, her breathing quickened as she tried to stay calm. But the pressure in the air was becoming unbearable. The black sedan accelerated, getting closer.

They turned sharply at an intersection, veering west. The tunnel was only a few feet away, but before they could reach it, another car, also black, appeared out of nowhere, blocking their way.

"Shit!" Emily screamed, slamming on the brakes.

Dr. James looked at the car blocking their way, his eyes cold and calculating.

"They're cornering us," he said quietly, his mind racing, searching for a solution.

The black Sedan lost their car while in the tunnel and abandoned the chase.

Chapter 17

The next day the cool evening air enveloped the outside of the café as Emily and Dr. James briefly embraced. They said nothing, but the weight of tension was palpable in the brief contact they shared. When they parted, Emily walked in the opposite direction as Dr. James headed toward his car, parked right in front of the café.

He paused for a moment before opening the door, looking back to where Emily had disappeared into the crowd. With a sigh, he stepped into his car and started the engine. The roar of the vehicle filled the silence of his thoughts, and without looking back, he pulled into traffic. The dark sedan that had been parked a few feet from the café also sprang into motion, following at a safe distance.

Dr. James tried to keep his focus on the road, but his mind couldn't help but return to Emily's words. The conversation they had had at the café kept echoing in his head. Had he made the right decision? The weight of what was at stake was crushing him, and the looming danger only made his worry worse.

He turned on the radio in a desperate attempt to distract himself. A soft melody began to fill the interior of the car, but it failed to appease the growing feeling of paranoia.

Instinctively, he glanced at the rearview mirror and there it was: the dark sedan, keeping a careful distance away.

"It can't be," he muttered to himself, adjusting his posture in the seat and gripping the steering wheel more tightly.

The music, which moments before seemed to be his refuge, was now an annoying noise. He slammed the radio off and looked back at the mirror. The sedan had changed lanes and was slowly approaching, like a predator stalking its prey.

Dr. James felt his heart racing. He pulled his phone out of his pocket with a shaking hand and began searching for Emily's contact. As the vehicle moved, his hand slipped, and the car swerved slightly, causing the horns of other drivers to alert him. With a quick movement, he righted the car and returned his gaze to the road. His hands were shaking, but his urgency to reach Emily overcome any fear.

Finally, he found her number and dialed it, placing the phone on speakerphone in the passenger seat. The ringing rang in a cadence that seemed to stretch out time, each second more unbearable than the last.

"Come on, please answer," he whispered impatiently.

The phone continued to ring, and when it finally stopped, it wasn't Emily who answered, but her answering machine.

"Hi, you've reached Emily. Leave a message and I'll call you when I have a moment. Thanks."

The beeping sound that indicated he could leave a message echoed through the car, but Dr. James didn't say anything. Instead, he slammed the steering wheel in frustration, glancing in the rearview mirror once more. The dark sedan was now dangerously close, as if to make it clear that it was purposely following him.

"Damn it," he growled, and without a second thought, he slammed on the accelerator, overtaking a car in front of him.

The sedan responded instantly, accelerating as well. Dr. James felt the adrenaline take over his body. He couldn't afford to be caught, not now, not when everything was at stake.

He decided to take a sharp detour, turning off the highway onto a side exit. The car skidded slightly, but he managed to control it. He turned onto a quieter street, away from the heavy traffic. He took a deep breath, believing that he might have managed to lose his pursuer. However, when he looked in the mirror once more, there was the dark sedan, turning the corner just as coldly as before.

"What the hell do they want from me?" he wondered aloud, fear mixed with frustration.

He turned the wheel to the left, turning into an even narrower side street. Buildings loomed tall around him, and the long shadows of the afternoon seemed to narrow over him. He turned again, this time onto a residential street. Houses lined up, children playing in yards, and cars parked on the sides gave him a false sense of normalcy.

He slowed down as he saw a small park with a basketball court. A few people were playing nonchalantly, oblivious to the danger lurking just a few feet away. Dr. James stopped his car in front of the park, engine still running as he looked in his side mirrors, searching for signs that the dark sedan was still following him.

The sedan appeared shortly after, slowly moving down the street. He stopped a few meters behind Dr. James' car, standing still for a few seconds that seemed like an eternity. Dr. James felt his heart racing. Would they attack him here, in broad daylight?

Finally, the sedan started up again, passing by Dr. James with a slight squeal from the tires. It continued on its way, disappearing into the distance.

Dr. James let out the breath he had been holding. He closed his eyes for a moment, leaning his head against the steering wheel. The feeling of relief was instant, but he knew it was temporary. Those following him would not stop until they got what they wanted.

****

The lab was silent, broken only by the hum of the equipment running. Dr. Reinhardt was deep in his work, looking through a microscope. He was concentrating, writing notes on a pad as the scans of the samples were carried out.

The doors to the lab slowly opened, but Reinhardt didn't notice. Two men, Antonio and JJ, entered. They looked dangerous, with looks that said they were there for a dark purpose.

As Reinhardt continued to work, JJ accidentally knocked over a row of test tubes to the floor. The sound of glass breaking made Dr. Reinhardt jump out of his chair, his face pale at the sight of the men.

"Who are you and what do you want?" he asked, trying to stand his ground.

"You've been busy, Doc. Too busy meddling in things that are none of your business," Antonio replied with a cold smile.

"I'm going to call the police," Reinhardt said, backing away to his phone.

But Antonio pulled out a gun, pointing it at Dr. Reinhardt.

"I don't think you're doing it," he said, as he sat down on a stool across from him.

Reinhardt stopped, paralyzed with fear.

"Who do you work for?" Antonio asked, keeping his gaze fixed.

Reinhardt gulped.

"I think that's something you should tell me."

"I'm the one with the gun, which means I'm the one asking the questions. Now, who are you and the other one?" Antonio demanded, not moving.

"No one," Reinhardt replied, feeling helpless.

JJ laughed, watching the chaos unfold.

"Very well," Antonio said, nodding to JJ. JJ grabbed a computer from the desk and threw it to the floor.

"No! Please stop!" Reinhardt screamed, helpless in the face of the destruction.

Antonio stood up.
He leaned on the desk, the gun still pointed at him.

****

After a couple of minutes parked in front of the park, Dr. James decided he couldn't stay there much longer. He was still shaky, but the urgency to act forced him to keep going. He started the car again and resumed his journey, but this time at a slower pace. He had to plan his next move carefully.

He pulled out his phone and tried to call Emily again. He knew he should warn her, but the call didn't go through, and he only got the damn answering machine again. He cursed under his breath and hung up without leaving a message. He didn't want to raise any more suspicion than he already had.

He turned right, heading into a more secluded area, where the houses seemed distant from each other, surrounded by tall trees. He needed to find a place where he could think without the constant feeling of being watched. Emily's words still echoed in his mind: "You can always let Reinhardt take the lead." He knew he couldn't trust this man, but maybe now he had no other choice.

As he drove to a remote location he used to seek out temporary shelter, paranoia continued to eat away at him. He knew this was just the beginning and that the shadows of the dark sedan could reappear at any moment.

After a few minutes, he came to a small cabin that he used as a temporary shelter. It was a remote place, isolated enough to think without distractions, but he still felt the

186

pressure in the air. Paranoia continued to eat away at him, and he wondered if he was really safe. **Was it smart to be there?

As he parked, a glow on his phone screen caught his attention. It was a message from an unknown number. He paused for a moment to read it. "Don't go to the cabin. They're looking for you." His heart stopped. The cabin, where he had made disturbing discoveries about lab experiments, had become a place of danger.

He decided he couldn't ignore the warning. Who had sent the message?** Curiosity drove him to check the contents of his phone, searching for more information, but there were no more clues. Keep it a secret, he thought. He couldn't trust anyone, and keeping his next move in the shadows seemed to be the only option.

Stepping out of the car, his gaze lingered on the forest surrounding the cabin. The shadows seemed to move, and a chill ran down his spine. Darkness enveloped him, and he was right in the center.

He entered the cabin and closed the door behind him. The air was permeated with a woody, damp smell. He walked over to the computer he had left there last time. "I must make sure no one accesses my data," he muttered to himself as he turned on the machine. The light from the screen illuminated his face, reflecting the concern in his eyes.

As he looked through the files, the screen flickered, displaying a message he had never seen before: "HELP ME! THEY'RE SEEING EVERYTHING." The handwriting was confusing, desperate. He wondered if it was one of the subjects he had been investigating. Was someone caught up in this conspiracy bigger than he could imagine?

Dr. James felt trapped in a web of secrets and lies. The call, the message, the warning… it all seemed like a puzzle to which he didn't have all the pieces.

He took a deep breath. "I can't let them catch me," he thought. He knew he needed to act fast. He decided he should return to the city and look for Reinhardt. "Maybe he has answers," he mused, though distrust of his colleague still weighed on him.

As he prepared to leave, a subtle sound stopped him. It was like a rustling outside, and his heart raced. Cautiously, he walked over to the window and looked out. The darkness of the forest seemed to have a life of its own, shadows slipping through the trees.

Without thinking, he turned around and closed the computer. He couldn't stay any longer. He left the cabin, making sure not to make a sound, and headed towards his car, heart pounding. The warning echoed in his mind: they're looking for you.

The car's engine roared to life. With one last glance at the cabin, he sped off, leaving behind the illusory safety he'd found there. He was now in a race against time, and he knew the only way out of this was to face the truth, no matter how terrifying it was.

The road stretched out in front of him, but his mind filled with questions. What was really going on? What was that shadow following him? As he walked deeper into the night, he knew that his life as he knew it would never be the same again.

****

Dr. Reinhardt still couldn't take his eyes off the mess JJ had caused. The debris of his equipment, which hours earlier had represented months of work, now lay scattered across the floor of the lab. His heart was pounding, and his breathing was becoming ragged as sweat ran down his forehead.

Antonio still had the gun pointed at him, his face breaking into a sardonic smile.

"Listen, Reinhardt," Antonio said, leaning even closer to the scientist. "This doesn't have to get any worse, but I need you to be honest with me. What do you know about James' project?"

Reinhardt gulped, not knowing how to react. He knew he couldn't reveal everything, but he didn't have many options either. His mind was racing, searching for a way out.

"I don't know anything about what you're talking about," Reinhardt replied, his voice shaky but firm.

JJ moved closer again, picking up a small vial from the floor and examining it under the fluorescent light.

"I think you're underestimating our patience," JJ said, not taking his eyes off the vial. "If you don't cooperate, we're going to destroy more than just your equipment."

Dr. Reinhardt felt fear creep up on him. He knew these men weren't there for mere intimidation. There was something much bigger at stake. His only hope lay in finding a way to stay calm long enough to come up with a plan. But who had sent them? And what did they know about the project he and Dr. James were developing?

"Okay," Reinhardt finally answered. "I know you're looking for information about a project. But it's not what you think. It's not a weapon."

Antonio frowned, but maintained his aggressive stance.

"Explain yourself," he demanded, without lowering his weapon.

Reinhardt took a deep breath, aware that any mistake could cost him his life.

"What James and I were developing wasn't a weapon to attack. It's a device to protect water sources from dangerous contaminants." It has nothing to do with what you guys think.

Antonio narrowed his eyes, clearly unconvinced.

"I don't believe you, Doc. The people we work for have told us that they are building something that can unleash chaos on the world. And honestly, I don't care if it's true or not. I just know that you can't keep doing this." Antonio paused, his eyes cold and calculating. "And I assure you that James isn't going to be around for long to clear things up."

Reinhardt's heart stopped for a second. James? Had they done something to him?

"What did they do to James?" he asked, his voice heavy with desperation.

Antonio laughed and looked at JJ, as if the situation was an inside joke.

"Don't worry about him, he already has enough problems. You should be more focused on what comes next for you."

Reinhardt knew he couldn't lose his mind now. He needed to keep these men talking, looking for any opportunity to escape or at least delay the inevitable. He knew James had mentioned something about a contact within the government, someone who could help them. But that information had to be kept secret, for now.

"Look," he said, his voice firmer, "I can't stop this. I don't even have all the information. James has it all in his head, and if you think eliminating me will solve it, you're wrong."

JJ dropped the vial he was holding and turned to Antonio.

"It seems Doc is giving us the runaround," JJ muttered, looking at Antonio with a sinister smile. "Maybe we should speed things up a bit."

Antonio tilted his head to the side, as if considering the suggestion. Reinhardt felt a wave of panic rise through his body. He had to act fast.

"Wait!" he shouted. "There's something else! But I need access to the files. They're in a different location, and without them, you won't know what's really going on."

Antonio stared at him, assessing his words. The tension in the room was palpable, like a taut rope about to snap.

"What location?" Antonio finally asked.

Reinhardt paused, his mind racing to improvise. He knew that if he gave a specific address, there would be no turning back. He would have to take them somewhere they could get lost or distracted.

"It's a warehouse. Near the research campus. It's hidden because it contains sensitive materials that can't be in the lab."

JJ chuckled.

"How convenient. But I believe you. We're going to pay a visit."

Antonio nodded.

"You're taking us there right now," Antonio said, waving the gun at the door. "And if you try anything, well, you know what's in store for you."

Reinhardt stood up slowly, his thoughts searching for a way to escape as the two men escorted him out of the lab.

As he stepped out of the building, the cold air hit his face, clearing his mind a bit. JJ and Antonio kept him under close surveillance.
a, but Reinhardt noticed something important: there were no other men waiting for them outside. It wasn't a big operation, at least not yet. That gave him a slight advantage.

They climbed into a dark van parked a few meters from the exit. Antonio sat in the passenger seat, while JJ took the wheel. Reinhardt was forced into the back, his mind still calculating all the options.

During the drive to the supposed "warehouse," Reinhardt tried to remember all the paths that could lead to some kind of help. He knew every street in the city, every corner of the research campus. But JJ wasn't driving slowly, and his time was running out.

Finally, they came to an intersection near the campus. Reinhardt pointed in a direction, aware that they couldn't stop there for long.

"It's this way," he said, trying to sound convincing.

Antonio looked outside, looking for something suspicious. Reinhardt knew that they couldn't spend much time in that area without attracting attention. With the local police patrolling frequently, he had to make something happen before it was too late.

Just as JJ turned the wheel onto the street Reinhardt had indicated, the sound of sirens could be heard in the distance. The scientist knew in that instant that his only chance was here.

Without a second thought, he threw open the van door and jumped onto the pavement, rolling across the ground with a sharp pain in his side. It took the men in the vehicle a few seconds to realize what he had done, giving him just enough time to get up and run towards the campus.

JJ screamed curses as he slammed the van on the brakes.

"Get him!" Antonio shouted, furious.

Reinhardt ran with all his might, zigzagging between the buildings, knowing that he had to get to a public place before he was caught. He knew his options were limited, but the presence of the sirens nearby gave him some hope.

As Reinhardt ran out of the building, the cold air hit his face, clearing his mind a little. The pressure he had felt inside didn't completely dissipate, but the shock of reality was a momentary relief. JJ and Antonio kept him under close surveillance, their gazes intense and distrustful, but Reinhardt noticed something important: there were no other men waiting for them outside. It wasn't a big operation, at least not yet. That gave him a slight advantage.

They climbed into a dark van parked a few feet from the exit. Antonio sat in the passenger seat, while JJ took the wheel. Reinhardt was forced to sit in the back, his mind still calculating all the options. The lights of the city faded as they drove away from the campus, and the tension felt like an added weight in the air.

During the drive to the supposed "warehouse," Reinhardt tried to remember all the paths that could lead to some kind of help. He knew every street in the city, every corner of the research campus. But JJ wasn't driving slowly, and he was running out of time.

"It's this way," Reinhardt said, trying to sound convincing as he pointed in the direction of a little-traveled street.

Antonio looked outside, looking for anything suspicious. Reinhardt knew they couldn't spend much time in that area without attracting attention. With the local police patrolling frequently, he had to do something before it was too late.

Just as JJ turned the wheel toward the street Reinhardt had indicated, the sound of sirens could be heard in the distance. The scientist knew in that instant that his only chance was there. The police. His heart was pounding, urging him to action.

Without a second thought, he opened the door of the truck and jumped onto the pavement, rolling on the ground with a sharp pain in his side. Adrenaline kept him moving, and it took the men in the vehicle a few seconds to realize what he had done, giving him just enough time to get up and run toward campus.

"Get him!" Antonio shouted, furious.

Reinhardt ran with all his might, zigzagging between buildings, knowing he had to get to a public place before he was caught. As he got further away, he could feel JJ and Antonio's presence behind him, their footsteps echoing in the night, but the promise of freedom kept him moving.

As he got deeper into campus, the light from the van's headlights faded. The sound of sirens grew closer and closer, and Reinhardt knew time was not on his side. Every step he took brought him closer to salvation or capture.

"Come on, come on!" he told himself as he ran. His breathing became heavier, but he couldn't stop. He needed to get to the main building, where there were more people. He knew that campus security wouldn't be able to ignore a disturbance in the middle of the night.

Finally, he reached the open area of the campus. The buildings stood like shadows against the starry sky. Reinhardt saw a group of students talking on a corner, and his heart raced. "If I can get to them, maybe they'll help me," he thought.

"Help!" he shouted as he approached, his voice filled with desperation.

The students turned, looking at him in surprise. One of them, a girl with curly hair and a leather jacket, frowned.

"What's wrong?" she asked, her tone changing to concern.

"They're chasing me. I need someone to call the police," Reinhardt replied, his mind still racing.

Before he could explain further, he heard the sound of the van approaching again. "I don't have time," he thought. He turned to see JJ and Antonio exiting the van, their faces tense and determined.

"Run!" Reinhardt shouted to the students, and they instinctively began to walk away.

But the panic in his voice caught JJ's attention, who was quickly advancing towards them.

"Don't let him get away," JJ shouted, raising an arm, as if he was about to use something.

Reinhardt knew he had to act fast. "This can't end like this," he told himself, looking around for an exit. In that instant, his gaze fell on a back door that led to an empty building. Without thinking, he darted towards it, throwing it open and closing it behind him.

The interior was dark and dusty, but he didn't care. His heart thundered in his ears as he searched for a place to hide. He crouched behind an old, dust-covered desk, hoping JJ and Antonio wouldn't find him.

From his hiding spot, he heard the sound of the door opening, and the men's voices echoed through the air.

"He can't have gone far," JJ said, his voice filled with frustration.

"We have to search everything. We can't afford to lose him," A replied.
ntonio, his tone   serious.

Reinhardt held his breath, his mind racing a mile a minute. What would he do if they found him? The situation was becoming increasingly dangerous. "I need a way out," he thought.

As he waited, he remembered something crucial: there was an emergency phone in the building. It wasn't the first time he had used it, but at that moment, it became his only hope. He crept slowly towards the door, each step calculated and silent.

Finally, he reached the phone, and his heart stopped for a moment as he saw that it was connected. Without hesitation, he dialed the emergency number. As the tone rang, his mind filled with uncertainty. "What if I don't get there in time?"

"Come on, come on!" he whispered to himself, each second feeling like an eternity.

On the other end of the line, a voice answered.

"911, what's your emergency?"

"They're chasing me!" "I need help at the research campus!" he shouted, feeling the pressure of time running out.

"Can you give me your exact location?" the operator asked, but before Reinhardt could answer, he heard footsteps approaching.

"I don't have time!" he exclaimed, knowing the situation was critical. Suddenly, the sound of a door was followed by a dull thud.

"Damn it!" JJ shouted, furious. "You can't hide here!"

Reinhardt felt a wave of panic, but decided to act with determination. "Send help, fast!" he shouted into the phone before hanging up and hiding again.

The men were approaching, their voices echoing in the empty space. Reinhardt felt the adrenaline rush through his veins as he searched for a way out. With one last glance at the door, he decided it was time to fight for his life. He wasn't going to let them catch him.

He crept towards the front door, making sure his movements were silent. Once he reached the exit, he pushed the door open and stepped out, feeling the cold air hit his face again. He had to find a place where people could help him, but the first thing he needed was to distract JJ and Antonio.

As he ran, he noticed the students still standing in the corner, staring at him in disbelief. "I must lure them over here," he thought. Reinhardt made his way towards them, shouting.

"They're behind me! Please help me!"

The students, shocked, began to move, their protective instincts kicking in. "Maybe this will work," Reinhardt thought as he turned his attention to the group, aware that JJ and Antonio were behind him, ready to catch him.

"Call the police!" he shouted to the group, his urgency evident.

JJ and Antonio began to move forward, but the group of students stood between them and Reinhardt. Confusion reigned, and Reinhardt seized the moment. **"I can't stay here," ** he thought, but he couldn't let them take him so easily.

With a sudden turn, Reinhardt darted to the other side of the group, running towards the nearest building. The sound of sirens continued to get closer, and his heart pounded with hope. He knew that if he could just keep his distance, he could reach safety.

But, as he ran, he felt a tug on his jacket. Antonio had made contact. Reinhardt stopped dead in his tracks, feeling himself being caught, but

in a desperate move, he slid to the side, breaking free from their grip.

"Let me go!" he shouted, feeling the fury and adrenaline surging within him.

Before he could react, JJ threw a punch at him. Reinhardt crouched down and, in a swift maneuver, pushed JJ aside, causing him to stumble.

"Run!" he shouted to the watching students.

The stunned group finally began to move, some screaming, others reaching for their phones. Reinhardt felt a little safer knowing there were people around him.

As the men tried to pull themselves together, Reinhardt took the lead, running toward the administration building. There, he could at least find a place to hide while he waited for help to arrive.

The sound of the sirens grew louder, and Reinhardt felt a mix of anxiety and relief. **"Maybe I'll make it out this time," he thought as he approached the main entrance, his footsteps echoing on the marble floor.

As he entered, he found the lobby empty. Lights flickered, and the feeling of being alone washed over him for a moment. However, he couldn't allow himself to hesitate.

He slid behind a group of chairs, trying to catch his breath as he listened to the murmur of JJ and Antonio's voices approaching. **"The police will be here soon," he kept telling himself, wishing help would come sooner.

Suddenly, the sound of the front door slammed open, and Reinhardt saw a pair of police officers walk in, their gazes quick and determined.

"Get down!" one of them shouted.

Reinhardt didn't hesitate. The cold hardness of the marble beneath him, as the officers took up positions, ready to face the men chasing him.

The tension in the air was palpable. Reinhardt stood still, pulse racing as he looked at the officers. "This is my moment," he thought, willing his plan to work.

Antonio and JJ walked in just as the police took up positions. The two men stopped dead in their tracks, their faces changing from shock to anger as they realized the situation had changed.

"You can't take him!" JJ shouted, pulling out a gun in determination.

"Let him go!" one of the officers shouted, pointing his gun at JJ.

Chaos broke loose. Reinhardt moved, sensing his chance had finally come. With the officers distracted, he ran into the back hallway, determined to escape this nightmare.

The sound of gunshots echoed behind him, and adrenaline propelled him even faster. He felt free, but he knew that freedom was only temporary. He had to find a safe place and contact someone who could help him untangle this situation.

Leaving through an emergency door, Reinhardt found himself in a dark alley. The rain was beginning to fall, turning the pavement into a slippery mirror. He looked both ways, unsure if the men were still following him.

With the rain soaking his hair and jacket, Reinhardt knew he had to act. "I can't stay here," he thought as he walked deeper into the maze of streets. He had to find a place where he could think, where he could make a plan.

As he ran, the lights of a nearby café called to him. Determined, he headed there. If he could get in and talk to someone he trusted, perhaps he could turn the situation around. Upon reaching the entrance, he pushed open the door and entered, feeling the warmth of the place contrast with the cold outside.

The customers looked at him in surprise. Out of breath and soaking wet, he approached the counter, where a blonde-haired woman was watching him with concern.

"Are you okay?" she asked, her voice soft but firm.

"I need help," Reinhardt replied, feeling his voice shaking. He had to find the right words. "I'm being followed by some men. I need you to call the police."

The woman frowned, but her gaze hardened. "Sure, I'll help. But first, come here," she said, leading him to a secluded table.

Reinhardt sat down, and she walked over to the phone. At that moment, he felt a mix of hope and fear. **"Maybe I'm finally safe," he thought as the woman dialed the number.

"Don't move, just a moment," she said, looking out the window. Reinhardt peered out, searching for any sign of danger.

"Do you think they'll follow me?" he asked, sensing the urgency in her voice.

"I don't know." But you must be prepared," the woman said, her tone grave.

Just as the call connected, Reinhardt felt a chill run down his spine. "Something's not right," he thought as he watched a black vehicle pull up on the street.

"I can't let them find me," he muttered.

The woman hung up and looked at him with concern. "What are you saying?"

"You have to help me get out of here," she replied, quickly standing up.

But before he could move, the door to the café swung open. JJ and Antonio entered, their eyes scanning the place until they landed on Reinhardt. Time stopped for a second, and chaos broke out again.

"You can't escape!" JJ shouted, his voice echoing in the space.

The woman moved quickly, standing between Reinhardt and the men. "Get out of here!" she shouted at them, firm and defiant.

Reinhardt felt fear take hold of him again. He couldn't let them catch him, not after he'd come this far.

"Let's go, Reinhardt!" Antonio shouted, trying to advance towards him, but the woman held her position.

"Get back!" ordered one of the officers, who had arrived at the café with reinforcements. "Get on the ground!"

The situation became even more chaotic. Reinhardt knew he had to take advantage of this moment. Without thinking, he ran towards the back exit of the café, feeling the adrenaline driving him to move faster than ever.

He stepped out into the rain, the cold enveloping him like a blanket. He didn't look back. He had to survive. As he ran, he knew the road was still long, but each step brought him a little closer to his freedom.

"I won't get caught," he told himself, as he disappeared into the darkness of the night, determined to find a way to undo all this chaos.

Chapter 18

The lab was a shadow of its former self. The air still smelled of burning, of melted plastic and scorched metal. Dr. James looked around, taking in the remains of his professional life, his masterpiece, now scattered across the floor as if it were worthless.

"What the hell happened here?" he asked, his voice barely controlled, trying not to give in to panic.

Dr. Reinhardt, a few feet away from him, was shaking. He ran a hand through his hair, nervous. His face was a mix of fear and shock.

"Two guys…" Reinhardt began, his voice cracking. "They came earlier, demanded to know who we worked for, and then did… all this."

James held up a piece of shattered keyboard. Wires hung from the walls like disjointed snakes, and the once-sophisticated lab equipment was now little more than trash. The blow was hard, but fury was beginning to gain ground in his mind.

"Did they take everything?" he asked as he inspected a broken computer.

"Everything," Reinhardt nodded, pointing at the shattered desks. "Hard drives, research files... even molecular samples."

James dropped the computer to the floor with a thud. The sound echoed in the silence, a somber echo of the disaster.

"They're trying to erase everything we've done... silence us," James said, his tone rising in intensity. "That means we're close. Very close."

"Did you take a look at them?" he asked as he turned to Reinhardt, searching for an answer that would confirm what he already suspected.

Reinhardt shook his head, his voice shaking. "Yeah, but they looked like... anyone you wouldn't want to cross paths with." His gaze remained fixed on the chaos around him.

Reinhardt's fingers trembled as he tried to gather his thoughts. It was clear he was disturbed by what had just happened.

"We're in too deep, Richard," he continued, sighing. "These people, whoever they are, if they're willing to do this—"

"We can't walk away from this," James interrupted, his fists clenched.

He'd come too far to back out now. This was more than a science project. It was the truth, and someone was desperate to bury it. But James had an ace up his sleeve.

"There's still something they didn't get," he said, determination returning to his voice. "I've got some of the original data backed up at home. It's locked away, safe."

Reinhardt looked up, worried.

"Are you crazy? If they did this to my lab, what makes you think your home is safe? None of us are safe."

James was silent for a moment, thinking. He knew Reinhardt was right, but he couldn't let fear paralyze them. This was too big. He raised a hand to his face, rubbing his eyes wearily. The stress was consuming him.

"We need more help," he finally admitted. "We can't do it alone anymore."

Reinhardt sighed, visibly exhausted. The magnitude of the problem seemed to overwhelm him, but James could see in his eyes that he understood. There was no turning back.

"What do you propose?" Reinhardt asked, his voice barely a whisper.

James walked over to the broken window of the lab. The sun was beginning to set, turning the sky a deep orange. It was a cruel contrast to the mess unfolding at his feet. His thoughts raced as he searched for a solution.

"I know someone," James finally said. "Someone who could help us. But it's risky."

"This is all risky," Reinhardt replied, still standing there. "If you leave here with that data, you'll be in danger."

"I know," James admitted, "but we have no other choice."

Silence settled between them, as the weight of what this decision entailed became more apparent. James turned to Reinhardt, who looked at him with a mixture of fear and resignation.

"We need to move quickly," James added. "They will soon discover that we still have information."

Reinhardt looked at him for a long moment, as if he wanted to say something, but in the end he just nodded, accepting the gravity of the situation.

****

A few hours later, night had completely fallen. The lab was empty, plunged into darkness. Outside, James and Reinhardt were moving quickly towards the car, with the lights of the city flickering in the distance. The engine roared as James turned the key. They both knew that what they were about to do would mark a before and after.

"Are you sure this is the right thing to do?" Reinhardt asked, looking out the window, as if he feared someone was following them.

James did not answer immediately. His mind was working at full speed, evaluating risks, possibilities and alternatives. But the reality was clear: they didn't have much of a choice.

"This is our only chance," he finally said, his jaw clenched. "We have to get in touch with her."

Reinhard
nodded slowly, resigned. The car glided through the deserted streets of the city, moving towards the unknown.

****

The cold night air was like a slap in the face as James stepped out of the car in front of a small house. The lights were off, but James knew she was there. He had been following her trail for years, waiting for the right moment to ask her for help. This was that moment.

"Do you think she'll be willing to help us?" Reinhardt asked, his face tense.

"I don't know," James admitted, "but we need to try."

He walked to the door and knocked. The seconds stretched out as they waited, until finally the door opened slightly, revealing a figure in the darkness.

"James," a female voice said from the gloom. "I knew you would come."

James gulped. He knew this meeting wouldn't be easy. But there was no turning back now.

The door swung all the way open, and she invited them in.

****

The interior of the house was simple, with bare walls and sparse furniture. The woman, in her thirties, watched them with an unreadable expression. Her eyes were dark and her presence filled the space.

"You and your problems…" she said, crossing her arms. "What have you done this time?"

James sighed and glanced at Reinhardt before answering. He knew he would need to be convincing if he wanted her to join his cause.

"We are in danger," he began. "And we need your help."

The woman, whose gaze never missed a single detail of James, remained silent for a long moment. Her name was Evelyn, a former colleague of James's from the early years of his career, when they were just beginning to delve into the depths of experimental biotechnology. She was brilliant, but there was also a reason she had stayed off the radar for so long. James knew that involving her meant dragging her into chaos from which there might be no return.

Evelyn took a step toward them, her eyes flashing in the dim light.

"When you say you're in danger," she said slowly, "what kind of danger exactly?"

James pressed his lips together, knowing she would understand better than anyone.

"The kind that destroys laboratories and erases years of research without a trace," he replied. "Someone is determined to bury us, and the worst thing is that they are close enough to do so."

Evelyn let out a sigh, moving toward the small kitchen where she turned on a dim light. The room filled with a warm, dim lighting that revealed the details of his exhaustion. He opened a cabinet and pulled out a small bottle of liquor, pouring two glasses.

"And what makes you think I can help you escape this?" he asked as he handed a glass to James and another to Reinhardt.

James stared at the liquid for a second, before downing it in one gulp.

"It's not just about escaping," he said, his voice firmer. "It's about fighting. We're close to something big, Evelyn. Enough that someone would spend a lot of money and effort to silence us. But I have the latest, most crucial data backed up. I hid it well.

Evelyn looked at him carefully, analyzing his words. It wasn't the first time she heard promises like that. However, something in James' intensity made her hesitate. After all, she knew that look, she had seen it before, when they were about to discover something monumental.

"And what do you want from me?" "What kind of ability?" she asked, slowly turning her glass in her hand.

Reinhardt, who had been silent all this time, spoke for the first time since they entered the house.

"We need someone with your ability," he said, clearly nervous. "Someone who knows how to navigate these kinds of situations. We can't do it alone."

Evelyn raised an eyebrow, leaning forward a little.

"What kind of ability?" she asked with a slight smile. "You know I stepped away from that whole world, right? I'm not a part of this anymore."

James leaned toward her, his tone serious, almost urgent.

"You say that now," he replied. "But this isn't just another investigation, Evelyn. This can change everything. You know what it means. And we need someone who not only understands the system, but knows how to manipulate it to our advantage."

Evelyn crossed her arms, her gaze fixed on James. She had been off the radar for a long time, but she knew exactly what they were talking about. Those with enough power and resources could wipe a person off the face of the Earth without anyone noticing. And if someone had gone so far as to destroy Reinhardt's lab, then this wasn't a simple attack out of revenge or competition.

"How serious are those guys?" she finally asked.

"Enough that this isn't a game," James replied, his voice low. "If we don't do something, they won't just destroy our research. They'll destroy us."

Evelyn dropped the empty glass on the table with a soft thud. She walked to the window, pulling back the curtain to look out onto the street. The city seemed asleep, quiet. But she knew that quiet was an illusion, especially when someone like James came to ask for help.

"I know someone who might be able to buy us some time," she finally said. "But if this goes wrong, if we're discovered…"

"We're already in danger," James replied. "This can't get any worse."

Evelyn let out a bitter laugh.

"It can always get worse, James." That's the one thing you must never forget.

There was a moment of silence before Evelyn turned around to face them again, her decision made.

"Okay," she said. "I'll help you. But we're doing this my way. There won't be any more surprises."

James nodded, relieved.

"Whatever you say," he replied, knowing he had no other choice. They would need it if they wanted to survive.

****

Hours later, as night continued to envelop the city, the three of them found themselves in a small room in the basement of Evelyn's house, a place where the technology seemed from another century, but which served its purpose of being invisible to anyone looking for traces. On the table were a couple of old laptops, connected to an encryption system that Evelyn had modified years ago.

"You can use this equipment to access your data safely," she said as she typed quickly on one of the laptops. They are encrypted in such a way that it will take more than a couple of thugs to crack them.

He pulled a small hard drive from his jacket and handed it to her. Evelyn inserted it into the port and began transferring the files as James and Reinhardt watched in silence.

"That data is our only guarantee," James said quietly, staring at the screen.

"It always is," Evelyn replied without taking her eyes off the monitor. "Now tell me, what exactly did you find?"

James hesitated for a second before answering.

"We've been working on a molecular restructuring project," he began. "Something that could change the way we understand living organisms. But not everyone wants that kind of power in the wrong hands."

"And who decides who the wrong hands are?" Evelyn asked with a grimace.

"That's the thing," Reinhardt said, sighing. "We're dealing with forces that want to monopolize it, control access before we can make public what we've really discovered."

Evelyn looked at them over the monitor, her gaze fixed on James.

"So... we're talking about something that could change the world, right?" she asked with a smile that didn't reach her eyes.

James nodded. There was nothing else to say.

Silence fell again as Evelyn continued working.

Dr. James closed the safe door with a dry click, his hands shaking slightly as he finished securing everything. Inside, the samples and the flash drive were his only insurance amidst the chaos. He took a deep breath, trying to calm himself, but the echo of Reinhardt's words still rang in his head: "We're not safe. No one is."

****

The knock on the door made him jump. He turned sharply, looking around the office, his mind already anticipating the worst. Quickly, he went to the window and looked out. He only saw the figure of a woman waiting patiently. He breathed a sigh of relief as he recognized Emily. He opened the door.

"Rich, are you okay?" Emily asked, frowning.

James nodded, but the concern on his face gave him away. He closed the door behind her and followed her into the living room. He knew that sooner or later he would have to explain everything to her.

"For now, yes." But things are getting worse," he said as he plopped down on the couch.

Emily sat down beside him, placing a hand on his shoulder.

"I know," she said. "Reinhardt called me. He told me what happened in the lab… how they destroyed both of you."

James clenched his fists, feeling frustration build. He had been left with nothing, or almost nothing. But he had saved something, enough to keep going.

"They haven't deleted everything," he said.

Emily raised an eyebrow, surprised.

"What?"

"I have a sample. And some data," he added, leaning toward her, his tone low. "I saved it all in a safe place."

Emily stared at him, trying to understand.

"You saved a sample? Where?"

James avoided her gaze, but the silence was answer enough.

"It's here, right?" Emily asked, her eyes scanning the room.

James looked away, but the expression on his face gave him away.

"You've always been terrible at hiding things," she said with a small smile. "But Rich, you need to put that somewhere safer. It's not safe here, not while you're being watched."

James knew she was right. He couldn't risk losing what little they had left.

"I'm not leaving him here," she replied with a sigh. "I already made a call. To someone I trust."

Emily looked at him, confused.

"A call? To who?"

"Mark Dawson," James said, as if it were an obvious thing. "An old friend from college. Now he works at the CIA."

Emily looked at him incredulously.

"The CIA?" she asked, almost in a whisper. "Rich, are you sure you can trust him?"

James nodded firmly.

"I trust him with my life. And if there's anyone who can get us out of this mess, it's him."

Emily leaned back on the couch, processing the information.

"What are we supposed to do when he gets here?"

James took a breath, then leaned toward her.

"I'll tell him everything," he said. "About the nanomaterials, about who's behind this, the cover-up... everything. He'll know what to do."

Emily crossed her arms nervously.

"And until he gets here?"

"We wait," James replied. "We keep our heads down, and make sure this information is safe until Mark gets here."

Silence fell between them as the gravity of the situation settled in.

****

Outside the house, the dark sedan was still parked a few houses away. Two figures stood silently inside the vehicle, watching the house with unwavering attention.

"There's no significant movement," one of them said, checking his watch.

The other, who remained silent, nodded. They knew they had to be vigilant. They had been given clear orders: keep an eye on Dr. James, don't let him out of their sight. If he tried to move, they had to be ready.

"How much longer are we going to wait?" the first one asked impatiently.

"As long as it takes," the other one answered, his eyes fixed on the house. "We were told not to move until we received the signal."

The first one snorted, looking back at the house. He knew something was about to happen, but he couldn't figure out exactly what.

****

Inside the house, Emily kept pacing back and forth, restless. She knew there was no turning back, but the idea of waiting without doing anything made her desperate.

"What if he doesn't get there in time?" she asked suddenly, breaking the silence.

James looked at her, understanding her concern.

"Mark will arrive. He always keeps his word."

Emily nodded, but she still had doubts. She knew they were in danger, and any delay could cost them more than they were willing to lose.

"I hope you're right," she said finally, stopping in front of the window and looking out.

James watched her for a moment, feeling the pressure on his shoulders increase. Everything depended on Mark arriving on time and his plan working.

****

A few days later, the sound of a plane landing echoed through the city's airport. Among the disembarking passengers, a tall, serious-looking man walked with a determined step towards the exit. Mark Dawson had arrived.

With a small suitcase in hand and a pair of sunglasses hiding his gaze

Using a calculator, Mark breezed through security. He knew every second counted.

He pulled out his phone and dialed a familiar number.

"I'm in town," he said when James answered. "I'll meet you at the agreed-upon location."

James breathed a sigh of relief on the other end of the line.

"Thanks for coming, Mark. I owe you one."

"We'll talk about that later," Mark replied curtly. "I'll see you in an hour."

Mark hung up and headed to his rental car, knowing the next few days would be crucial.

****

An hour later, James and Emily sat in a small, discreet café, away from prying eyes. They both remained silent, awaiting Mark's arrival.

Finally, the door to the café opened, and the man they had been waiting for entered. Mark Dawson approached their table with the same calm that had always characterized him.

"Rich," Mark said, shaking his hand firmly. "It's good to see you."

"Likewise, Mark," James replied, making an effort to smile. "This is Emily."

Mark nodded at her before sitting down.

"Tell me what the hell is going on," he said, getting straight to the point.

James took a breath and began to tell him everything. From the research they had been conducting on nanomaterials, to the attack on the lab and the disappearance of their findings.

Mark listened intently, his expression unchanging.

"And you have the data backed up," he finally said, nodding. "That's what we need to expose all of this. But I need to know exactly who is behind this before I move."

James exchanged a glance with Emily before answering.

"We don't know for sure," he said, "but they are well connected and they won't stop until they destroy all traces of our research."

Mark leaned back in his chair, assessing the situation.

"Okay," he said after a moment. "This is going to be complicated, but there are ways to handle it." The first thing is to secure that data.

Mark nodded, his expression serious and focused. He knew the situation was more delicate than James and Emily had imagined. Although he trusted his old friend, this was no longer simply a matter of stolen scientific data; it involved something far more dangerous.

"The first thing is to secure that data," Mark repeated, but this time with a firmer tone. "We can't risk them finding it. Are they with you now?"

James shook his head, lowering his voice as he looked around.

"I have it at home, in a safe. No one else knows of its existence… at least I don't think so."

Emily, arms crossed, looked at Mark suspiciously.

"And now that you know, don't you think we increase the chances that they're watching your movements as well?"

Mark looked straight at her, his calmness seemingly unbreakable.

"That's a possibility, yes. But if they're watching me, they haven't given me any signs yet. The important thing is to act fast. We need to move that data as soon as possible."

James nodded, but there was something else that worried him more at the moment.

"Mark, I saw a car parked near my house the other night," he said, cautiously. "I'm not sure if I was being watched, but it didn't seem like a coincidence."

Emily opened her eyes, clearly alarmed.

"Why didn't you tell me before?"

James sighed, knowing he couldn't hide anything from her anymore.

"I didn't want to alarm you, but we can't ignore it now. We're being followed."

Mark narrowed his eyes, quickly processing the information.

"That makes it complicated, but it doesn't stop us. What we're going to do is this: I'll go with you to your house, we'll collect the data, and we'll get it out of there as quickly as possible. But we have to do it in a way that we don't attract attention."

"What do you suggest?" Emily asked, her arms still crossed.

"First, we need to make sure we're not being followed directly. We'll do a little maneuver to throw off anyone watching the house," Mark replied. I have a team at the CIA that can help us monitor the surroundings in real time. I don't want to use my connections in an obvious way, but in cases like this, it's necessary.

James looked at Emily, who finally nodded, resigned.

"Okay, then… when do we do it?" James asked, his voice tense.

Mark stood up, ready to move.

"Right now. There's no time to waste."

****

An hour later, the dark sedan was still parked near Dr. James's house. The two figures inside the vehicle were growing tense.

"It's been over two hours and there's been no movement," said one of them, the younger one. "I'm not sure he's still inside."

The other, an older man, looked at his watch and then pulled out a small device. It was a signal tracker.

"It doesn't matter," he replied, as he fiddled with the device. "We've got everything under control. If he comes out, we'll know."

What they didn't know was that Mark had foreseen this possibility. As he and James approached the house, he had made a detour down a side street, where a black vehicle was waiting for them. There they switched cars, under the supervision of an agent Mark had quietly coordinated.

"Everything is clear," the agent reported through a small earpiece. "No one has detected the maneuver."

Mark nodded, driving slowly toward the house in a car the vigilantes would not recognize. He knew any mistake could cost them dearly.

"We're there," he said, parking a block from James's house.

"Are you sure about this?" James asked, his nervousness evident.

"As sure as I can be in this situation," Mark replied, looking around. "Come on, move quickly."

They both got out of the vehicle and walked silently toward the house. Emily had insisted on staying behind, keeping safe in a different location, under the protection of another Mark agent.

James cautiously opened the door, his heart racing. The atmosphere inside the house was heavy, as if something was out of place, but nothing looked different at first glance.

"Let's go straight to the safe," Mark ordered quietly. "Let's not waste any time."

James nodded and quickly led them towards his office. They reached the safe, which was well hidden behind a cabinet. With shaking hands, James began to enter the combination.

Mark, meanwhile, kept watching every corner of the room, making sure there were no hidden cameras or listening devices. He knew how careful the people responsible for all this were, but he couldn't afford to let his guard down for even a second.

Finally, the safe clicked open. James pulled out the small box with the samples and the USB stick.

"Here they are," he said, handing them to Mark.

Mark carefully took the box, making sure it was tightly closed.

"Good. Now let's get out of here."

However, just as they were about to leave the office, a sound of heavy footsteps at the entrance made them freeze.

"What was that?"

The dark night enveloped the neighborhood as Mark and James ran through the backyard, the shadows of the trees creating eerie shapes around them. Mark stayed one step ahead, moving with the agility of someone used to this kind of situation, while James followed close behind, his breathing labored by the mix of fear and adrenaline.

"Where are we going?" James asked quietly, fighting to control his panic.

Mark didn't stop.

"We have to get away from the house as quickly as possible. There's a car waiting for us on the corner. We only have a few minutes before they realize we've escaped."

The lights in the neighboring houses were off, everything was silent. However, they both knew that didn't mean safety. Behind them, the sound of doors opening and whispered voices confirmed that they weren't alone.

As they reached the corner, a black car without license plates waited with the engine running. The driver, a burly man wearing sunglasses despite the darkness, gestured for them to get in quickly.

"Did you have any trouble?" the driver asked, as he accelerated without waiting for an answer.

"Nothing we couldn't handle," Mark replied, turning to look back, watching carefully for any sign of being followed.

James, still trying to catch his breath, leaned forward.

"Who were those men? Why did they know where we were?"

Mark shook his head.

"I don't know, but it's clear we're not dealing with a random group. Those guys knew what they were doing. This just confirms that we're on the radar of someone much bigger."

James gritted his teeth, trying to come to terms with what had just happened.

"Mark, if this is as serious as it seems… what are we going to do?" he asked, his voice cracking slightly with uncertainty.

Mark looked at him in the rearview mirror, his expression more serious than ever.

"First, we need to make sure that data doesn't fall into the wrong hands. These people are willing to do anything to destroy any trace of your research. What you have on that flash drive is the only thing we have left to expose them."

James nodded, understanding the weight of his words.

"But if they already know where I live, how safe are we now?" James continued, looking at the box he still held firmly in his hands.

Mark turned into a side street, moving away from the main road.

"For now, we're out of danger. This car has no trace they can follow, and we have a safe place where we can plan our next move."

The driver remained silent, but Mark motioned to him.

"Head to the safe house," he ordered, glancing sideways at James. "We're going to need some time to decide what we do next."

****

The safe house was on the outskirts of town, hidden in a rural area. Upon arrival, the car stopped in front of a modest cabin surrounded by tall trees, almost invisible from the main road.

"We'll be fine here for now," Mark said, getting out of the car and helping James out. "No one knows about this place."

They quickly entered, and Mark closed all the windows and doors behind them. The cabin was equipped with the basics: a small kitchen, two bedrooms, and a living room with old, but functional furniture. It was a temporary, but safe shelter.

"How much time do we have before they find this place, too?" James asked, still uneasy as he set the box down on the living room table.

"Long enough to think about our next move," Mark replied, checking his phone for trackers. "I've already put some extra security measures in place. If they come close, we'll know in advance."

James sat on the edge of the couch, his mind filled with questions and worries. The weight of the box in front of him reminded him of how fragile his situation was. If they lost that data, all of their research, everything they had worked for, would be gone. But what worried him most was who was willing to go to such lengths to stop them.

"Mark, there's something I haven't told you," James said, his voice low, almost as if he feared the very words might invite danger.

Mark looked up from his phone, watching his friend warily.

"What are you talking about?"

James ran a hand through his hair, nervous.

"When we first started this research, I didn't think we'd get this far. But once we discovered the potential of nanomaterials, I started getting anonymous emails. At first I thought it was spam, but then they started getting more specific. Threats, warnings… They were telling me to stop researching, that what I was doing was dangerous."

Mark frowned.

"Why didn't you tell me this before?"

James sighed, lowering his head.

"I didn't want to involve you." I thought that if I ignored the threats, he would eventually give up.
 But now I know I was wrong. They're closer than I imagined.

Mark was silent for a moment, processing the new information. Then, he stood up and began pacing back and forth, clearly upset.

"This changes things," he finally said. "If they've been after you this whole time, then they've been a lot closer than we thought. They have resources, contacts... this isn't a simple covert operation."

James nodded, knowing he'd made a grave mistake in underestimating the gravity of the situation.

"So what do we do now?" James asked, feeling the ground crumble beneath his feet.

Mark stopped and looked him straight in the eyes.

"First thing is to make sure this data gets to the right person. And as for who's behind all this... let's give them something to distract themselves from."

Chapter 19

The night was growing longer and the small basement room was feeling increasingly claustrophobic. Evelyn found herself trapped between the brick walls and the palpable fear that surrounded her. The agents, in their protective suits, looked like something out of a science fiction movie, but their seriousness was anything but fictional. Each of them exuded an intensity that made it clear they weren't there to ask polite questions.

"Who are you?" Evelyn exclaimed, her arms crossed, displaying a mix of defiance and fear.

One agent, taller than the others, took a step closer, the glow of his visor reflecting the dim light of the room.

"We're not here to argue," he replied, his deep voice echoing in the space. "We're here for you, Evelyn. We know what you've been investigating."

Evelyn felt a chill run down her spine. The agent's words made her feel uncomfortable, causing her to look at herself. which also seemed to be dealing with their own uneasiness.

"What do you want from me?" Evelyn asked, keeping her voice steady, though the tremor in her hand betrayed her nervousness.

"We're offering you the chance to work with us," the agent said, dropping his words like an axe. "Or, if you prefer, you could die here."

The words echoed through the room, and an awkward silence fell over everyone. .

"What kind of work are we talking about?" Her voice sounded more defiant than he felt.

The agent smiled, though his gaze was cold.

"We know you have access to information that could change the world. We want you to collaborate on our project."

"What kind of project?" Evelyn asked, crossing his arms suspiciously.

"One that interests you." We're looking for ways to manipulate biology on a large scale. What you and James have been researching is crucial to us.

Evelyn felt the air escape from her. She knew what that meant. Their research had been a mix of impressive and dangerous discoveries. How much did they really know about them?

"And if we refuse?" Evelyn challenged, though She knew her bravado was just an attempt to show control.

"Then this conversation ends here," the agent replied, and the rest of his team stepped forward, their posture menacing.

Evelyn looked around, trying to find a way out, but there was none. The pressure in the room was becoming unbearable. Reinhardt's words echoed in her mind: "We're not safe. No one is."

"We can't trust you," Evelyn said, trying to remain calm. Her eyes met the agent's, and in an instant, the power play became more evident.

"You're right. You can't trust us." But you don't have any options either," the agent replied, crossing his arms.

Evelyn felt the room spinning around her. The implications of what was happening were too big to grasp.

"Why don't you explain it to us better?" Another agent said, trying to buy time. "Maybe we can come to an agreement."

The agent moved even closer, his voice now a menacing whisper.

"There's no room for agreements, doctor. There's only one decision here: cooperate or die."

Evelyn swallowed, her mind racing. She knew they had to get out of there, but her instincts told her that any wrong move could be fatal.

"Okay," she finally said, her voice barely a whisper. "I'm willing to hear what you have to offer."

The agent's eyes shone with a mix of satisfaction and triumph.

"That's what we wanted to hear. Now, if you'll come with me, I'll show you what we have in mind," the agent said, gesturing for her to follow.

Evelyn followed the agent into a dark hallway, each step echoing in her mind like an echo of her decision. She knew she was entering uncharted territory, and every fiber of her being screamed at her that she was making a mistake.

"What are they really after?" she asked, trying to keep her voice steady.

"We want you to use your knowledge to develop a new kind of technology. Imagine having control over the biology of any organism. That's what we aim to achieve."

The sight of such absolute power sent shivers down her spine. She knew that, in the wrong hands, it could lead to the destruction of everything she knew.

Finally, they reached a control room. Screens lit up the space with images of various investigations.

"This is where the magic happens," the agent said, pointing at the screens. Your data is just the tip of the iceberg.

Evelyn looked at the images, a mixture of horror and fascination. There were the experiments, the data that had never been

They had seen the light of day.

"This is not what we want to do," she protested, trying to stand her ground.

"What do you mean?" the agent asked, his interest piqued.

"We can't play gods. Science should be used for good, not to control humanity," she replied, feeling her voice rise.

The agent laughed, a cold, calculating sound.

"Evelyn, humanity is not in control. It never has been. But you, you can be part of something bigger."

Evelyn felt the atmosphere closing in around her. It was as if she were trapped in a spider web she couldn't escape from.

"Give me some time to think," she said, searching for a way to buy time while she came up with a plan.

The agent smiled confidently.

"Take your time, but remember that the clock is ticking against us. The longer you wait, the fewer options you'll have."

Evelyn returned to the room, her mind boiling. Two of her friends were waiting for her, worry painted on their faces.

"What happened?" The first friend asked, his tone urgent.

"They offered me a deal," Evelyn replied, feeling betrayal building in her chest. "They have plans to use our research."

"You can't trust them!" The second friend shouted, his voice echoing in the enclosed space.

"I know," Evelyn replied, her voice barely a whisper. "But I have no other options. They are determined to obtain our technology, and if I don't cooperate, not only will I lose my life, but it could cost you yours as well."

The first friend took a step forward, her gaze intense.

"So what are we going to do? Are they going to force you to work on something that could be devastating?"

"I don't know. I need a plan. I will inform a colleague of mine," Evelyn said, feeling the pressure mounting. She had to act fast.

Suddenly, the sound of footsteps echoed down the hall. The three of them fell silent, aware that they were not alone.

"You have to go," Evelyn whispered. "If you find me here with you, you won't hesitate to end it all."

The two friends exchanged desperate glances.

"We can't leave you here," The second said, concerned in her voice.

"It's the only way," Evelyn insisted, determined. "You must find a way to expose this."

The first nodded, resignation visible on her face.

"Be careful, Evelyn. We don't know who we're dealing with here."

Evelyn felt a lump in her throat as she watched her friends walk away. Each step they took brought her closer to a terrifying reality.

"And you be careful," she said, her voice breaking.

With one last glance, the men disappeared down the hall, leaving Evelyn alone. Darkness seemed to close in around her, and in the back of her mind, she knew she was about to step down a path from which she might not return. Decisions were made in seconds, and the fate of the world was in her hands.

As she turned to face her captors, Evelyn realized her fight had only just begun. Night had fallen, and the real challenge was yet to come.

Chapter 20

The airport was bustling with activity, but for Mark Dawson, every move was calculated. He walked among the travelers with his briefcase held tightly under his arm, his gaze alert but unobtrusive. His work at the CIA had taught him to move in the shadows, always one step ahead. But this time, something was bothering him. He knew the people behind all this weren't amateurs.

He paused briefly to look at the departure screen. His flight was on time, but he couldn't afford any mistakes. He looked around, searching for anything out of the ordinary.

Meanwhile, at James's house, the atmosphere was tense. Emily watched him from across the room, trying to understand what was happening, but fear was beginning to overcome her.

"Do you really think you can hide?" Emily asked, crossing her arms. "You know they're not going to stop."

James rubbed his temples, trying to calm himself.

"I don't know, Emily. But if I make one wrong move, they'll come after us. We have to be smart."

"You can't just stand still forever, James. Mark is risking a lot for us. We can't just wait for it all to blow over."

James stood up and started pacing the room, the weight of the situation falling on him like a slab.

"I know, but I need time. If we go out now without a plan, they'll destroy us. And not just us… think about it, this goes way beyond you and me."

Emily stared at him, her hands shaking slightly.

"So what do you propose? We can't just hide and hope they forget about us."

James paused for a moment, looking at the safe he'd locked just hours ago. He knew the flash drive and the samples were all that remained of his work. And he also knew that made them targets.

"I'm going to do something, but it won't be what they expect," he said finally, his voice firmer.

Emily looked at him skeptically.

"What does that mean?"

"I'm going to contact someone else. Someone who can help us keep this safe while we find a way out."

"More help? Who do you have in mind?"

"I know someone in Europe. A scientist who's been working on something similar. We've kept in touch for years, and if anyone can protect this under the radar, it's him."

Emily frowned, clearly worried.

"Are you sure we can trust him? We've already risked a lot."

"I trust him as much as I trust Mark. And if what I suspect is true, he'll be in danger too. He better know what's going on before it's too late."

Emily nodded slowly, still looking into his eyes.

"Okay. But don't do this alone, James. We've been through too much already. I can't lose you now."

James took Emily's hands, sensing her worry but also her determination.

"I won't." This is bigger than the two of us, but I'm not going to let them destroy us without a fight.

****

At the airport, Mark made his way to the gate, taking one last look around. He sat down in one of the waiting chairs, pulled out his phone, and dialed a number. He knew he'd only have a few minutes before boarding.

"Everything in order?" a voice on the other end of the line asked.

"Yes. I'm boarding in a few minutes." Mark glanced at his watch. "But this isn't over. They know too much."

"Do you have what we need?"

Mark paused, looking at his briefcase.

"I have it. But it won't be easy to keep him safe."

"What about James?"

"He's in a tough spot. I think he has a plan, but this is far from over. Those behind this aren't going to stop just because he goes into hiding." Mark sighed. "He's going to need our help."

"We'll deal with it." Make sure you get there safely. I'll see you on the other side.

Mark hung up and put the phone away. He knew he was entering dangerous territory, but he had no other choice. He stood up when his flight was called and walked towards the gate. As he walked forward, an uneasy feeling washed over him. Someone was watching him.

He didn't turn his head. He had learned that the best way to handle pursuers was to stay calm. He got on the plane, knowing that the next few days would be crucial.

At the airport, Mark made his way to the boarding gate. He took one last look around, aware that he wasn't alone. The fluorescent lights illuminated the place, but they couldn't erase the feeling that someone was watching him. He sat down in one of the waiting chairs, pulled out his phone, and dialed a number. He knew he would only have a few minutes before boarding.

"Everything okay?" a voice on the other end of the line asked.

"Yes. I'm boarding in a few minutes." Mark glanced at his watch. "But this isn't over. They know too much."

"Do you have what we need?"

Mark paused, looking down at his briefcase. Tension built up in his chest. "I have it. But it won't be easy to keep it safe."

"What about James?"

"He's in a tough spot. I think he has a plan, but this is far from over. Those behind this won't stop just because he hides." Mark sighed. "He's going to need our help."

"We'll take care of it. Make sure you get there safely. I'll see you on the other side."

Mark hung up and put the phone away. He knew he was entering dangerous territory, but he had no choice. He stood up when his flight was called and walked toward the gate. As he walked forward, a feeling of unease washed over him. Someone was watching him.

He didn't turn his head. He had learned that the best way to handle pursuers was to stay calm. He boarded the plane, feeling the piercing gaze on his back. He placed his briefcase in the overhead compartment and took a seat, trying not to show his nervousness. He stared out the window as the plane began to roll. The outside world was fading away and with it, the shadows of his past.

As the plane ascended, his mind filled with thoughts of what he was leaving behind. The decisions he had made, the lines he had crossed. The reason he was on this flight had to do with a discovery that could change everything: a report on clandestine experiments at the lab where he worked, research that had led him to the truth behind a secret government project.

Mark had been working on developing new biological materials, but he soon realized there was something more sinister at play. Someone had been using those advances to create biological weapons, and he had found proof of it. But the information hadn't just put him in danger; it was also his colleague, Dr. James, who was more involved than he had admitted.

A chill ran down his spine as he remembered his last conversation with James. The warning about the men in black, the shadows lurking in the halls of the lab. Mark knew time was running out. He had to act fast.

A few minutes later, the pilot announced that they were on their way to their destination. Mark relaxed slightly, but the discomfort lingered. He looked around, searching for distractions. A couple of seats behind him, a woman was watching him. Her gaze was piercing, as if she could read his thoughts. Mark looked away, his instinct telling him something wasn't right.

He decided to open his briefcase, taking out a file with the crucial information he had saved. It was a set of documents and recordings that proved the connection between the lab and the deadly experiments being carried out. He had to make sure these got into the right hands.

As he was looking through the documents, the woman came over, sitting next to him. "Are those classified documents?" she asked in a soft, but firm voice.

Mark was startled, quickly closing the briefcase. "It's nothing that concerns you."

She smiled, but it wasn't a friendly smile. "You and I both know that's not true. You're in a dangerous game, Mark. People are looking for what you have."

"How do you know my name?" Mark frowned.

"There's no time for that. What you have could cost you your life. And not just yours." She looked at him seriously. "You have to be more careful. There's a lot at stake."

"And who are you?" Mark felt increasingly uneasy.

"Someone who wants to help, but I don't have time to explain. You need to get to wherever you're going, but most importantly, don't talk to anyone about what you're carrying. You can't trust anyone." Her tone was serious, almost pleading.

"What are you suggesting?" Mark looked at her, aware that every word was a risk.

"Just follow your instinct. Sometimes, the answer is closer than you imagine." The woman stood up from her seat. "Take care, Mark."

With that, she walked away, disappearing into the crowd of passengers. Mark sat there, feeling a mix of confusion and fear. He knew he had to act quickly. The truth was a powerful weapon, but also a dangerous one. He had to find a way to protect himself and make sure the information got to hand.

****

Back at the house, James had begun to pack his things. He had decided that they couldn't stay any longer. Emily was silently helping him, both aware that every minute they spent in that place brought them closer to being discovered.

"Do you think they'll be watching?" Emily asked, as she put some paperwork into a backpack.

"Probably. But if we move quickly, we could be one step ahead of them."

The sound of a car pulling up outside made them freeze. Emily looked at James with fear written on her face.

"Do you think it is...?"

James walked over to the window, barely pulling the curtain aside toShe glanced over. Her heart began to pound.

"I don't know," she whispered. "But we can't stay here to find out."

Emily nodded and they both hurried to the back of the house. James opened the back door, but before they could get out, a loud knock on the front door stopped them dead in their tracks.

"Police! Open the door!"

Emily turned to look at James with a mix of disbelief and panic.

"What do we do?"

James closed his eyes, trying to think quickly. If it was the police, how did they know they were there? What if it wasn't the police?

"Let's go. Now," he said, grabbing Emily by the hand and pulling her into the backyard.

The sound of the front door being forced open filled the house as they both ran into the darkness of the garden. They knew they only had seconds before they were found.

The two of them ran to the car they had hidden on a side street, out of sight. When they arrived, James climbed behind the wheel, starting the engine as fast as he could. Emily looked out the back window, watching the flashlights begin to illuminate the garden.

"They're following us," Emily said, her voice shaking.

James stepped on the accelerator, speeding away through the dark streets, knowing his options were running out.

Chapter 21

The bookstore was filled with the comforting aroma of freshly brewed coffee and fresh ink from new books. The faint bustle of shoppers turning pages and whispering to each other filled the air, providing a backdrop for what, at first glance, looked like just another conversation between two old friends. But nothing was as it seemed.

Dr. James, sitting on a comfortable leather couch in the reading section, kept a steady hand on a small, discreet-looking briefcase. In front of him sat Mark Dawson, a CIA agent who radiated calm, though his ever-alert eyes scanned every corner of the bookstore. He was a man accustomed to secrets and betrayals, and today, his neutral expression left no room for error.

"Most people think you're on a wild goose chase," Mark commented, glancing sideways at the briefcase he had just received.

James did not respond immediately. He knew what he was about to say implied, and he knew there would be no turning back once the truth was out.

"It's real, Mark. You just have to look at the data," James replied, his voice low but firm.

Mark closed the briefcase, securing it on his lap as if it were a delicate artifact, his face impassive.

"I'm doing this as a favor to an old friend, but I'm not promising anything," the agent warned, his tone making it clear he was treading into dangerous waters.

James nodded, knowing that was the most he could ask of him. Anything else would depend on what Mark found when he went through the files.

"That's all I ask."

Mark took another quick look around, unable to shake the feeling that something wasn't right. The tension in the air was palpable, and though the bookstore was still a quiet space, he knew that at any moment they could be under someone else's scrutiny.

"If all this is true, Rich, you could have prevented a catastrophe of global proportions," Mark said quietly, not taking his eyes off the door.

"And if it's not enough?" James asked, clearly exhausted by the weeks of uncertainty.

"I need to know who else is aware of this," Mark insisted, his tone hardening.

James hesitated for a moment, evaluating whether he should reveal more than necessary. In the end, he realized he had no other choice.

"Aside from us, there's Dr. Reinhardt… and Emily," he admitted, his voice dropping even lower.

Mark frowned, clearly surprised.

"Your ex-wife? Really?" he asked, incredulous.

James sighed, knowing what his old friend was thinking.

"I had no one else to turn to. No one in the lab would listen to me, and she helped me contact Reinhardt. It was the safest thing I could do at the time."

Mark rubbed his chin, clearly uncomfortable with the idea.

"No one else can find out about this, got it? No one."

Before James could respond, a familiar figure appeared in his field of vision. Emily, with her purposeful gait, approached from the other side of the store. James immediately stood up, surprised by her presence.

"Emily, what are you doing here?" he asked, trying to remain calm.

She glanced briefly at Mark, then turned her attention to James.

"I tried calling you, but you weren't answering." She turned to Mark with a firm expression. "You must be the famous Mark that Rich told me so much about."

"Mark Dawson," he replied, shaking Emily's hand, though his smile was barely perceptible, more a formality than a show of confidence.

They studied each other briefly, each trying to read the other in that short exchange.

"Is everything okay here?" Emily asked, crossing her arms.

James nodded, trying to appear nonchalant.

"It's all good, Emily. Don't worry, I'll call you when I'm done here."

But Emily didn't seem willing to wait.

"I have some news," he said quickly. "I've arranged a meeting with a representative from BioCore for Wednesday at three in the afternoon."

James frowned, confused by the unexpected turn of events. Mark, for his part, tensed at the name.

"BioCore? The military contractor?" Mark asked, with a mix of disbelief and alarm.

Emily nodded.

"Yes, I have a colleague who heard rumors about your research, Rich. They're interested in hearing what you have to say. They can help us."

Mark looked at her suspiciously.

"And how do you know them?"

Emily looked at him in surprise, not expecting an interrogation. She turned to James, looking for backup.

"I told you, he's a colleague of mine. Nothing more."

"What kind of work are you in, Emily?" "Mark asked, now in the tone of someone making a very serious assessment.

Emily frowned at him, feeling cornered.

"This is starting to feel like an interrogation, Mark," she replied coldly.

James, sensing the tension, stepped in.

"Emily is a consultant in the technology field. She has contacts."

"In several industries," he explained.

"Exactly," Emily added, regaining her composure. "BioCore has resources and connections that could be useful in exposing what you've discovered, Rich."

Mark shook his head, clearly disagreeing.

"I wouldn't recommend it. BioCore is too involved with the military. If what you have is as dangerous as you say, they're not going to help you expose it. They'll want to control it," he warned, his tone grim.

James was caught between the two, hesitating. He looked at Emily, who was watching him expectantly, and then at Mark, who shook his head slightly, warningly.

Finally, Mark stood up.

"I'm going to review all this information. I'll get back to you later, Rich. But be careful. This is far from over," he said, with one last glance at both of them before exiting the bookstore.

Emily fell silent, watching as Mark disappeared into the crowd of customers. She then turned to James, her face serious.

"I should be going too. Talk to you later?" she asked, her tone softening.

James nodded. Emily placed a hand on his shoulder, letting go of the contact for a moment before pulling back. James watched her walk away, his mind filled with doubt.

The weight of what had begun to reveal itself was plunging them all into a plot more dangerous than any of them could have anticipated.

James stood still for a moment, staring at the door where Emily had just exited. He felt like the world around him was closing in more and more, compressing him with each new turn. He was now not only worried about the information he had given Mark, but also the implications of BioCore's intervention. Was he making the right decisions? Could he fully trust Emily?

His thoughts overwhelmed him as he stared at the clock on the wall of the bookstore. Time was ticking, and the pieces of the puzzle didn't seem to fit together as he expected. Suddenly, reality hit him hard: there were now too many players involved. Too many hands on the board. Each with their own interests and, worse yet, their own agendas.

The soft sound of a notification on his phone interrupted his reverie. He pulled it out of his pocket quickly, expecting it to be Mark, but instead it was an encrypted message from Dr. Reinhardt. James' pulse quickened as he unlocked the message.

"Urgent. We've been tracked. Abandon the plan and disappear. Details encrypted in the attachment."

James felt cold sweat begin to form on his forehead. He read the message over and over again, hoping he had misinterpreted something. But the meaning was clear. They were in danger. They had been found.

He quickly put his phone away and stood up from the couch. His eyes scanned the bookstore for any sign of threat. Everything seemed normal, but now, every anonymous face could be a latent danger. He grabbed his coat and hurried out of the bookstore, avoiding eye contact with others.

The cool evening air hit his face as he walked through the city streets, feeling like every second was another step into the unknown. His mind went over the options, the moves he had to make. He couldn't stay in the city any longer. He needed an escape plan, and he needed it now.

As he quickened his pace, he pulled out his phone again, dialing Emily's number.

"Emily, it's me. We need to talk," he said quickly when she answered. "Something's happened. We can't wait for that meeting with BioCore. They've tracked us."

There was a brief pause on the other end of the line, and then Emily's voice came through, low and strained.

"What? How do you know?"

"Reinhardt sent me a message. He's in danger. They tracked us, Emily. I don't know how, but they did."

James could hear Emily's breathing quicken.

"What do we do?" she asked, clearly frightened.

James paused, weighing his options. Could he trust her? Up until now, Emily had been his ally, but Mark's words kept echoing in his mind. "I wouldn't recommend it," he'd said about BioCore. Was Emily being naive, or was there something else behind her contacts?

Finally, he made a decision.

"Meet me in the hotel's underground parking lot in an hour. We'll grab everything we can and leave right away."

"Okay. I'll be there."

James hung up and put the phone back away. He stopped at a corner, watching the traffic in front of him. He had to move fast, but he couldn't afford to make any more mistakes. He decided to call Mark.

"Mark, it's me," he said as soon as the agent answered. "They've tracked Reinhardt. We're in danger. I need to know if you've found anything in the data."

The silence on the other end of the line was brief, but it seemed like an eternity.

"I'm still going through everything," Mark finally answered, his voice steady. "But if they've tracked you, this is more serious than I thought. Do you have a plan?"

"We're leaving town in an hour. There's no time for a meeting with BioCore."

Mark took a deep breath, and James could picture the agent analyzing the situation instantly.

"I'll meet you at the hotel." Don't do anything stupid, Rich. And don't trust anyone too much," he added in a tone that could only be interpreted as a warning.

James nodded, though Mark couldn't see him.

"See you soon."

He hung up the phone and continued walking with quick steps, though more carefully now. Every face in the crowd seemed to be hiding something, every car stopped at the traffic light seemed suspicious to him. He knew that once they entered the game of disappearing, there would be no turning back.

****

An hour later, James arrived at the hotel's underground parking lot, his heart pounding in his chest. He parked the car in a dark corner and turned off the engine. He looked around, expecting to see Emily arrive. Anxiety was eating away at him, and he wondered if Mark was already on his way, too.

Suddenly, a car pulled into the parking lot. It was Emily. She pulled up next to her vehicle and quickly got out, her expression reflecting the same mix of fear and determination that James felt.

"Do you have everything?" "She asked, as James got out of his car.

"The essentials," he replied, opening the trunk and showing her a small suitcase. "We can't take much if we have a lot of things."
We want to disappear quickly.

Emily nodded, but before they could continue, the sound of another car pulling into the parking lot echoed in the darkness. James tensed at the sight of the car's lights, wondering if it was Mark or if his time was up.

The car stopped near them and Mark got out, his face as serious as ever. He didn't say anything at first, just looked at the two of them before approaching.

"We have to go now," he finally said, not wasting time on greetings. "They're closer than you think."

James exchanged a glance with Emily, but they both knew there was no turning back now. The three of them climbed into Mark's car and sped away from the hotel, not looking back.

As they drove out of the city, Dr. James felt the weight of the decisions they had made. All that was left now was the hope that the truth, however dangerous, could be their salvation. But in a world full of betrayal and secrets, he knew that hope was anything but safe.

Chapter 22

Emily walked out of the bookstore, the sun shining on her face. She adjusted her sunglasses and took a deep breath, trying to stay calm. There was an eerie feeling in the air, like someone was watching. She paused for a moment on the sidewalk, her gaze sweeping the street. Everything seemed normal, but she had learned that normal was just a facade.

Her heart pounded as she walked forward, feeling more and more exposed. She wasn't alone in this; Rich and Mark were aware of the situation, but that didn't ease her anxiety. There was the dark sedan parked across the street, which she had noticed as she left. Now, as she glanced at it out of the corner of her eye, the car's engine started and it began to move slowly, following her.

"No," she muttered to herself, quickening her pace.

As she walked away from the bookstore, her mind filled with doubt. Why was she being followed? Was it just paranoia or was there something more? She looked back and saw that the sedan was getting closer, its driver seemed impassive, but the way he was following her made her nervous.

Emily walked to her car, a small blue hatchback, and opened it quickly. She got inside and slammed the door shut, trying to calm her breathing. Her hands shook slightly as she searched for her keys. Was it safe to start the engine? Could it be a trap?

The dark sedan turned the corner and stopped at a safe distance, as if its driver was waiting. Emily felt a chill run down her spine. She knew she had to act quickly.

With a determined move, she started the engine and pulled out of the parking lot. She looked in the rearview mirror and noticed that the sedan was still there, keeping the same distance. Her mind was racing, looking for solutions. She couldn't alert Rich or Mark of what was happening. If they were really following her, any contact could put them in danger.

"Think, Emily, think," she said quietly to herself, her mind wandering through options.

As she turned the next corner, she decided the best option was to head to the small café where they usually met. It was a place they knew, a haven where they could talk without worry. But what if the sedan followed them there, too?

She made a risky decision. Instead of following her usual route, she turned down a side street, looking to lose her pursuer. She entered a residential neighborhood, and as she moved between the houses, she felt increasingly nervous. Adrenaline kept her on her toes.

"Come on, please don't follow me," she muttered as she drove into an alley. At the end of the alley, she turned right and stopped in an empty spot, trying to look nonchalant.

The dark sedan passed her by and continued down the street, not stopping. Emily felt momentary relief, but her heart hadn't calmed down yet. She pulled out her phone and sent a quick text to Rich: "I'm still being followed. I need to see you now."

She waited a few moments, looking around warily. Seeing that the sedan didn't return, she decided to come out of hiding. When she saw that there were no cars in the rearview mirror, she turned around and headed to the cafe.

****

The cafe was relatively quiet. The aroma of fresh coffee and the murmur of conversation greeted her, and Emily felt a little more relaxed. However, she knew she couldn't let her guard down. She sat down at a table in the back, facing the door, and pulled out her laptop.

She began looking up information about BioCore as she waited for Rich. Her mind couldn't stop thinking about the dark sedan and what it meant. The connections she had with BioCore could be dangerous, but the thought of losing the chance to talk to them made her uneasy.

Rich arrived shortly after, his face serious. He walked over to her, looking around before sitting down.

"What's going on?" he asked, his voice low.

Emily frowned, feeling like everything was rushing in.

"I was being followed. The dark sedan. I saw it right after I left the bookstore."

Rich leaned forward, worried.

"Are you sure?"

"Yeah. I keep thinking about what Mark said about not trusting anyone, but I can't pass up this opportunity with BioCore. Maybe they can help us expose what we've discovered."

Rich ran a hand through his hair, his expression reflecting tension.

"Do you realize how risky this is? If BioCore has connections to whoever is behind this, we could be in serious trouble."

Emily crossed her arms, determined.

"I know it's risky, but I have no choice. I don't want to be the only one left out of this. Besides, I have a colleague there, someone I trust."

Rich sighed, clearly conflicted.

"Okay, but first we need to make sure we're safe. We need to talk to Mark."

Emily nodded, feeling her heart sink a little. She couldn't let her fear get the better of her. This was a crucial moment.

"Okay, okay, but first we need to make sure we're safe. We need to talk to Mark."

Fine, but first, we need a plan. We can't be surprised.

As they argued, the atmosphere of the café changed. A familiar figure walked through the door. It was Mark, his expression tense and determined. He quickly approached their table.

"Everything okay?" he asked, looking at both of them with concern.

"No, not really," Rich replied. Emily was followed.

Mark leaned in, his voice low but firm.

"This is getting complicated. We need to act fast. BioCore is not a safe option. If they have even the slightest suspicion that you are involved, they will face serious problems."

Emily felt her stomach turn. She knew Mark was right, but she couldn't let the opportunity to get close to BioCore slip away.

"We can't let them get away," he said, his voice full of determination. "I need to talk to them."

Mark looked at Rich, who was clearly frustrated.

"Okay, but we need to be careful. We don't know how far their influence reaches." And if they're looking for information, they might have someone on the inside.

Rich looked at Emily.

"How do you plan to approach them?"

"My colleague at BioCore, his name is Adam. He's a good guy, he can help us. I just have to be careful not to raise suspicions."

Mark crossed his arms, assessing the situation.

"What if he's not trustworthy? We can't risk getting caught."

Emily felt time running out. Every moment that passed brought them closer to being caught.

"I understand, but this might be our only chance. I just need a meeting, I don't have to reveal everything we know right away. I just want to hear what they have to say."

Rich looked at Mark, who nodded slowly.

"Okay. If you decide to do this, you'll need protection. I don't want you to expose yourself to more danger than you already are."

Emily felt a knot in her stomach. She knew they were in dangerous waters, but she couldn't pass up the opportunity to find answers.

"Okay." I'll meet him.

Mark leaned towards her, his eyes serious.

Don't risk it. Keep your contacts secret. If the situation gets tense, back off.

Emily nodded, knowing the risk was high, but the desire to do justice kept her going.

I will, trust me.

After a tense exchange, the group dispersed, each returning to their role in this intricate web of secrets and danger. Emily knew the game was just beginning and every move could be her last. The fight for the truth was pushing her beyond her limits, but she was determined to keep going.

Emily walked out of the cafe, feeling the pressure of the air on her chest. She looked out at the street, keeping her mind clear. She couldn't let fear take over. Her mind was on the next move.

As she drove away, the dark sedan appeared again, this time parked closer. The driver watched her. Without missing a beat, Emily hurried into her car, her heart pounding.

She glanced in the rearview mirror. The sedan continued to move, its engine roaring as loudly as before. Emily knew she couldn't stay there. She started the engine and took off, looking for a path that would take her away from surveillance.

Chapter 23

Dr. James walked through the front door, the dim light of the living room illuminating the shadows dancing on the walls. He dropped his keys on the table and took off his coat. Everything seemed calm, but that quietness made him uneasy.

As he walked into the kitchen, he noticed a slightly ajar drawer and a half-open window. He froze, his breath catching in his throat. Something wasn't right.

He pulled out his phone, ready to dial, when a cracking sound from another room made his head spin. His heart raced, a rush of adrenaline coursing through his veins.

"Is anyone there?" he called, trying to keep his voice steady.

A shadow moved quickly at the end of the hallway. A crash was heard from a room beyond. Dr. James didn't wait any longer; he dialed 9-1-1 as a car engine roared outside, followed by the screeching of tires.

OPERATOR (VOICEOVER)
9-1-1, what is your emergency?

"Someone is in my house," Dr. James replied, his voice shaking. "I need help."

The hotel room was modest, shadows lengthening under the dim light of the desk lamp. Mark sat, absorbed in Dr. James' research. On his laptop screen, graphs and molecular models glowed. He took the USB drive, inserted it into his computer, and a file titled "PROJECT H20 CONTROL" opened.

Mark's face tightened as he scanned the information. Hydrogen disruption technology. Strategic Targets for Water-Based Manipulation. Each word seemed more alarming than the last.

But before he could dig any deeper, all the lights in the room went out, plunging him into darkness. Instinctively, Mark grabbed his phone, turned on the flashlight, and tension washed over his face. Something was very wrong.

From the hallway, a faint humming sound echoed. Cautiously, he moved toward the door, placing his ear against it. He could hear footsteps, a distinct sound that chilled him.

Quickly, he grabbed his gun from the drawer of the nightstand, his eyes scanning the dark room for an exit.

A knock on the door.

Mark didn't answer.

He moved to the window, peering through the blinds, his mind racing. He had to get out of there, but the only way out was through the door, and he knew he was getting close to danger.

****

Dr. James waited for the operator's response. The sound of footsteps echoed closer.

"Are you sure you're in danger?" the operator asked, her calm voice contrasting with the growing tension.

"Yes, I heard noises in my house. I think someone's inside," she replied, panic beginning to creep into her voice.

"Stay calm, we're sending someone." The voice on the phone became more urgent. "Can you get out of your house?"

Dr. James looked down the hallway, his mind racing. He needed to get out, but what if the intruder was blocking the door? In that instant, the sound of breaking glass filled the air, followed by a deep voice.

Unfamiliar voice
"Rich, I know you're here."

Dr. James froze. That voice... who was it?

"Who are you?" —he asked, his voice firmer than he felt.

Unfamiliar Voice
It doesn't matter who I am. It matters what you know.

As the voice came closer, Dr. James knew he had to act. He followed the escape route he had planned, carrying his phone in hand, waiting for a moment to run out.

****

The dark sedan was parked just outside the hotel. Two men, austere looking and well dressed, stood near the vehicle, staring at the building. One of them, wearing a wide-brimmed cap, was checking a wristwatch, his impassive expression revealing his impatience.

"How much longer are we going to wait?" the other asked, his tone a tense whisper.

"The contact should have gone out by now. We can't afford for this to get complicated." The man in the cap glanced sideways, making sure no one was paying attention.

***

The knocks on the door became deafening. Mark felt fear take over him, but his determination was stronger. He took a deep breath, aware that he couldn't let them catch him.

With shaking hands, he made his way to the window and carefully opened it, making sure it didn't make a sound.

Without wasting a second, Mark jumped towards the fire escape. He landed hard, the cold metal under his feet reminding him of the urgency of his situation. Hearing the door open behind him, his survival instincts kicked in and he began to quickly descend the stairs.

His breathing became heavy, heart pounding, and sweat was pouring down his forehead. Adrenaline pulsed through his veins as he wondered if they had seen him.

Mark landed in the dark alley behind the hotel. He paused for a moment, seeking shelter, and looked around, making sure no one was around. The street was deserted, and a cold wind made his skin crawl. He moved quickly towards the alley exit, aware that the danger had not yet passed.

As he turned the corner onto the main street, his mind raced. Who were these people? What did they want from him? Questions raced through his mind as he cautiously moved forward.

The street was lit by flickering street lights. Mark felt exposed, but knew he couldn't stay there. He needed a plan. He stepped into the darkness of a closed shop, looking for a place where he could think.

The air was thick with dust and the smell of old wood. Mark peered out the window, hoping the figures in the hotel wouldn't follow him. Moments passed that seemed like hours, and the silence was deafening.

His phone vibrated in his pocket. Cautiously, he pulled it out and saw it was a text from Rich.

RICH: "Where are you? I'm worried."

Mark typed quickly.

MARK: "Leaving hotel. Forces unknown. Catching up."

He made sure the shop remained quiet and prepared to leave.

Mark walked out of the store and into the night, determined to find Rich. Yet every shadow seemed to threaten him, every noise a reminder of impending danger.

As he turned the corner, he saw a dark sedan parked. The same sense of danger washed over him again. He kept his distance, moving in the opposite direction.

****

At Rich's house, the atmosphere was tense. Rich looked at his watch, uneasy. He had contacted Mark, but time was passing and he had heard nothing from him. He decided he couldn't wait any longer.

"If Mark doesn't show up soon, I'll have to go out and look for him," he muttered to himself.

Meanwhile, Mark was moving quickly. His thoughts were focused on how he had gotten into this situation. The research, the discovery of BioCore... it all felt like a whirlwind. Suddenly, he heard a noise behind him and stopped dead in his tracks.

Footsteps were approaching quickly, and his heart raced. He couldn't allow himself to be caught again.

Without looking back, he began to run. Sweat was pouring down his forehead, but fear was driving him on. To his left, an entrance to a building beckoned to him. He slipped inside just as figures emerged from the darkness.

The interior was dim, covered in rubble. Mark hid behind a wall, trying to calm his breathing. From his hiding spot, he watched the shadows pass by. They were three men, all in dark suits. The tension in the air was palpable.

"There's no sign of him here." One of them muttered, looking around.

'He's probably gone into the neighborhood. We need to find him before he talks to anyone. The leader gestured, indicating that they should move away.

Mark felt a pang of fear. He couldn't let them find him, but he knew he couldn't stay there for long. He listened to their conversation, looking for any clue that could help him.

'Dr. Reinhardt must know more about the project. If we can get her to collaborate, this could be resolved quickly. —The leader crossed his arms, showing confidence.

Rich decided he had to act. He couldn't wait any longer. He pulled out his phone and called Mark.

'Where are you, buddy? —he asked, concern evident in his voice.

'I'm... in a tough spot.

Chapter 24

Mark turned the corner, his heart still pounding. He looked back, searching for any sign of the men chasing him. Body tense, he raised his hand and a taxi passed just in time.

"Taxi!" he shouted, voice shaking a little from adrenaline.

The taxi stopped, and Mark yanked open the door, quickly getting into the backseat. He glanced out the window just as the dark sedan pulled out of the hotel parking lot, his breath quickening again.

"Where to, buddy?" the taxi driver asked, looking in the rearview mirror.

"Anyone that's as far away from here as possible," Mark replied, trying to remain calm.

The taxi driver nodded and put his foot on the accelerator. Mark slumped back in the seat, trying to catch his breath. He pulled the USB drive out of his pocket, held it tightly, and closed his eyes, allowing himself a moment of relaxation after having escaped such a dangerous situation.

This is just the beginning.

The taxi zigzagged through the streets, and Mark peered out the window, watching the city speed by. The bright lights and sounds of the night seemed a world away compared to the chaos he had left behind.

"Are you okay?" the taxi driver asked, noticing his passenger's tense expression.

"Yeah, just… a long day," Mark murmured, his face still pale.

The taxi driver nodded, but Mark could see him looking at him sideways, as if he was evaluating whether or not he should be worried. To Mark, that look was uncomfortable, so he decided to divert his attention.

"How's the night going?" he asked, forcing a smile.

"Same as always. People going out, some fun. But there are also those who don't know when to stop," the taxi driver replied, shrugging.

Mark felt the taxi driver's words resonate with him. There were too many entanglements in his life now, and the line between right and wrong had become blurred.

"You know," the taxi driver continued, "I've had my rough days. Sometimes, it seems like things just come together. But there's always a way, right?"

Mark looked at him, surprised by the depth of his words.

"Yeah, there's always a way. You just have to find it."

The taxi driver smiled, and Mark felt the atmosphere in the taxi relax a little. However, the tension inside him didn't go away.

The cab stopped in front of a dimly lit bar. Mark looked around, making sure there was no danger in sight.

"It's okay here," he said, pulling out some bills and handing them to the cab driver.

"Be careful, buddy. The world can be a tricky place."

Mark nodded, feeling a mix of gratitude and sadness. He got out of the cab and watched it drive away, taking a part of his fear with it.

****

The bar was small and cozy, with a relaxing atmosphere. Music played softly, and a few patrons were engrossed in conversation. Mark sat at the bar, ordering a drink to calm his nerves.

"What can I get you?" asked the bartender

"A whiskey, please," Mark replied, feeling safer in that environment.

As he waited for his drink, he pulled the USB drive out of his pocket and looked at it. He knew it contained crucial information, but it also put him in danger.

"You new around here?" the bartender asked, placing the glass in front of Mark.

"Something like that. Just… needing some fresh air."

Mark took a sip of his whiskey, enjoying the warmth it gave him. As he did, his mind wandered back to the men at the hotel. What did they want from him? He felt caught up in a game bigger than himself.

"Sometimes a drink is just what you need. But be careful. Things can get intense quickly." The bartender added.

Mark looked at the bartender, nodding slowly. The night was a reflection of his life, full of surprises and unexpected twists.

"I know. I'm in the middle of a… problem."

"Problems, huh." The bartender frowned. "We all have those days. But remember, there are always people willing to help."

Mark sighed, feeling the man's words resonate within him. Perhaps there was more at stake than he could handle alone.

'Thanks. Sometimes it's good to talk to someone'. Mark appreciated.

'That's the key. People aren't always as alone as they think.' The bartender asserted.

Mark finished his drink, feeling a little lighter. He needed to act soon, and knowing there were people who cared was a relief.

As Mark pondered, a group of men entered the bar. Instantly, his instinct told him they weren't the type to be easily intimidated. They settled in at a table in the corner of the bar.

Chapter 25

Dr. James sat on his couch, leaning forward, lost in thought. The dim light from the lamp illuminated his face, revealing the worry that kept him restless. Across from him, Emily showed signs of tension; her hands moved nervously in her lap, as if she wanted to release the energy that weighed her down.

"You're pushing so hard for this BioCore meeting. You've made me wonder why it's so important," Dr. James said, his deep voice echoing in the room.

Emily looked up, searching for the right words. Her eyes darted between the floor and his face, as if that way she could find the courage she was lacking.

"I need you to do this," she finally answered, her voice weak.

"Why? Why is this so important to you?" "He insisted, with a mix of curiosity and concern.

"Because..." The word caught in her throat. She paused, hesitating before continuing. "Because it's not just about you! It's about me, too."

She stood up from her seat, pacing back and forth nervously, trying to find stability. Dr. James, sensing her distress, approached slowly, concern etched on his face.

"Talk to me, Emily. Are you overstepping your bounds or something?" he asked, his tone gentle.

"No. Nothing like that." She took a deep breath, searching for a way to convey what she felt. "BioCore promised me a job… a permanent one if I could get you to meet with them."

The words fell like a weight on Dr. James. He froze, processing what he had just heard.

"But you already have a job," he replied, surprised.

"Yes. I work on a contract basis as a consultant." And let's be honest, Rich, we all want something permanent.

"You could have said that from the beginning," he said, frowning.

"You're right, and I'm sorry. But I don't want to seem desperate. I need something solid, something real. And BioCore said if I could have you in the room with them, they'd give it to me. No more jumping from job to job."

Dr. James watched her, the weight of her confession weighing on him. Emily's gaze, full of hope and fear, disarmed him.

"I hate to put you in this position, but I really want this. And I thought, after everything we've been through, maybe…"

She paused, her voice cracking a little, vulnerability creeping into her tone.

"Maybe you'd help me. Like I helped you with Reinhardt."

"So, you're using me?" he asked, feeling caught between disbelief and affection.

"No!" "I really think they can help you, and yes, it's important to me too," he explained, resting his hand on her shoulder. His soft smile was meant to calm the storm raging between them. "You know how hard I've worked just to stay afloat. And I didn't want to ask this, I really didn't, but I'm asking you now. Please. For me."

Dr. James looked at her, feeling conflicted. The woman in front of him had been a crucial part of his life, someone who had held him up when he was at his lowest.

"I know it's risky. But we're already in deep, and you said yourself that we can't turn back. At least if you go, you can hear what they want. You might even learn something," Emily said, determination shining in her eyes.

"But…" he tried to object.

"I know. You're afraid they might be involved in some way because of their job. Believe me… they're not, or I wouldn't want to work there."

Dr. James sighed, running a hand over his face. He turned around, staring out the window. The city glittered in the distance, but the darkness in his mind wouldn't dissipate.

Emily watched him, her anxiety mixing with hope. Finally, he turned to her, the decision taking shape within him.

"Okay. I'll do it."

Emily's shoulders instantly relaxed, and a flash of relief crossed her face.

"Thank you," she murmured, emotion in her voice.

"I'll go to the meeting, but I don't promise anything more than that," he warned, feeling his words carry more weight than intended.

"That's all I ask."

"You were always good at convincing me to do things," Dr. James said, his smile half-hearted.

Emily laughed softly, the tension that had dominated the room beginning to dissipate. However, deep in his mind, James couldn't help but wonder what kind of dangers he might face by joining BioCore.

"Trust me, Rich. What you're doing is important, more than you can imagine," Emily said, her gaze fixed on him.

"I've always been wary of big corporations. Especially in this field," he replied, his voice gravelly.

"Me too, but this is an opportunity. Sometimes, we must take risks to get what we want."

"The risk isn't just mine, Emily. It's yours too," he replied, reminding her of the gravity of the situation.

Emily paused, her determination
She grew stronger.

"I'm willing to take it on. If I don't, I'll always be stuck in this cycle."

Dr. James looked at her, the weight of his decision beginning to press down on his chest.

"When's the meeting?" he asked at last.

"Tomorrow at three. At BioCore headquarters," she replied, her voice filled with anticipation.

James nodded, knowing that time was running out.

"Okay. We'll do this."

They stared at each other intently, an unspoken understanding forming between them. It was a leap of faith, a step into the unknown.

****

The sun was shining brightly as James and Emily approached the imposing structure of the BioCore lab. The modern architecture, cold and calculated, looked intimidating, like a monster awaiting their arrival.

"Remember, just listen to them and keep an open mind," Emily advised, her eyes shining with nervousness.

"I'll try," he replied, feeling the knot in his stomach grow.

As they entered, an atmosphere of frenetic activity enveloped them. Scientists and employees bustled about, immersed in their work. Advanced technology surrounded them, every corner of the lab reflecting innovation and promise of the future.

***

The sun was shining brightly as James and Emily approached the imposing structure of the BioCore lab. The cold, calculated, modern architecture looked intimidating, like a monster waiting for their arrival.

"Remember, just listen to them and keep an open mind," Emily advised, her eyes shining with nervousness.

"I'll try," James replied, feeling the knot in his stomach grow. Emily's words echoed in his head. It was the first time he had entered such a place, and the mix of excitement and fear overwhelmed him.

As they entered, an atmosphere of frenetic activity enveloped them. Scientists and employees bustled about, immersed in their work. Advanced technology surrounded them, and every corner of the lab reflected innovation and promises of the future. But beneath that shiny surface, James couldn't help but feel that there was something else, something hidden in the shadows.

"Are you sure this is what you want to do?" Emily asked, breaking his reverie. Their eyes met, and for a moment, concern was evident.

"It's my chance, Emily. I've been waiting for this for years," James replied, trying to instill confidence in his voice. But as he spoke, a part of him hesitated.

"Just be careful. You know there are rumors about BioCore," she said, her voice barely a whisper.

"Rumors. They're nothing more than that." James shrugged. "Science advances, and this is the place to be."

As they moved forward, they stopped in front of a conference room. A glass door swung open and a group of scientists stepped out, arguing heatedly. James felt a chill run down his spine as he noticed their tense faces.

"Did you know Dr. Mason is in charge of this project?" Emily asked, her voice filled with wonder.

"Yes, but that shouldn't be a problem," James said. "He's one of the best in the field."

"I know, but he's also known for his unorthodox methods. There are those who say he has no limits." Emily looked around, as if expecting someone to be listening.

James frowned, feeling frustrated by Emily's warning. "It's just rumors. Come, we need to register."

As they entered the room, they were met by a group of scientists. Dr. Mason, a middle-aged man with an authoritative air, stood at the front.

"Welcome! I'm delighted to have you here," he said, a smile that didn't reach his eyes. "What you're about to see will change the world."

"Really?" James muttered, though doubt still loomed in his mind.

"Today, we'll witness the latest advancements in nanotechnology and biomedicine. We're on the cusp of something incredible," Mason continued, as a screen lit up behind him.

The lights dimmed, and the presentation began. Images of cells and nanostructures filled the screen. James felt fascinated, but also uneasy. As Mason explained the benefits, a group of scientists at the back of the room murmured among themselves, exchanging worried glances.

"What do you think they're saying?" Emily asked, discreetly pointing toward them.

"I don't know," James replied, turning his head to hear better. "They seem to disagree about something."

As Mason talked about the achievements, a graph showed promising results. "With this technology, we will be able to cure previously incurable diseases, improve the quality of life, even prolong life itself," Mason said, his enthusiasm brimming over.

"It sounds too good to be true," Emily commented quietly.

James nodded, but curiosity kept him glued to the screen. Suddenly, a flash of information caught his eye: a project labeled "Aegis Code." His skin crawled at the term, a reference he had heard in his previous research associated with conspiracy theories about secret experiments.

Suddenly, a crash interrupted the presentation. The door to the room slammed open, and a nervous-looking man rushed in. "Dr. Mason! We need to talk, now," he said, almost out of breath.

Mason frowned. "What is it, Anderson?"

"There is a problem with security in the lab. Someone has been accessing restricted data," the man replied, his face pale.

James and Emily exchanged glances. The atmosphere in the room instantly changed, tense. Mason dismissed the audience with a wave, and most of the scientists began to file out, leaving James and Emily feeling uneasy.

"Do you realize what this means?" Emily said, her voice shaking. "You are not alone here. Something is not right."

"Maybe it is just a mistake. We have no proof of anything," James replied, but doubt was beginning to creep into his mind.

a. As they reached the door, James felt cold sweat running down his forehead. They barely managed to close the door behind them before the sound of footsteps echoed again.

"We don't have much time," James said, looking back. "Come on."

They ran down the halls, their hearts pounding. They knew they couldn't be discovered. Adrenaline gave them strength as they searched for a way out.

"There! The emergency exit!" Emily shouted, pointing towards a lit door at the end of the hall.

With each step, the feeling of danger grew. The door was only a few feet away, and the echo of their footsteps grew more and more deafening.

Finally, they reached the door and pushed it open hard. Cool air hit their faces as they stepped outside. Sunlight enveloped them, and for a moment, everything seemed fine.

"We did it," James exclaimed, taking a deep breath.

"But what do we do now?" Emily asked, her eyes filled with concern.

James looked out at the horizon, knowing this was just the beginning. "First, we must analyze what we have. Then, alert those who can help us. We can't let what we've discovered stay here."

As they walked away from the lab, a new determination took hold of them. The fight was just beginning, and they knew they would have to face forces they couldn't imagine. But together, they were ready to uncover the truth hidden within the bowels of BioCore.

Chapter 26

James and Emily were greeted by a group of BioCore executives. The tension in the room was palpable, every glance wary and every smile too wide.

"Welcome, Dr. James, Emily. We're excited to have you here," one of the executives said, his tone almost rehearsed.

James studied the executives. Their smiles were wide, but there was something in their eyes that made him hesitate. A spark of distrust lit up inside her.

"We've heard a lot about your work, Dr. James. We believe that together we can do something really great," the executive continued, his voice filled with enthusiasm.

"I hope so. But first, I'd like to understand more about your intentions," James replied, his gaze fixed on them.

"Of course. What we do here at BioCore is revolutionary. We work on nanomaterials that could change the world," another executive explained, gesturing enthusiastically.

The conversation intensified, each word weighing more than the last. Emily watched anxiously, feeling the atmosphere becoming more and more tense.

"What we're proposing is a collaboration. We believe that your experience can be key to taking this to the next level," the first one said, with an air of confidence.

"And what about the ethics behind this? Science can be dangerous if not handled properly," Dr. James interrupted, his voice firm.

Silence fell over the room. The executives exchanged nervous glances.

"We understand your concerns, but we have taken all necessary precautions," one of them replied, but his tone lacked the assurance he intended to convey.

James was not convinced. Something inside him told him there was more than they were revealing.

"Maybe we could see some results before making a decision," Emily suggested, trying to keep the dialogue in a constructive direction.

"Of course. We will show you some of our progress," the second executive promised, although

his tone was less certain.

As the meeting progressed, James felt increasingly uneasy. An inner voice warned him that danger might be closer than he imagined. The tension in the air was almost tangible, and Dr. James knew he had to be careful.

"I am willing to listen, but I need assurances. The safety of my job and of everyone involved is paramount," he declared, feeling that each word carried weight.

The executives nodded, but skepticism was still palpable.

"We are committed to working with the best. And you are one of them," the chief executive said, but his eyes did not reflect the sincerity his words intended to convey.

****

As they continued the presentation, James watched as the lab vibrated with energy, but at the same time, a shadow of doubt followed him. The atmosphere was charged with ambition and secrets. What was hidden behind the walls of that place?

Emily, at his side, remained firm, her eyes fixed on the executives. She believed in the possibility that this opportunity could be a change in their lives, but every time Dr. James looked at her, he saw the shadow of his doubts reflected in her.

"This is not just about science," James intervened. "It is about ethics, about the consequences of our actions. And we must be responsible."

"We understand that, Dr. James." We are committed to maintaining our standards," the second executive said, trying to calm his concerns.

Deep in his heart, however, James knew that in the world of science, ethics were often overlooked in the name of progress.

Chapter 27

The sleek, modern glass building stood majestically in the center of the city. The sun shone brightly, reflecting off the glass and creating dazzling sparkles. A large sign on top, bearing the word "BioCore," gave the place an air of grandeur, as if promising a radiant future.

The room was a model of modernity, decorated with chrome and glass. Dr. James sat at a long glass conference table, feeling a little nervous. Beside him, Emily kept her hands carefully folded on the table, her expression professional and unfazed.

Mr. Hartman, a corporate representative in his fifties, dressed in a smart suit, stood before them. His smile was wide, but his eyes showed no sincerity. Flanked by two other BioCore executives, their gazes were fixed on Dr. James, as if trying to see through him.

"We've been waiting for this conversation. Your discovery is intriguing. It definitely caught our attention," Mr. Hartman said, his tone brimming with interest.

James nodded politely, but a shadow of distrust hung over him.

"So what exactly is this all about?" he asked, his voice firm.

"A man who likes to jump right into business. I like that," Hartman replied, sliding a folder toward Dr. James. The folder, labeled with the BioCore logo and the word "Confidential," came to rest on the table.

"As I was saying, we're very interested in your research. From ecological stabilization to defense systems revolving around this hydrogen-based nanoparticle." It's exactly the kind of innovation we thrive on here.

Dr. James opened the folder, scanning the pages as Hartman continued to speak.

"You would have full autonomy to continue your research, and of course a very substantial financial package," Hartman continued.

James looked up from the documents.

"What's the catch?"

Mr. Hartman's smile faltered for a moment before he regained his composure.

"Uh, well, there's no catch."

"There's always a catch with you corporate guys," James replied, feeling increasingly wary. The executives shifted in their seats, adjusting their suits. A worried Emily gave him a look that said he needed to be more diplomatic.

"It's not really a catch, but the contract states that BioCore would own the research," Hartman said, still smiling.

"In exchange for?" Dr. James interrupted.

"In exchange, you would be a key part of our research team. You, Emily, and Dr. Reinhardt would lead the project together."

Emily, hope renewed, said, "Working together, Rich. Isn't that great?"

Dr. James frowned, sensing that the proposal had a dark undertone.

"So, you want me to hand over all of… my work, so you can pass it off as your own?" he asked, his voice filled with disbelief.

"But you would be part of something much bigger. With our resources, we could take your discovery to places you could never go on your own. It's about expanding it… something you can't do without help like ours."

James paused for a long time, considering the proposal. His eyes darted to Emily, seeking her support.

"I appreciate the offer, but I don't feel comfortable handing over my research. And who's to say I want to pursue this? I want to find out who's behind this," he said, his voice firm.

Emily frowned, worried about the direction the conversation was taking.

"Rich, think about it. This is a real opportunity. We could control how the research is used. We can't let it pass us by."

"Once BioCore owns it, we lose control. They decide how it's used, not us," James replied, sensing the tension rising.

"Dr. James, I assure you that BioCore is committed to using this technology responsibly. You would have a seat at the table. You would have influence," Hartman said, trying to calm him down.

Dr. James looked him in the eye, not budging.

"But I wouldn't be in control. And I'm not willing to give that control up. Not to a corporation like BioCore… or any corporation, for that matter."

Emily shifted in her seat, her frustration mounting.

"Rich, don't do this. This is the best chance we have to take your research to the next level. You can't do it alone. Please…"

"No!" "James exclaimed, abruptly standing up.

Mr. Hartman, sensing that the decision was final, pulled the folder toward him with a sigh.

"I'm sorry you feel that way. BioCore would have been a strong partner. But the decision is yours."

James stood up, his determination clear.

"Thank you for your time."

He turned and walked out.
He walked out of the room with a determined step. Emily, after a moment of indecision, jumped up and quickly followed him.

****

The fresh air of the city hit his face as they left. James stopped on the sidewalk, taking a deep breath to calm his agitation.

"Rich, why didn't you let me talk?" Emily said, running to his side. Her voice reflected a mix of anguish and frustration.

"Because I couldn't let you walk into that trap, Emily. What they're offering is a poisoned candy," he replied, his eyes fixed on the horizon.

"But we could have done something great. I know it. I've seen what your research can achieve. It's not just a job; it's a step towards the future," she insisted, trying to meet his gaze.

"I'm not willing to give up my job. It's not just mine; it has implications that I can't ignore," James said, remembering his mentor's warnings about corporations manipulating science.

Emily took a deep breath, her hands shaking slightly.

"I understand your reservations, but BioCore could be our ticket out of this cycle of uncertainty. We need it, Rich. And I know, you do too."

He looked at her, a whirlwind of emotions in his eyes.

"It's not just about us. It's about the science. If BioCore is in control, what's stopping them from using it for purposes we don't approve of?" he replied, recalling the stories of past research gone wrong.

"But we also have to think about the future. About what it could be. If we don't, someone else will," Emily said, her voice now a whisper, almost as if she feared his answer.

James felt a pain in his chest as he listened to her. He knew she was right, but he couldn't give in to the pressure.

"You have to understand, Emily, I don't want us to be a part of something we can't control. I'm not comfortable with this," he said, his words firm.

****

They decided to enter a nearby cafe to clear their minds a bit. The familiarity of the place offered them a respite from the tension they carried. They sat at a table out of the way, the soft lights creating a warm atmosphere.

"What are we going to do now?" Emily asked, pouring herself a coffee. Her voice sounded calmer, but the nervousness was still evident.

"I don't know. Maybe we need to talk to Dr. Reinhardt. He may have more information about BioCore," James suggested, scratching his head in thought.

"Rich, you know that Dr. Reinhardt has also been looking for funding. What would happen if he joined them? It might be our only option," Emily said, her gaze worried.

"I can't risk losing everything, Emily. What we've built can't be sacrificed on the altar of money and resources. Sometimes, it's better to fight alone," he replied, feeling more determined.

"What if the price of that fight is our careers?" she asked, her voice rising in frustration.

The café began to fill with people. The atmosphere changed, and the noise intensified, but for them the outside world faded away. They sank into their thoughts, both knowing that the decision they made could change everything.

As they headed to their cars, a dark figure appeared in the alley. James felt a chill run down his spine. It was a man dressed in black, watching them from the shadows.

"Rich, do you realize we're being watched?" Emily whispered, noticing the presence as well.

James nodded, his instinct telling him to be careful.

"Maybe we should go," he said, quickening his pace toward his car.

As they reached the vehicle, the man approached, his gaze piercing them.

"Dr. James, Emily... I have something important to tell you," the stranger said, his deep voice echoing in the cold evening.

James looked at Emily, and they both knew the night still had surprises in store for them.

"Who are you?" James asked, his voice defiant.

"Someone who knows more about BioCore than they want you to know. You're in danger, and you must act fast."

Chapter 28

Dr. James pushed open the glass doors of the building and stepped outside, leaving the cold modernity of BioCore behind. The fresh city air hit him like a relief, but the tension inside him wouldn't go away. Emily was right behind him, her face a mix of anger and desperation.

"Rich, wait!" she yelled, running to catch up.

James stopped and turned around, his expression blank, a flash of sadness in his eyes. He didn't want to face what was happening between them, but the words were already in the air.

"Why are you doing this? This is the best deal we're going to get! You can't just walk away!" Emily said, her voice filled with frustration.

"Why? Because it's not about what's best for us. It's about what's best for you," Dr. James replied, his tone firm.

"You're insisting on this because you want that job, that security. And I get it, but I'm not going to sell my research for your career."

Emily's jaw dropped, feeling like the ground was falling out from under her feet.

"I'm trying to help you!" he replied, his voice a whisper.

"Stop lying. You're trying to help yourself," he said, his words sounding like a blow.

Emily felt taken aback, as if James had stripped her of her most genuine intention.

"How can you say that? I've supported you through all of this," he said, fighting back the tears that threatened to spill out.

"I'm not selling out, not to BioCore, not to anyone else. And if that puts your career at risk, I'm sorry," James replied, the determination in his voice unwavering.

Without another word, he turned and walked away. The distance between them grew, a gap that felt more personal than ever. Emily watched him walk away, feeling the air escape from her lungs.

****

Emily leaned against a wall, feeling the world around her fade away. Everything she had worked for, all the sacrifices, felt in vain. She needed a solution, but James' decision had left her trapped in her own frustration.

A sound behind her snapped her out of her thoughts. Turning, she saw the dark man from the previous alley, now closer than she would like.

"I found you, Emily," the stranger said, his tone grave.

"Who are you? What do you want?" he asked, feeling vulnerable.

"I am someone who knows more about BioCore than you think. Your friend is in danger, and so are you," the man replied, his gaze deep.

****

Dr. James entered the cafe, trying to clear his mind. Emily's words echoed in his head, but he knew his decision was the right one. He sat at a table in the corner, ordering a coffee and trying to ignore the chaos of his personal life.

As he waited for his drink, he looked out the window. Traffic flowed, and people walked past aimlessly. He wondered if he could ever find that same sense of direction.

His phone vibrated on the table. It was a text from Emily: "I don't know what to do. We'll talk later. "James' stomach tightened. He wanted to help her, but he knew he couldn't betray his principles

When he stepped outside, the sun was beginning to descend, turning the sky orange. The city was preparing for the night, but inside, a storm was brewing. He realized he had to return to his lab, to his shelter.

The lab was dark and quiet, but James knew the research needed him. He turned on the lights and made his way to his desk, where a stack of papers awaited his attention. Amidst the confusion, a small vial of nanoparticles glinted in the light.

As he leaned over his work, he remembered the look in Emily's eyes. She wasn't just looking for a job; she was looking for stability, a path to rely on. But he couldn't let his desire for security lead him into a commitment he wasn't willing to make.

Suddenly, the sound of a knock interrupted his concentration. James started and looked toward the door. The stranger's figure appeared in the doorway, his face half hidden in the shadows.

"What are you doing here?" James asked, feeling uncomfortable.

"We need to talk," the man said, moving toward the table. His voice was low and serious. "What you discovered at BioCore is not what it seems."

James frowned, unsure if he should trust him.

"What do you mean?" he asked, his tone challenging.

"There's more at stake than you imagine. BioCore is involved in something dangerous. Your research… it's just the tip of the iceberg," the stranger said, his gaze fixed on James.

James felt a chill run down his spine. What did that mean for him and Emily?

"Why should we believe you?" he replied, but his voice sounded less certain.

"Because "What you want to protect could be what destroys you," the man replied, and James felt caught in a dilemma he hadn't expected

****

The stranger stood in the room, the light illuminating his face. James, still seated, felt the tension rising in the air. The man's statement about BioCore echoed in his mind like a disturbing echo.

"What are you saying?" James asked, trying to keep his voice steady, even though his heart was pounding.

"Evelyn," the stranger said, his eyes intense. "She's been murdered. During one of her trips to China, a group of nano scientists were stalking her. They weren't there to help her.

James felt as if the ground had opened beneath his feet. The mention of Evelyn hit him with the force of a storm. His mind filled with images: the conversations in the basement, the gleam in her eyes when she talked about her research, the last time they said goodbye.

"No..." he murmured, his voice shaking. "It can't be."

The man nodded, his expression grave.

"She is. She was in the wrong place at the wrong time. What you discovered at BioCore was related to her work, and that made her a target."

"And who are you?" James demanded, fear turning to fury. "Why should we trust you?"

"My name is Adam. I've been investigating BioCore for some time now. They're not just manipulating biology. They're in the business of death, and you, James, are on their list."

James felt the air drain out of him. The revelation of Evelyn's death, an echo of the dangers he'd always wanted to avoid, hung over him like a shadow.

"Why are you telling me this?" he asked, his voice barely a whisper.

"Because you have to be prepared. The threat you faced at BioCore hasn't disappeared. On the contrary, it will intensify."

James stood up, his mind spinning. He couldn't accept what he was hearing. Evelyn, his colleague and friend, dead.

"How do you know this is true?" he insisted, his disbelief crossing with desperation.

"I've had access to confidential information. Evelyn's team was being watched. If you don't do something soon, you could be next."

"What kind of information?" he asked, his voice cracking.

Adam took a step closer, his gaze steady.

"There's a project at BioCore that's beyond what you imagine. Nanotechnology applied to human biology. If it falls into the wrong hands, there could be devastating consequences."

James felt overwhelmed. He knew his research could have major implications, but he'd never imagined it would also make him a target.

"And what do you suggest I do?" he asked, looking the stranger in the eye.

"You need to get out of here. You can't be alone. I can help you, but you have to trust me first."

James hesitated. The danger seemed real, but the thought of running away was heartbreaking. He had dedicated his life to research, to finding answers. Was he willing to leave it all behind?

A sound echoed from the hallway, a distant echo that made James jump. He approached the door, holding his breath.

"There is no time to waste," Adam said, urging him to act. "If they find you here, it will be too late."

James knew he had to act, but the thought of leaving his life behind terrified him. He looked around his lab, at the notes, the samples, his world, and felt himself crumbling.

"Where will I go?" he asked, feeling the pressure in his chest.

"I know a safe place. But you must decide quickly."

Adam's voice brought him out of his lethargy. Without thinking any further, James nodded.

"Okay. Let's go."

They both hurried out of the lab. Night had fully fallen, and the city was lit up with a mix of flickering lights. But to James, everything seemed bleak. The thought of Evelyn's death and the danger that lurked around him enveloped him like a fog.

Adam led him through dark alleys and paths James had never walked. As they went on, the feeling of being watched increased.

"Who's behind this?" James asked, trying to find answers as they ran.

"BioCore has allies in the shadows. Scientists, mercenaries, all with an interest in keeping this secret under control," Adam replied. "They want you and your research."

"I don't understand why," James said, feeling his mind on the verge of collapse. "What do they have to do with me?"

"Because what you discovered could expose their plans. What they know about you and your research, what they did with Evelyn… it's all part of a puzzle you're just beginning to see."

James gulped, each word Adam said hitting him with the force of a revelation.

Finally, they came to an old, uninhabited building. Adam gestured for James to enter, making sure no one followed them.

"You'll be safe here for a while," Adam said, closing the door with a click that echoed in the darkness.

The interior was dark.

Simple, but there was a sense of security. A couple of lights flickered, and maps and documents were scattered on the walls.

"What is this place?" James asked, looking around.

"It's a safety net. We've gathered information here about BioCore and other actors who are playing with fire," Adam replied, his tone serious.

James sat down, feeling the weight of the world on his shoulders.

"I can't believe Evelyn died. She believed in this work," he said, his voice heavy with pain.

"I know," Adam replied. "But this is bigger than you think. We need to find out what they've done with their research and stop them before it's too late."

"How?" James asked, hopelessness creeping into his voice.

"You have to go back to the lab," Adam said, determined. "We need that data. It's the key to dismantling their plans."

James felt a knot in his stomach. Going back to the place where it all began was terrifying. But he also knew that this was his only chance. He had to do something for Evelyn.

"Okay. I'll do it," he said, finding a spark of determination amidst his grief.

Adam began to map out a plan, explaining each step. James listened intently, absorbing every detail. They had to infiltrate BioCore, get the information they needed, and get out before they were discovered.

"First, we need secure access," Adam said, looking through a couple of documents. "There's a meeting scheduled for tomorrow. If we get in, we can access Evelyn's files."

James felt nervous, but the thought of revenge for his friend's death pushed him forward.

"What if we get caught?" he asked, anxiety weighing on his chest.

"We'll have to be sneaky. If we get caught, we'll lose not only the information, but our lives," Adam admitted, staring at him. But if we manage to get the data, we could make the truth about BioCore public.

James nodded, adrenaline beginning to flow through his body. The thought of taking action, of fighting for what was right, gave him strength. He knew this was bigger than him. It was a battle for the future.

As the night deepened, they both began to prepare. James gathered his things, making sure he had everything he needed. The nanoparticles, the information about Evelyn's research, everything was at stake.

"We're not just fighting for our lives, but for everyone else's," Adam said as he checked his equipment.

James looked at him, his resolve solidifying.

"I'm not going to let Evelyn's sacrifice be in vain."

Adam smiled, the spark of hope shining in his eyes.

James felt fear turn into resolve. This was a fight that had only just begun, but he knew he couldn't take a step back. The lives of many people depended on his next move.

Chapter 29

Emily walked down the street, trying to clear her mind. The conversation with the stranger still echoed in her thoughts. The thought of Rich being in danger filled her with anxiety. What if he didn't understand the magnitude of what they were facing?

As she passed by a park, she saw a group of people gathered together. Her curiosity led her to approach. A demonstration against BioCore was underway, and banners filled with defiant slogans floated in the air.

"BioCore is not to be trusted!" some shouted.

Emily felt drawn to the energy of the crowd. She knew they were right. There was something unsettling about the way BioCore operated, and her intuition told her that James was right to be wary.

****

Back in the lab, James was trying to process the information the stranger had given him. His mind was filled with questions. Who was this man really? What did he want from him?

"Listen, you don't have much time. There's something you need to do," the stranger said, interrupting his thoughts.

"What do you want me to do?" James asked, now feeling like he was trapped in a game he didn't understand.

"Investigate. Find the truth behind BioCore. And take care of yourself. You're not alone in this. There are others who won't hesitate to remove any obstacle," the stranger warned.

James nodded, feeling the weight of the world fall on his shoulders. He knew he couldn't do this alone. He had to talk to Emily, even though the distance that had been created between them seemed insurmountable.

As the demonstration continued, Emily looked around, feeling like the truth was closer than she thought. She realized she had to act and not let her future depend on a corporation she didn't trust.

Making a decision, she approached a group of protesters.

"Can I help?" she asked, feeling like this was her moment to act.

A young man with a sign looked at her.

"Sure. We're trying to gather evidence of BioCore's practices. Do you have any information?"

"I know something. Maybe I can help," Emily replied, feeling stronger.

The night continued to progress, and with each decision they made, they came closer to a dangerous truth. In a game of shadows and secrets, they both knew the future was at stake.

Chapter 30

A grim inn stands on the edge of the road on the outskirts of town. The tattered sign flaps in the wind, and a few old cars are parked outside, silent witnesses to secrets lurking in the gloom. The place seems frozen in time, a stopping place for lost souls.

The motel room is dingy, with stained carpets and peeling wallpaper. The overhead light flickers occasionally, creating eerie shadows on the walls. Mark Dawson sits on the edge of the unmade bed, his face tense as he talks on the phone.

"General, you need to know what's going on," Mark says, his voice tense and laden with urgency. "There's something bigger here than I thought. There's a cover-up." I'm not sure who, but they're following me.

General Cortez, a gruff, stern man in his sixties, stares ahead as he sits behind his desk. His tone is menacing, like a gathering storm.

"Dawson, I didn't send you there to get killed. I allowed you to go help a friend... give him advice and not get involved," Cortez replies, his voice firm

Mark narrows his eyes, feeling anger creep into his voice.

"They're manipulating hydrogen molecules, General. If they control this technology, they control the world's water supply."

Mark paces back and forth, feeling the air grow thicker.

"Stand back." "This isn't your fight," Cortez replies, his tone hardening. "This case isn't on file and you're sticking your nose where it doesn't belong."

"What's going on, General? Why are you covering this up?" Mark asks, his voice now filled with desperation.

General Cortez's voice turns cold and authoritative.

"I'm not covering anything up. And everything else is not for you to worry about. I'm giving you a direct order… finish the investigation and go home. Now."

Mark feels adrenaline rush through his veins.

"Are you serious? You know what's at stake!" he exclaims, gripping the phone tightly.

"If you stay, then you'll be on your own. But I strongly suggest you come back here or there will be consequences, Dawson. If you stay, you're disobeying a direct order."

Mark feels rage boil inside him.

"You think you can just close this? Sweep this under the rug?" I'm not going to back down. Not when I know what's really going on.

General Cortez sighs, frustrated.

"Alright. You've made your decision."

There's a click on the phone as General Cortez abruptly hangs up. Mark stands there for a moment, staring at the phone in his hand, feeling the pressure of the situation closing in around him.

"Damn," he mutters, dropping the phone onto the bed.

****

Mark walks out of the room with a frown, his mind buzzing with the conversation. The sunlight hits him, and he blinks, trying to clear his thoughts. He needs to act quickly; every second counts.

As Mark walks down the road, a couple of cars whiz by, but he pays them no mind. Suddenly, a black vehicle pulls up beside him. The window slowly rolls down, revealing a suspicious-looking man wearing dark sunglasses.

"Dawson?" the man asks, his tone curt.

Mark stops, feeling a pang of caution.

"Who are you?" he asks, trying to remain calm.

"I'm someone who can help you. But you need to get in the car."

Mark hesitates, weighing his options. A survival instinct screams at him not to get in, but curiosity and desperation push him forward.

"Why should I trust you?" he says, crossing his arms.

"Because time is running out and they're watching you. BioCore doesn't play fair, and you're on their list," the man replies, his tone urgent.

Mark feels a chill run down his spine. Despite his reservations, he knows he needs answers.

"Okay," he finally says, and opens the door, getting in the vehicle.

****

The man starts the engine, and the car speeds away from the inn.

"What do you know about BioCore?" Mark asks, feeling anxious.

"I know they are manipulating technology that could change the world. And not only that, they are willing to kill for it," the man says, keeping his gaze fixed on the road.

"Why didn't you tell me this before? Who are you?" Mark asks, intrigued.

"I am an ex-employee of BioCore. I got rid of them before they destroyed me. Now I am here to warn you."

Mark feels his heart pounding. Was this his chance to find out the truth?

"What?
"What kind of warnings?" he asks.

The man stops at a red light, and turns to face him.

"What you're investigating isn't just a research project. It's a weapon, and they're willing to do whatever it takes to keep it a secret," he says.

Mark feels the gravity of his words crush him. He needs to act, but how?

"Do you have proof?" he asks, his voice barely a whisper.

"Yes, but not right now. I need you to help me get something they can't let come to light."

Mark feels caught between duty and loyalty. The conversation with Cortez and the man's warning are two sides of the same coin. Was he willing to risk it all?

"What do you need from me?" she asks, determined to act.

"I need you to break into BioCore and gain access to their files." They have everything you need to expose them," the man replies, his eyes intense.

Mark nods, feeling a spark of determination.

"I will. But I need to know you're on my side."

"I'm the only one who can help you on this. But there's something else you need to know: you can't trust anyone, not even those you think are on your side."

****

The black vehicle pulls up into a dark alley. Mark steps out, feeling the adrenaline rush through his veins.

"How will we communicate?" he asks.

"Use this," the man says, handing him a cell phone. "Stay alert, and don't go near BioCore until I tell you to."

Mark nods, feeling the responsibility on his shoulders. He turns and walks away, feeling the weight of the decision he just made.

****

Later, Mark enters a small cafe and sits in a dark corner. He watches the people walk by, feeling like the world is moving on as he is caught in a dangerous game.

A group of suspicious-looking men enter, their gazes scanning the room until they stop on Mark. He tenses, feeling his heart beat faster. Had they found him?

As Mark leaves, he tries to act normal, but his instincts scream that he is in danger. The men follow him, their footsteps echoing on the sidewalk behind him.

Mark quickened his pace, feeling sweat soaking his back. He needs to lose them. As he turns a corner, he realizes he can't look back. The pressure intensifies, and his mind searches for a way out.

****

He finds himself in a narrow, dark alley, the walls seeming to close in around him. He knows he needs to find shelter, but the silence is deafening.

Suddenly, he hears voices behind him. Without thinking, he hides behind a dumpster, his heart pounding. He watches the men walk by, their faces serious and determined.

"Where is he?" one of them asks.

"We'll find him. He can't go far," another answers.

Mark holds his breath, feeling time stop. What will they do if they find him? Adrenaline courses through his veins, and he knows he needs to be sneaky.

As the men walk away, Mark emerges from his hiding spot, feeling more determined than ever. If he had to risk everything to stop BioCore, he would do it. He heads toward the lab, knowing the truth was waiting to be discovered.

****

The atmosphere in the lab is thick, full of tension. Mark looks around, feeling like every corner might be under surveillance. He moves forward slowly, searching for any clue that will lead him to the truth.

His footsteps echo on the floor, and the echo reminds him that he is not alone. Every second counts, and the feeling of being watched follows him like a shadow.

Chapter 31

Dr. Reinhardt's lab had been a mess, but now, in the darkness of the night, it was in precarious order. Tables were straightened, salvaged equipment sat in place, and a pile of broken glass and other debris piled up in the center. Despite the cleanup, the air was still thick with tension and memories of what had happened.

Dr. Reinhardt sat at a table, his head propped up on one hand. The dark circles under his eyes revealed the accumulated exhaustion of sleepless nights. The door swung open, interrupting his thoughts.

Dr. James walked in, a six-pack of beer in his hand. Without a word, he sat down across from Reinhardt and opened a can, sliding it toward him. Reinhardt quickly took the beer, raised it in a half-hearted toast, and downed it in one gulp. The refreshing drink gave him a slight relief.

"You need to drink faster to get it to do what we need it to do," Reinhardt said, with a half-smile.

Dr. James took a sip of his own beer, thoughtful, his face reflecting the internal struggle he was carrying with him.

"Emily got me a meeting with BioCore," he said, his deep voice echoing in the air.

Reinhardt frowned, getting up to go to a cluttered desk. He began to sort through papers and finally pulled out an envelope with "Dr. Richard James" printed on the front. In the corner, "BioCore" was also written in clear letters.

"That arrived for you a few hours ago," Reinhardt said, offering the envelope to James.

James looked at the envelope, confused. They remained silent, the air heavy with awkward expectation. Finally, James pushed the envelope aside, uninterested.

Reinhardt quickly opened the envelope and scanned the typed words. His expression changed as he read.

"Interesting," he murmured, sensing that something bigger was at play.

James snatched the envelope from him and read it quietly, frowning as he took in the contents. His eyes darkened with concern.

"I take it they didn't like your answer," Reinhardt commented, watching his colleague's reaction.

"Why would they want me to attend a government-sanctioned trade mission to Japan?" James asked, his tone filled with disbelief.

At that moment, the door opened again. Mark walked in, a tired expression on his face, and quickly sat down next to James. He grabbed a beer, nodding in thanks before drinking.

"I don't know about you two, but I've had an interesting few hours," Mark said, glancing around the lab, which now looked less cluttered, but just as tense.

Mark sensed the tension in the air and took the envelope, reading it carefully. The words echoed in his mind, creating an echo of unease.

"Tokyo… what is this about?" he asked, his voice shaking slightly.

"BioCore," James replied, feeling his skin crawl.

"Of course it is. It sounds like a trap," Mark replied, his voice laced with distrust.

"A trap I should accept," James said, looking at Reinhardt determinedly.

Reinhardt crossed his arms, thoughtful. He knew the situation was dangerous.

"Aren't you seriously considering going? Look what they did to this place. It's not safe, and if—"

"It may be our only way to find out who's behind this," James interrupted, urgently.

Reinhardt leaned forward, his gaze fixed on James.

"What does Emily say?" he asked, searching for clarity in the confusion.

"She's not worried," James replied, a little unsure.

Mark and Reinhardt exchanged glances, intrigued by Emily's answer. It was an indicator of what was at stake.

"If I go to Japan, then I could do exactly what they want. But not if I go prepared," James said, his voice full of resolve.

"I'll go with you," Mark stated, without hesitation.

"I can't ask you to do that, Mark," James replied, feeling the weight of the decision.

"I volunteered. Besides, it's not like I'm employed by the government right now," Mark said, with a slight smile.

"What?" James asked, confused.

"I'll tell you about it later," Mark replied, leaving curiosity hanging in the air.

A long silence followed. The three of them looked around, the tension palpable as the weight of the pending decision tightened on their chests. Each knew their next move could change everything.

Suddenly, the door to the lab swung open with a bang. A man in a dark suit entered, his expression serious and determined.

"Dr. James?" "I need to talk to you," he said, his voice echoing in the tense air.

The three of them looked at each other, surprise on their faces.

"Who are you?" James asked, frowning.

"I'm from the CIA. We need you to cooperate with us," the man replied, taking a step forward.

Tension rose in the lab. Reinhardt and Mark exchanged worried glances.

"What do you know?"
"Is this about us?" Mark asked, keeping his guard up.

"More than you imagine. What happened here is no accident, and time is running out," the man said, his voice low and urgent.

"What are you talking about?" James asked, feeling increasingly intrigued and frightened.

The man took a step closer, his gaze intense.

"There's a plot afoot, involving nanomaterials. We need your help to stop it."

Reinhardt leaned forward, his voice firm.

"And what assures us that we can trust you?"

"I can't assure you of anything, but if you don't act soon, there will be catastrophic consequences," the man said, his seriousness filling the lab with a sense of impending danger.

The three men looked at each other, each sensing that they were on the verge of something bigger, something that could change the course of their lives.

"What do you have in mind?" James asked, his heart pounding.

"We must go to Japan. That is where everything is brewing," the man replied.

Mark took a deep breath, trying to process the information.

"So, we are caught in a web of conspiracies," he said, sensing the gravity of the situation.

Reinhardt nodded, acknowledging that the mission could be more dangerous than they had ever imagined.

"But we cannot sit idly by," he said, determined to act.

James stood up, his resolve burning.

"I will go, and this time I will be prepared," he stated, a gleam of determination in his eyes.

"If you go, I will go with you. I will not let you face this alone," Mark declared, determined to accompany his friend.

The CIA man's gaze lit up with a mixture of respect and urgency.

"Good. Then, you must prepare. Time is running out," he said, as the weight of the decision began to settle on his shoulders.

The three men looked at each other, knowing that the darkness of the lab was only an echo of the shadows lurking outside. They were preparing for a journey that would not only be physical; it would also be a descent into the unknown.

Chapter 32

The plane lifted off the runway, its engines roaring loudly as it slowly rose into the air. Inside the cabin, the passengers exchanged nervous glances, some with pale faces, others with a mix of excitement and anxiety. Among them, Dr. James, staring out the window, watched the city lights fade away, feeling like he was leaving more than just a place behind; he was leaving a part of himself behind.

"Are you ready for this?" Mark asked, sitting next to him. His voice was a whisper amid the hum of the plane.

James turned his head and smiled weakly at him.

"I don't know. Sometimes I feel like this is bigger than us."

"That's because it is," Mark replied, leaning forward. "But we have to. What we saw in the lab can't go unanswered."

James nodded, but his mind kept wandering. The meeting with the CIA had left a weight on their chest. They had to uncover the truth about BioCore and the dark web that had been woven around it. What secrets would they keep in Japan?

The flight was long and tiring, but finally the plane landed at Narita International Airport. The lights of the airport flickered, and the bustle of travelers filled the air. James and Mark walked through the terminal, their suitcases rolling behind them, while excitement and anxiety mixed in their stomachs.

"Do you have the contact yet?" Mark asked, breaking the silence that had settled between them.

James nodded, taking out his phone to check the message he had received from the CIA. His gaze stopped on the screen, where an unknown number waited.

"Yes, we should meet him in an hour. He said he will be waiting for us at a cafe near Shinjuku."

Mark smiled, a spark of excitement lighting up his eyes.

"Perfect! I always wanted to see Shinjuku."

As they headed out of the airport, the cool morning air enveloped them. The contrast between the tense atmosphere of the lab and the vibrant energy of Tokyo was palpable. The streets were full of life; pedestrians ran, bicycles zigzagged, and bullet trains glided smoothly across the horizon, like steel snakes.

"Look at that," Mark said, pointing to a cluster of neon lights illuminating a nearby building. "This is amazing!"

James smiled despite the anxiety that consumed him. The city was a sea of colors, noises, and aromas, and in the midst of it all, he and Mark had a mission to accomplish. However, the beauty of Tokyo made him forget, if only for a moment, the danger that awaited them.

As they reached the café, a cozy little place surrounded by skyscrapers, the atmosphere became more serious. They sat at a table by the window, from where they could watch the people pass by. Mark fiddled with his drink, while James looked nervously toward the door.

"What do you think he'll say?" Mark asked, breaking the silence.

"I don't know," James replied. "But I don't think we have time to waste."

Just then, a dark-haired man in a well-fitting suit entered the café. His gaze was intense, and he walked toward them with determination.

"Dr. James, Mark Dawson," he greeted, extending a firm hand. It was Agent Takashi, the CIA contact in Tokyo.

"Thank you for coming," James said, squeezing his hand firmly.

"I've been looking forward to meeting you two. Time is of the essence, so let's get down to business," Takashi said, taking a seat.

"What do we know about BioCore?" Mark asked, directly.

Takashi opened his folder and began to speak in a deep voice.

"BioCore has been working on developing nanomaterials. They're not just commercial products; they're potential weapons. What they've done in their lab is just the tip of the iceberg." There are rumors that they plan to use these materials in a clandestine project in Japan.

Worry crept across James' face.

"So what do we need to do?" he asked, feeling the pressure mounting.

"We need to infiltrate their facility here in Tokyo. I've gotten information about a company event at a luxury hotel. An important presentation is being held there," Takashi explained. "It's meant to attract investors and partners, but it's the perfect place to gain vital information."

Mark leaned forward, his eyes shining with interest.

"What about us? How do we get in?"

"You'll need to pose as BioCore employees. I've already prepared the necessary credentials," Takashi replied, handing them two ID cards.

James looked at the card, feeling torn between the excitement of the adventure and the fear of what might happen. He knew that every decision they made could have serious repercussions.

"This sounds risky," James said, sensing the gravity of the situation.

"It is," Takashi admitted. "But if we succeed, we can find out who is behind it."
BioCore and stop it before it's too late.

Mark nodded, determined.

"We're in. We can't let this become a bigger threat."

James felt his heart pounding. There was a spark of determination within him. This was the path they had chosen, and while it was dangerous, it was necessary.

The conversation continued as Takashi gave them more details about the event and how they would proceed. As the plans took shape, the energy in the cafe grew more intense. The bustle outside faded as they focused on what was to come.

When they were done, James and Mark left the cafe with a mix of nerves and adrenaline. Tokyo enveloped them with its light and noise, but in their minds, there was only one goal: to unravel the mystery surrounding BioCore.

As they walked through the illuminated streets, James paused for a moment, looking around. Everything seemed so vibrant, so full of life, but he knew that beneath that surface there were dangers lurking. The mission ahead of them was more than a job; it was a fight for the truth.

"Are you ready for this?" Mark asked, patting him on the shoulder.

James took a deep breath and smiled.

"Yes. I'm ready."

Chapter 33

The streets of Tokyo vibrated with energy as the sun shone brightly on the towering skyscrapers. Pedestrians filled the sidewalks, moving in a constant flow between neon signs flashing in every direction. The sound of bullet trains echoed in the air as they glided smoothly across the city skyline, like a stream of steel connecting lives.

The hotel room was a modern refuge amidst the chaos of Tokyo. The floor-to-ceiling windows offered a stunning view of the skyline, where skyscrapers rose like steel giants. Inside, however, the atmosphere was fraught with tension.

Dr. James entered first, feeling his heart pounding. The mission was getting closer, and with each step, anxiety grew. Mark followed, closing the door with a soft click that echoed in the silence.

"Alright, let's go over this one more time," Mark said, taking the lead as he moved to the table near the window.

James let out a sigh, placed his briefcase on the bed, and opened it. He pulled out a number of documents, organizing them carefully. The room might be elegant, but the reality of his mission was anything but comfortable.

"We went over it on the flight. We need to sleep," James replied, trying to hide the tension in his voice.

"Sleep comes next. Now we need to make sure you're ready," Mark insisted, his voice gravelly like the sky in a storm.

James sat on the edge of the bed, his eyes scanning the list of attendees Mark had handed him. He knew each of them could be a potential ally or an enemy.

"Who should I pay attention to?" he asked, his mind churning as he focused on the names and photos.

Mark pinpointed several key names on the list.

"These three. Li Wei, a representative of China's trade sector, with ties to shady business dealings. Katsuro Yamada, a high-level executive at BioCore, deeply invested in military contracts. And Mila Petrova, a Russian diplomat interested in advanced technology. If any of them come close, stay alert."

"But they shouldn't come close to me, right?" James frowned, trying to take in the information.

"Wrong! BioCore has likely already briefed them on you." And don't forget that someone, maybe more than BioCore, is following us," Mark explained, his gaze fixed on James.

Dr. James listened intently, nodding as he imagined various scenarios that could unfold. He knew that their mission involved not only infiltrating an event, but also avoiding detection.

Mark grabbed his earpiece and mini surveillance camera, quickly checking the connections.

"I'll be conducting surveillance from outside. If anything looks strange, I'll be nearby. But you'll be alone there. If any of these people make a move or try to corner you, stay calm. Always watch your corners, stay alert," Mark said, his voice deep and clear.

James leaned back slightly, feeling the weight of the situation. This wasn't just a mission; it was a game of life or death. Sweat was beginning to build up on his forehead as he contemplated what was to come.

"They'll be watching you, but I'll be watching all of them," Mark said, looking at him seriously. We stick to the plan, okay?

"We'll be ready," James replied, feeling the knot in his stomach.

"If something goes wrong, get out. There are no second chances," Mark added, his voice firm and determined.

Both men finished packing their things. The silence in the room was almost deafening, but the energy of the city continued to flow through the windows. The sense of impending danger seemed to be palpable in the air. They mentally prepared themselves for the event, each dealing with their own fears and determinations.

Mark checked his equipment once more, making sure everything was in order. James walked over to the window, looking down at where Tokyo life continued unabated. In his mind, one question spun relentlessly: what would happen if they failed?

"What will you do if you encounter any of them?" Mark asked, interrupting his thoughts.

"I'll stick to the plan." "I'll just have to remember what we rehearsed," James replied, though he wasn't sure he could keep his cool in a real situation.

"That's what I hope. Remember, every second counts. If you see something you don't like, back off. Don't take any chances," Mark insisted, taking a deep breath.

The tension in the room was palpable, and both men knew they couldn't afford to fail. They looked at each other, a silent understanding between them.

"We're going to do it," James said, determinedly.

Time passed quickly. As the day progressed, the city prepared for the event. The sounds of traffic, the voices of the crowd, and the hum of technology combined into a frantic background noise. Everything seemed to have a purpose, and every step they took brought them closer to their goal.

"Time to leave," Mark announced, looking at his watch. His face had hardened, reflecting the seriousness of the situation.

James nodded, feeling like every part of his body was on high alert. They headed for the door, each carrying their own burden of proof.

As they stepped out of the hotel, the cool Tokyo air enveloped them. They headed towards the event venue, the crowd moving in a frenetic pace around them. James could feel his pulse racing, but he knew he had to keep his composure.

"Remember, stay focused," Mark whispered as they made their way through the crowd.

As they approached the event venue, a sleek, modern building, the energy in the air intensified. There was a slight murmur, a mix of excitement and anticipation, which only heightened their anxiety. They knew that what was at stake was much more than just them; the future of many lives could depend on their success.

"Remember, don't get separated. I'll be outside keeping watch," Mark said before they entered.

James nodded, one last look of determination passing between them before they parted. With a deep breath, James stepped into the building, feeling like destiny was waiting for him.

The lobby was spacious and luxurious, with bright lights and an air of sophistication. The crowd moved with purpose, exchanging greetings and smiles as James mingled with them. His heart was pounding as he made his way into the main hall.

Looking around, his attention was drawn to a group of people in a corner, a lively conversation piqued his curiosity. James knew he had to remain calm and act like he belonged in that world. He couldn't give them the satisfaction of showing his nervousness.

Then, suddenly, he felt a presence behind him. He turned to find Li Wei looking at him with a sly smile. The man looked composed, but his eyes held a glint of cunning.

"Dr. James?" Li asked, extending his hand. James felt his heart stop for an instant.

"Yes, it's me. Nice to meet you," James replied, squeezing his hand firmly as his mind raced.

"I've heard a lot about you." "I hope you enjoy the BioCore presentation. It will be… interesting," Li said, his tone almost mocking.

James forced a smile, feeling like every word they exchanged was a game of strategy.

"I'm certainly looking forward to seeing what they have in store," he replied, trying not to give anything away.

Li Wei smiled, and although his words were friendly, James could feel the tension between them. Around them, the crowd was still moving, but at that moment, time seemed to have stopped.

Meanwhile, Mark remained outside, keeping a watchful eye. He knew that every second counted and that any mistake could cost them dearly. He was in constant contact with James through the earpiece, ready to act at any moment.

"Stay alert," Mark whispered in his ear. "If you see anything suspicious, act fast."

James nodded, concentrating on the conversation with Li. However, the feeling that they were being watched was growing inside him, a shadow he couldn't ignore.

Chapter 34

Emily leaned against the cold wall of the alley, feeling her body give way under the pressure. Everything she had fought for was beginning to crumble before her eyes. James' decision had been the final blow, the one that had plunged her into this maelstrom of frustration and uncertainty. He didn't understand her, he didn't understand the magnitude of what she was trying to achieve. It wasn't just ambition, it wasn't just power. It was much bigger than that.

A thud, the crunch of a foot on a stone, interrupted her thoughts. Turning her head, she saw a familiar figure emerging from the shadows. The dark man from the alley she had seen before was now much closer than she was comfortable with. Her heart skipped a beat.

"I found you, Emily," the man said in a deep, gravelly voice, almost as if he had been waiting for this moment for a long time.

Emily straightened up, her gaze hardening, but she couldn't stop her insides from filling with anxiety. Who was he? Why was he following her? She had thought she had lost him after the previous encounter, but here he was.

"Who are you? What do you want?" she asked, her tone firm, but her mind was working a mile a minute.

The man took a step forward, completely emerging from the shadows. His face, now visible under the dim light of a nearby streetlamp, revealed features that seemed calm and calculating. Dark eyes, an impeccable haircut, and an air of someone who left no loose ends.

"I'm Takashi," he said, his gaze fixed on her. "And I know more about BioCore than you can imagine. Your friend is in danger, and so are you."

The name sounded vaguely familiar, but Emily couldn't place it in her memory. BioCore, the company she had worked for alongside James and Reinhardt, was the epicenter of all this. But Takashi... she didn't remember ever hearing about him within the organization. Yet something in his voice, in his posture, told her he wasn't lying.

"What do you know about BioCore?" Emily asked, showing no more than a hint of unease.

"I know you've been playing with fire," Takashi replied, his tone leaving no room for interpretation. "And I know that if you go through with it, you'll not only destroy BioCore, but you'll put everything you think you control at risk."

Emily narrowed her eyes, evaluating every word. This wasn't just a casual encounter. He knew more than was good for him, and if he was talking about James, then it could be related to Dr. James and Mark Dawson's efforts to stop her.

"Are you working for James?" Emily asked, her voice sharp as a knife.

Takashi took a step closer to her, closing the distance. The tension between them was palpable.

"James and Mark asked me for help," he confessed, without any hesitation. "They both think you're playing with something you can't handle. And now, they want to stop you before this gets out of hand."

Emily crossed her arms, her mind spinning rapidly. James had always been too cautious, too risk-averse. And now he had brought in an outsider to interfere with his plans.

"James doesn't understand what's at stake," Emily snapped, her voice shaking slightly with rage. "This isn't just about nanotechnology. This is about rewriting the world, about controlling essential resources. It's bigger than us."

Takashi watched her in silence for a few seconds before speaking again.

"You may be right about one thing, Emily. This is bigger than all of us. But the methods you're using won't lead to the future you desire. Only chaos."

Emily let out a bitter laugh.

"So what do you suggest? That I just give myself up and wait while they ruin everything I've built?"

Takashi didn't answer right away. His gaze hardened, as if trying to pierce through Emily's shell and get to what was really going on inside her mind. He knew she was on the verge of something big, something dangerous, but he also knew it wasn't too late.

"You don't have to do it alone," he said finally. "If you give up Reinhardt and give up, you might have a chance to save everything you love."

Emily stared at him, and for a brief moment, something akin to doubt crossed her mind. But that instant quickly faded, replaced by her determination to keep going, to see her vision fulfilled.

"It's too late for that," she murmured. "I've already gone too far."

Takashi took one last step toward her, until they were face to face.

"You still have a choice, Emily," he said quietly. "Think about what you're risking. Not just your life, but the lives of everyone around you."

Emily stared at him for a few seconds, her face hardened, before turning around.

"I don't need your advice, Takashi," she replied as she began walking toward the dark alley. Tell James that if he really wants to stop me, he'll have to do it himself.

Takashi watched her walk away, knowing that things were about to get a lot more complicated.

Chapter 35

The night in Tokyo was a display of light and shadow. The imposing glass facade of the mission building shone brightly, reflecting the vibrant colors of the city skyline. High-end cars pulled up to the entrance, where diplomats, executives, and government officials alighted, flanked by security personnel watching every move.

A large sign hung above the entrance, proclaiming: "INTERNATIONAL TECHNOLOGY AND TRADE SUMMIT." Armed guards and surveillance cameras were everywhere, watching as guests mingled and greeted each other in an atmosphere of ostentation and power.

The grand hall was overflowing with opulence, with crystal chandeliers hanging from the ceiling and marble floors reflecting the light. The tables, elegantly draped with fine linens, were the focus of a lively array of conversations. The air was filled with the murmur of diplomats, executives and scientists exchanging ideas and banter.

Dr. James stood in the doorway, anxious, his eyes darting around the room. His body, rigid with tension, gave away his uneasiness as he searched for the right people in the crush of guests.

A discreet earpiece in his ear crackled, interrupting his thoughts.

"Mark, do you read me?" he whispered, his voice barely audible.

MARK DAWSON (V.O.)
Remember to stay calm, watch your six at all times and be natural. Find out what you can and get out.

James adjusted his suit jacket, taking a deep breath before moving further into the room. His eyes widened as he spotted a small group standing near one of the tables. There was Li Wei, the Chinese trade representative, who immediately spotted him and headed toward him before James could react.

"Li Wei is coming," he whispered into the receiver, his voice thick with nerves.

MARK DAWSON (V.O.)
Be cool.

Li Wei, with a shrewd look, sized Dr. James up and down as he approached. He extended his hand confidently.

"Dr. James, is it?" he asked, his smile affable but calculating.

"Yes. And you are…" James felt himself caught in his gaze, searching for a way to remain calm.

"Li Wei. BioCore has told me a lot about your work. Interesting, to say the least. And a remarkable discovery," Li replied, squeezing Dr. James' hand firmly.

"Thank you, sir," James replied, feeling the tension build in his chest.

"I'm sure you'll find much interest in what we're working on as well." I'd love to have a chat with you about it later... if you have time.

James nodded, though his nerves were evident in his stiff posture.

MARK DAWSON (V.O.)
He's connected to the Chinese military. Be careful what you say around him.

"I hope to learn more. But you'll excuse me for a moment; there's someone I need to say hello to as well," James replied quickly, backing away quickly, his heart pounding in his chest.

He grabbed a glass of water from a passing waiter, seeking to calm his nervousness. His eyes darted to the bar, and, sensing that he needed something stronger, he moved through the crowd towards it.

Leaning against the bar, he grabbed a glass of champagne, sipping it slowly before gulping down the rest in an attempt to calm himself. Just as he placed the glass on the bar, Mila Petrova appeared, moving gracefully and seductively beside him, holding her own glass of champagne.

Her eyes locked on him, and she smiled, drawing his attention. James felt a chill run down his spine, nervous and enthralled.

"You're not bored, are you?" Mila asked, her accent thick and polished.

"No, I just needed a drink," James replied, trying to sound relaxed.

"I understand. I prefer vodka, but the occasion calls for a celebratory drink." Mila picked up her glass and drank elegantly, smiling at James as he raised his glass in a toast.

"If I'm not mistaken, you are Dr. Ricardo James," Mila said, her gaze fixed on him.

"I seem to be popular here," James replied, sensing the conversation heating up.

"More than you know. I was hoping to have the pleasure of speaking with you," Mila said, her voice soft and inviting.

"And you are…?" he asked, aware that he should be cautious.

"Mila Petrova. I'm a fan of your research," she replied, leaning slightly towards him.

"You and a few others take it," James said, trying to keep the conversation light.

"Of course. Your work could change the world, Dr. James. People will do everything they can to control it. You must be careful who you trust," Mila warned, as she nodded toward Li Wei. "Never trust them."

Mila moved closer and put her arm around his shoulder, speaking almost in a whisper.

"I would love to know more about this. Maybe you can trust them."
"We can go back to my room," she suggested, her eyes shining with hidden intentions.

MARK DAWSON (V.O.)
It's time to finish, Rich. Don't linger.

James felt sweat trickle down his forehead as she caught him in her gaze.

"Some other time," she replied, forcing a polite smile as she walked away.

Mila grabbed his arm firmly, catching James off guard. He felt a chill run down his spine as she pushed him against the bar, her aggression now evident.

"Don't be afraid, Dr. James. I won't bite you… unless you ask me to," she whispered, her voice sweet but menacing.

Just then, Samuel Jennings, a suave and elegant man, arrived at the bar, interrupting the tense conversation. He stumbles slightly and spills his drink all over Mila.

"What's wrong?" "Disgusting animal," Mila muttered in Russian, horrified, as she wiped her dress with a napkin.

Samuel watched with a mischievous grin, enjoying the show.

"Sorry to interrupt or come on so loud, but my boss would like to talk to you," Samuel said, looking at James.

"Your boss…" James repeated, feeling a growing unease.

"Follow me," Samuel gestured, and James felt his stomach twist.

MARK DAWSON (V.O.)
Stay in sight.

Dr. James's eyes widened, unsure of what to do as Samuel walked away, looking back at James.

"Come on," Samuel insisted, gesturing for him to follow.

James calmed his nerves and joined Samuel as they moved through the crowd. Each step they took felt heavier than the last, a mix of anticipation and dread.

"Who's your boss?" "James asked, trying to keep the conversation light while his senses were on high alert.

"Someone who is very interested in your work has sent me to find you," Samuel said, leading him towards a set of ornate double doors.

James felt sweat trickle down his forehead. Every time he thought he could relax, something new kept him on his toes.

"What does he want?" James asked, trying to hide his nervousness.

"Trust me, you'll like it. Just keep up with me," Samuel replied, pushing open the doors and revealing a more private, quiet area, away from the bustle of the event.

****

The hallway was decorated with contemporary artwork, softly lit by warm lights. As they moved forward, James realized that the murmurs and laughter of the great hall gradually faded away. His mind was on high alert; each step took him deeper into unfamiliar territory.

"Why are you so interested in me?" "James asked, trying hard to remain calm.

Samuel stopped, looking him in the eyes seriously.

"Your work is not only innovative, it is dangerous. You know things that many would like you not to know," he said, his tone now serious.

James felt a chill run down his spine. The conversation with Mila and the interaction with Li Wei took on a new meaning.

"Did you mean BioCore?" James asked, trying to connect the pieces.

"Yes, but not just them. There are other players in this game. People who will stop at

nothing to get what they want," Samuel stated, and for a moment, the tension became palpable.

"And what do you propose?" James challenged, feeling the adrenaline flow.

"I want to help you. My boss wants to protect you and offer you an opportunity that could change the course of your research," Samuel said, crossing his arms.

"Why should I trust you?" James replied, distrustful.

"Because there's more at stake than you can imagine. Come, listen to what my boss has to say. It might be the only chance you have to get out of this mess alive," Samuel suggested, pointing towards a door that led to a private room.

James hesitated, but curiosity and survival instinct pushed him to follow Samuel. A moment of decision, and everything would change.

Chapter 36

As he entered, the atmosphere felt tense, full of expectations. As the door closed behind Samuel, an assistant who had brought James here, a chill ran down his spine. The only light came from a dim lamp that illuminated the face of Katsuro Yamada, an enigmatic man, whose aura emanated both power and mystery.

Katsuro sat behind his desk, his expression serene but intense. A samurai sword hung behind him, a reminder of the legacy and discipline he represented.

"Thank you, Samuel. You may wait outside now," Katsuro said in an authoritative tone.

Dr. James felt like a fish in a fishbowl, caught in curiosity and expectation. He approached Katsuro, gulping, feeling the tension in the air.

"Dr. James," Katsuro began. "As I'm sure you know, my name is Katsuro Yamada. I've been curious about your research. Sorry for the drama in bringing you here, but I'm not one for parties."

"It's okay, sir," Dr. James replied, trying to maintain his composure despite the nerves that were taking over him.

Katsuro watched him closely before gesturing for him to sit down. Dr. James settled back in his chair, trying to hide his shaking hands, a sign of his growing anxiety.

"Are you enjoying the party?" Katsuro asked, his voice calm as a pond.

"It's okay. It's not really my style either, but it's necessary to mingle," Dr. James replied, sensing the conversation becoming awkward.

"Seeing and being seen. Indeed, that's right," Katsuro nodded, tilting his head slightly.

Dr. James felt the situation growing tense. He cleared his throat and, in a firmer voice, asked,

"I'm not trying to sound too direct, but... what can I do for you, Mr. Yamada?"

Katsuro leaned back in his chair, his eyes fixed on Dr. James, as if he were trying to read his every thought. Without looking away, he poured a glass of sake and offered it to Dr. James, who shook his head with a polite smile.

"Your research. The possible applications in nanotechnology are quite revolutionary, aren't they?" Katsuro said, his tone suggestive.

At that moment, a voice resonated in Dr. James' mind, like an echo warning him:

"Careful. Yamada's firm is linked to defense. He will want to investigate your technology."

Dr. James forced a smile, although an uneasiness began to form in his stomach.

"Yes, sir, but it's too early to tell where it will lead," he said, trying to remain calm.

Katsuro nodded, intrigued.

"And you are a dentist, right?"

"That's right," Dr. James replied, sensing the topic of conversation changing direction.

Katsuro smiled slightly, as if the information gave him satisfaction.

"Impressive. After this, I imagine you will be in high demand, so you must choose your partners wisely."

Dr. James felt uncomfortable at Katsuro's insinuation.

"I never said I was looking for a partner," he clarified.

"Perhaps an investor," Katsuro replied, his tone more serious.

"I haven't thought about it, sir," Dr. James said, sweating slightly.

"Well, if you ever need guidance in such matters, you know where to find me," Katsuro concluded, looking at him with an intensity that made him feel small.

Dr. James nodded, smiling nervously as a bead of sweat formed on his forehead. The pressure of the situation was palpable.

"Is everything okay, Dr. James? You look… nervous," Katsuro said, his eyes deep and penetrating.

"I'm not feeling too well. Is there a bathroom I can use?" Dr. James asked, trying to escape the gaze that was stalking him.

"You can use my private facilities. Outside this office, down the hall and around the corner," Katsuro replied, not taking his eyes off him.

Dr. James stood up, grateful for the chance to get out of that oppressive atmosphere.

"Thank you," he said, trying to keep his voice steady.

"I look forward to continuing our conversation," Katsuro said as Dr. James walked away, his tone now more somber.

As he left, Dr. James felt a slight relief, though uneasiness followed him.

The hallway was dimly lit and decorated with paintings that seemed to follow him with their eyes. James took a deep breath, trying to calm himself as he walked. The pressure of the conversation had left him reeling.

"Don't relax. We need to know what this guy is up to," said the voice of Mark Dawson, his friend and colleague, sounding from the earpiece.

Dr. James headed toward the bathroom, his mind spinning with questions. What was Katsuro really looking for? Why was there so much interest in his work?

Reaching the bathroom, he looked in the mirror and noticed the trace of anxiety in his own.
reflex. He washed his hands, thinking about what Samuel, Katsuro's assistant, had said. The warning weighed on his mind like a stone.

A deafening noise interrupted his thoughts. A sound of breaking glass echoed from the hallway.

"What was that?" Dr. James muttered, alarmed.

Determined to find out what was happening, he stepped out of the bathroom, his heart pounding. The light from the hallway enveloped him, creating shadows that danced around him

The hallway was silent, but the air was heavy with tension. Dr. James moved forward cautiously, his senses alert. When he reached the corner, his heart stopped. Samuel stood there, pale and wide-eyed.

"Dr. James!" Samuel exclaimed, his voice shaking. "You have to go. Now!"

"What's going on?" "Dr. James asked, feeling a chill run down his spine.

"They're coming for you. I've heard things." Samuel looked around, as if danger was lurking.

Dr. James felt adrenaline rush through his veins.

"What do you know?" he asked, urged by the need to understand.

"I can't talk here. Just... stay away from Katsuro. He doesn't mean well." Samuel looked more scared than ever.

"Why? What does he want from me?" Dr. James asked, but Samuel could only shake his head.

"You have to get out of here. If Katsuro finds out, there's no turning back," he said, pressing Dr. James' hand firmly.

"I can't leave without understanding what's really going on." Dr. James felt caught up in his own curiosity.

"Then play your cards right, Dr. James." Don't let him catch you in his game." Samuel stepped back, his expression grave.

Dr. James was overwhelmed by the information and the imminent risk. Before he could formulate a response, a group of men in dark suits appeared at the end of the hallway, advancing quickly towards them. Katsuro stood in front, his gaze unwavering.

"Where do you think you're going?" Katsuro asked with an icy smile.

Dr. James felt his stomach drop. The trap had snapped shut.

"Samuel, we have to—"

"Run!" Samuel shouted.

Without a second thought, Dr. James turned and began to run, his mind in a whirl. The truth became a maze from which he didn't know if he could escape.

"This doesn't end here. You have to find out the truth," Mark's voice sounded again through the earpiece, a reminder that he was in for a much bigger fight than he had imagined.

Chapter 37

Dr. James stood by the sink, cold water splashing his face as he tried to stifle the panic rising in his throat. He leaned against the sink, feeling the cold edge against his palms, taking deep breaths to calm himself. The echo of the party noise faded behind him, and the solitude of the bathroom became oppressive.

The door creaked open, and in an instant, his eyes met those of JJ, a man whose presence had always had an eerie air about him. James noticed him approaching the adjacent sink, turning on the faucet with slow, deliberate movements.

"How are you, Dr. James?" JJ asked, keeping his gaze fixed on the water, avoiding eye contact.

James felt a knot in his stomach. Something about the way JJ moved, too calm, too calculating, told him there was something off about him. He gripped the sink, feeling the atmosphere closing in around him.

JJ finished washing his hands, drying them with a paper towel, and as he did so, James felt the urgency push him to get out of there. He didn't want to stay to find out what JJ planned to do. Without a word, he grabbed a towel, dried his face, and quickly left the bathroom.

Dr. James walked quickly, casting glances over his shoulder, feeling like he was being watched. The pounding beat of his heart thundered in his ears. He walked over to the elevator and pressed the button, expecting it to arrive quickly.

The doors opened, and Antonio was there, standing, staring at him with cold intent. James felt himself freeze. The warnings in his mind screamed at him that this was a bad situation.

"Dr. James. We've been looking for you," Antonio said, taking a step forward.

James took a step back, his breathing quickening. The situation was becoming more dangerous as JJ appeared behind him, cutting off his only way out.

"It's time for you to come with us, Doctor," JJ said, his tone firm and authoritative.

"What do they want from me?" James asked, trying to keep his voice steady as panic began to wash over him.

Mark Dawson's voice echoed through his earpiece, like an anchor in the storm.

"Rich, what's going on? Talk to me."

James couldn't answer. His eyes darted back and forth, searching for a way out, but every direction seemed to close off.

Without thinking, he lunged forward, pushing Antonio aside, his survival instincts taking over.

"Shit!" —JJ shouted, running after him.

Dr. James moved fast, adrenaline propelling him forward. The lights in the hallway flickered, creating shadows that seemed to lengthen and stalk him.

James pushed open the door to the stairs and took them up two at a time, the sound of footsteps behind him echoing like an echo of his impending capture.

"Don't let them catch you!" Mark's voice echoed in his mind, a constant reminder of the need to keep moving.

The footsteps behind him grew closer, a palpable threat urging him onward. Reaching the final step, Dr. James burst into a lower hallway, desperately searching for an exit. His heart was pounding, but he forced himself to focus, to stay calm.

He saw a service door at the end of the hallway, dimly lit by a flickering light. Without thinking, he ran towards her, feeling the thick, hot air around him, as if the pressure of danger was following him.

Dr. James pushed open the service door forcefully, stepping into a small supply room. Inside, shelves were filled with boxes and equipment that seemed forgotten, as if time had passed without touching the place.

All around him, the silence was absolute, but he couldn't afford complacency. He walked over to a small window, trying to see if there was any way to escape. Through the dirty glass, he could see the dim lighting of the street.

"There's no time," he whispered to himself.

With every passing second, danger came closer. He turned, looking for another exit. Around the corner, a smaller door seemed to lead to another hallway. Without hesitation, he darted towards it, feeling cold sweat run down his forehead he entered a toilet.

****

Dr. James stood by the sink, cold water splashing his face as he tried to stifle the panic rising in his throat. He leaned against the sink, feeling the cold edge against his palms, taking deep breaths to calm himself. The echo of the party noise faded behind him, and the solitude of the bathroom became oppressive.

The door creaked open, and in an instant, his eyes met those of JJ, a man whose presence had always had an eerie air about him. James noticed him approaching the adjacent sink, turning on the faucet with slow, deliberate movements.

"How are you, Dr. James?" JJ asked, keeping his gaze fixed on the water, avoiding eye contact.

James felt a knot in his stomach. Something about the way JJ moved, too calm, too calculating, told him there was something off about him. He gripped the sink, feeling the atmosphere closing in around him.

JJ finished washing his hands, drying them with a paper towel, and as he did so, James felt the urgency push him to get out of there. He didn't want to stay to find out what JJ planned to do. Without a word, he grabbed a towel, dried his face, and quickly left the bathroom.

Dr. James walked quickly, casting glances over his shoulder, feeling like he was being watched. The pounding beat of his heart thundered in his ears. He walked over to the elevator and pressed the button, expecting it to arrive quickly.

The doors opened, and Antonio was there, standing, staring at him with cold intent. James felt himself freeze. The warnings in his mind screamed at him that this was a bad situation.

"Dr. James. We've been looking for you," Antonio said, taking a step forward.

James took a step back, his breathing quickening. The situation was becoming more dangerous as JJ appeared behind him, cutting off his only way out.

"It's time for you to come with us, Doctor," JJ said, his tone firm and authoritative.

"What do they want from me?" James asked, trying to keep his voice steady as panic began to wash over him.

Mark Dawson's voice echoed through his earpiece, like an anchor in the storm.

"Rich, what's going on? Talk to me."

James couldn't answer. His eyes darted back and forth, searching for a way out, but every direction seemed to close off.

Without thinking, he lunged forward, pushing Antonio aside, his survival instincts taking over.

"Shit!" —JJ shouted, running after him.

Dr. James moved fast, adrenaline propelling him forward. The lights in the hallway flickered, creating shadows that seemed to lengthen and stalk him.

****

James pushed open the door to the stairs and took them up two at a time, the sound of footsteps behind him echoing like an echo of his impending capture.

"Don't let them catch you!" Mark's voice over sounded a constant reminder of the need to keep moving.

The footsteps behind him grew closer, a palpable threat urging him onward. Reaching the final step, Dr. James burst into a lower hallway, desperately searching for an exit. His heart was pounding, but he forced himself to focus, to stay calm.

He saw a service door at the end of the hallway, dimly lit by a flickering light. Without thinking, he ran towards her, feeling the thick, hot air around him, as if the pressure of danger was following him.

Dr. James pushed open the service door forcefully, stepping into a small supply room. Inside, shelves were filled with boxes and equipment that seemed forgotten, as if time had passed without touching the place.

All around him, the silence was absolute, but he couldn't afford complacency. He walked over to a small window, trying to see if there was any way to escape. Through the dirty glass, he could see the dim lighting of the street.

"There's no time," he whispered to himself.

With every passing second, danger came closer. He turned, looking for another exit. Around the corner, a smaller door seemed to lead to another hallway. Without hesitation, he darted towards it, feeling cold sweat run down his forehead.

As he opened the door, he found himself in a darker hallway, the lights flickering intermittently. At the end, a flash illuminated a staircase leading up. He knew he had to go up, that his only chance of escape was to find a place to hide.

The footsteps of Antonio and JJ echoed closer, like an ominous beat threatening to catch him. He hurried toward the stairs, his mind spinning with fear.

As he opened the door, he found himself in a darker hallway, the lights flickering intermittently. At the end, a flash illuminated a staircase leading up. He knew he had to go up, that his only chance of escape was to find a place to hide.

The footsteps of Antonio and JJ echoed closer, like an ominous beat threatening to catch him. He hurried toward the stairs, his mind spinning with fear.

Chapter 38

The night was cold and enveloping. The air thick with moisture clung to Dr. Richard James' skin as he stumbled, almost staggering, through the darkness. His mind was clouded with panic, and cold sweat covered his forehead. He didn't dare look back. He knew Antonio and JJ were following close behind him, their footsteps echoing like a constant threat behind him.

His lungs burned from the effort, but he couldn't stop. As soon as he reached the shadows of the side street, he quickly crouched behind a parked car. The cold metal under his shaking hands didn't reassure him in the slightest. His eyes scanned the street, looking for any trace of his pursuers. Antonio and JJ were soon out of the building, their silhouettes outlined by the dim lights. Both looked around, scanning the area like predators sniffing out their prey.

Dr. James stifled a gasp, his breathing erratic and shaky as he brought a hand to his ear, activating the small earpiece he was carrying hidden away. He whispered desperately, fear latent in his voice.

"I'm being followed," he said, his tone almost cracking as he tried to remain calm.

On the other end, Mark Dawson's voice came through with a slight crackle, tense but controlled. Mark had always been the type of person who kept a cool head under pressure, the opposite of how James felt at the moment.

"Stay low. Where are you?" Mark asked, his tone direct.

James took another quick look around the car, making sure Antonio and JJ hadn't seen him yet. Both men seemed to lose interest in that part of the street and began backing up towards the building, but James knew the danger hadn't passed.

"I took a service door outside... behind the building," James replied, his voice barely a whisper.

Mark took a few seconds before answering, his voice lower, almost as if he could see the panic in James' eyes through the earpiece.

"Stay still. I'm on my way."

Dr. James leaned against the cold surface of the car, his heart pounding in his chest, each beat a countdown as he watched Antonio and JJ slowly retreat. Shadows were shrouding the scene again, but he knew it wasn't safe to trust the darkness. These men wanted him. They needed him.

As he tried to calm his breathing, his mind began to race with disturbing thoughts. How had he ended up in this situation? It had all started with the nanotechnology research he had been developing for the government. What had seemed like a promising breakthrough had soon turned into something much more sinister. Something involving people like Antonio and JJ, and names he had heard in whispers, like Katsuro Yamada, a Japanese businessman involved in shady dealings involving high-tech weapons. Dr. James never imagined that his work would lead him to this nightmare.

Since he had become involved in the project, more and more dark details had come to light. The technology he was working on was not used solely for medical purposes, as he had initially believed. Nanomaterials had devastating applications in the military field, and someone in high places was very interested in taking full control of these advances.

A nearby noise brought him out of his thoughts. A car passed slowly down the street, and James felt his entire body tense. He barely raised his head to look sideways, and for a second, he thought it was Mark. But it wasn't. The vehicle continued on its way, disappearing into the distance. James swallowed, anxiety bubbling up inside him again.

"Come on, Mark. Where are you?" he thought, feeling time running out.

Silence was once again his only company. Although Antonio and JJ had returned to the building, he couldn't shake the feeling that they were still looking for him. They were there for him. They knew too much. They knew what he had discovered. And now, they needed to make sure James didn't talk to anyone else.

A few minutes passed that seemed like hours. Dr. James remained crouched in his hiding place, listening for any movement in the shadows. Every night sound seemed amplified, as if the city itself was conspiring against him.

Finally, the earpiece emitted a soft crackle, and Mark's voice broke the awkward silence.

"Rich, I'm close. Are you okay?"

"I don't know..." James struggled to keep control of his voice. "They're still close, I'm sure they're looking for me."

"Listen, I have a plan. I'm going to have you picked up on the other side of the street. There's an alley around the corner, see? Head there as soon as I tell you. Not before."

James raised his head slightly to see the alley Mark was talking about. It was dark and seemed narrower than he would have liked, but it was his best option.

"I see it."

"Wait for my
Signal. Stay hidden for now.

James nodded, though Mark couldn't see him. He returned to his position behind the car, his body shaking, but he tried to focus on the plan. His mind was torn between fear and hope. If he managed to escape, maybe he'd have a chance to find out the truth behind all this. But if he got caught... he didn't want to think about the consequences.

The minutes passed slowly. Mark hadn't given the signal yet, and every second made James' anxiety increase. The sound of a door opening in the distance made him jump. He peeked over the edge of the car and saw JJ coming out of the building again, talking on a phone.

"Shit," James whispered.

JJ seemed to be giving orders to someone. Something in his posture gave him away; he was getting impatient. They knew James couldn't have gone far, and they were intensifying the search.

"Mark, they're moving again..." James whispered, panic growing in his voice.

"Hold on, Rich. Just a few more seconds. They're preparing to leave."

James took a deep breath, trying to stay calm. But everything inside him screamed that he had to run, that he had to move before it was too late.

Suddenly, JJ hung up the phone and turned, his gaze scanning the street in the direction of the alley. He seemed to have smelled something, as if he knew James was nearby.

"Mark!" James whispered urgently. "I think he saw me!"

Mark's voice was quick and firm:

"Run, now!"

Without a second thought, Dr. James stood up and ran into the alley, his legs moving faster than he thought possible. He could hear footsteps behind him, JJ and Antonio reacting almost instantly.

Chapter 39

Tokyo was a city that never slept, but on that night, the usual bustle seemed to be drowned out by the tension that dominated the minds of Dr. Richard James and Mark Dawson. As they walked down the hotel hallway, their swaying bodies showed the weight of the past few hours. Their breaths were short, laden with anxiety, knowing that what was at stake went beyond their own lives.

The door to the room slammed shut behind them, the thud echoing in the silence. Mark dropped his body to the edge of the bed, exhausted. Meanwhile, Dr. James didn't waste a second. His shaking hands searched his bag for the flash drive with the data he had so painstakingly extracted and inserted it into his laptop. He needed to verify the information, confirm that what they had was enough to stop the coming storm.

Graphics and data appeared on the screen quickly. The complexity of the information was overwhelming, but not for someone like him. He had spent the last five years developing the technology that was now about to be used for purposes he had never imagined. Every number, every graph, reminded him of the sleepless nights, the sacrifices, and most of all, the original purpose of his research: to save lives, not destroy them.

As Dr. James sifted through the files, his phone vibrated on his desk, breaking his concentration. He glanced at the screen: "Dr. Reinhardt." His stomach immediately tightened. He knew something serious was going on.

"What's going on?" he asked bluntly, answering the phone.

On the other end, Dr. Reinhardt's voice was a frantic whisper, barely able to keep his cool.

"What the hell have you done, Richard?" The accusation-laden question landed like a lead slab.

Dr. James frowned, bewildered.

"What do you mean? I haven't done anything."

"Nanotechnology!" Our research is out there, in the wrong hands!

James froze. He felt his stomach sink as he tried to process what Reinhardt had just said.

"What? We knew the technology was available, but the research… how?"

Reinhardt's voice cracked in frustration.

"Two Chinese military officers, posing as students, have stolen the research. They're reverse engineering it as we speak!"

The shock of that statement left James breathless. His fingers stopped moving across the keyboard. The air in the room seemed to become thick and suffocating.

"No… that's impossible. We've been so careful… How could they…?"

Reinhardt didn't let him finish.

"The Chinese government is already racing to develop the technology as a weapon! Richard, they have it all. Everything!"

James stood up abruptly, panic gripping him. Mark, who had been silently watching from the bed until then, sat up, noticing the change in tone of the conversation.

"No… it can't be," James muttered, almost to himself, his breathing labored as he tried to understand how it had all gone so wrong.

Suddenly, Mark's phone began to ring, breaking the tense silence. He exchanged a glance with James before answering, knowing the bad news wasn't over.

"General?" Mark said, trying to keep his voice steady.

General Cortez's voice, from the other end, was cold, unforgiving.

"Dawson, what the hell is going on? I've just been informed that the Chinese have taken over nanotechnology. Are you aware of the situation?"

Mark clenched his jaw, holding back his frustration as he began to pace back and forth.

"We didn't know, sir. This is the first time we've heard this. How did they gain access?"

General Cortez didn't bother to soften his answer.

"I don't know, but it's under your watch. I don't need to remind you of the consequences if this becomes public."

Mark felt a knot in his stomach. The pressure was palpable. He knew what was at stake, and it wasn't just technology. The entire agency's reputation and international relations were hanging in the balance.

"I'm aware, sir," Mark replied, his jaw set.

The General paused, his tone hardening even further.

"I'm giving you one chance to fix this. Or you're finished."

"So I have orders now? Officially?" Mark asked, searching for clarity amidst the chaos.

"Yes!" was the General's curt reply before he abruptly hung up.

Mark lowered the phone slowly, his mind already beginning to work on what the next step would be. He knew he couldn't afford any mistakes. Not this time.

Dr. James, still holding the phone, listened to Mark's conversation, and although he couldn't hear every word, he caught the tone and knew the situation was even more serious than he thought.

Mark walked over to the desk, his gaze fixed on the computer screen.

James.

"What do we have?" he asked, knowing that time was against them.

Dr. James began to sift through the computer logs again, his fingers shaking as he scrolled through the data. He knew there had to be some clue, some sign of how everything had fallen apart so quickly.

Then, a warning message appeared on the screen. In bright red, the words "MALWARE DETECTED" stood out like a cry of alarm.

"Damn it!" James exclaimed, a fist slamming down on the table.

Mark stepped closer, his brow furrowed as he read the message.

"They've been watching us this whole time," Mark said, his tone grave.

Dr. James leaned back, his hands clutching his head, stress etched into every line of his face. The feeling of being trapped, of having failed, was suffocating him.

Mark, on the other hand, didn't lose focus. He knew that hanging around moping wasn't an option. He walked over to the hotel window and pulled the curtains back a little to see the street below. The lights of Tokyo were still bright as if nothing had happened, but inside that room, they knew the fate of a dangerous technology was at stake.

"We have to act fast," Mark said, moving back to the center of the room. "We can't let this get out of here."

James nodded slowly, though he was still processing the gravity of everything that had happened.

Mark stood in the middle of the room, making quick decisions in his mind. They didn't have much time before the consequences became something bigger than them. With the malware revealing that they had been watched for some time, it was clear that this wasn't just a robbery. Someone had been following their every move, and they probably knew they were both in Tokyo.

"You have to delete those files," Mark said, his tone firm, leaving no room for objection.

Dr. James looked at him, his face still pale from the news he had just received from Reinhardt. The data he had on his computer was all his work, years of research, but he now understood that the danger of leaving that information in the wrong hands outweighed any other feelings.

"No… we can't just destroy it," James replied, his voice low but tense. "There are things in those files that we need. If we delete them, we lose any trace of how they are using it. We could be blind in this technological war."

Mark shook his head.

"I know, but if they've already accessed it, those files could be anywhere right now. The priority is to stop them from getting any more. Delete them and then we can come up with a plan."

James hesitated for a few seconds, but eventually, Mark's words echoed in his consciousness. With shaking hands, he began deleting the files. As he did so, he felt how each pulse of his fingers on the keyboard took away a part of his life, but there was no choice. Time was against him.

"Done," he said, closing the laptop with a dry click. Mark walked back to the window, looking out at the illuminated streets of Tokyo as he thought of his next move.

"We have to get out of here," he finally said, his words breaking the heavy silence of the room. "If they've been watching us, we're not safe in this hotel. They probably already know we're here."

Dr. James nodded, knowing that the paranoia he felt was more than justified. Anyone could be outside waiting for them. Antonio and JJ weren't the only ones.

Suddenly, Mark's phone vibrated again. He looked at it with a mix of surprise and alert, not expecting another call so soon. It was an unfamiliar number, which only added to his unease.

"Who is it?" James asked, eyeing the phone warily.

Mark watched him for a second before answering.

"Dawson?" a gruff voice said on the other end of the line.

Mark recognized the voice immediately. It was someone he hadn't expected to hear.

"Blake?" he asked, surprised. "What the hell are you doing calling here?"

Blake was an old acquaintance, someone who had worked in the shadows of the intelligence world, a man with no clear loyalties. If he was contacting Mark, it meant something much bigger was afoot.

"Listen, there's no time for questions. I know you're in Tokyo, and I know what's going on with nanotechnology. You're not the only one behind this." Blake's voice sounded more urgent than usual, and that wasn't a good sign. I've been tracking you, and believe me, I'm not the only one.

Mark looked at James, who was still listening intently to every word.

"What do you mean?" Mark asked, walking to the window again, feeling the weight of the situation intensify.

"The Chinese aren't the only ones interested in your little investigation. There are other hands moving the pieces on this board, and if you don't get out of Tokyo soon, you'll be caught between several forces you don't even know about. They're closer than you think." Blake paused, as if he was hesitant to say the next thing. "I left something for you at the hotel reception. You're going to need it if you want to get out of there alive."

Mark closed his eyes for a moment, knowing he didn't have many options. Blake wasn't someone he fully trusted, but if he said there was something waiting for him, it had to be important. The risk of ignoring him was greater than that of following his advice.

"Understood," Mark finally replied. "We're leaving right now."

Blake ended the call without further ado, leaving him alone with his thoughts. Mark turned to James, who was looking at him with a mix of curiosity and fear.

"What happened?" James asked, slowly getting up.

"Blake left us something at the front desk. I have no idea what, but we'll figure it out on the way. We need to get out of this place before things get worse."

James nodded, beginning to quickly gather his things. He knew Mark was right. Any second they stayed in that hotel brought them closer to danger.

They both left the room in a hurry, going down the elevator in tense silence. The walls of the small cubicle seemed to close in on them as the floor numbers slowly dropped. Dr. James' heart was pounding, and every time the elevator doors opened on a floor, they both held their breath, waiting to see if anyone else got in.

And, the doors swung open in the lobby, revealing the spacious, carefully decorated space. Mark and James walked briskly toward the front desk, trying not to appear too obvious, even though they knew discretion was probably no longer an option.

The receptionist gave them a curious look as they approached.

"Mr. Dawson," she said, "we received a package for you a few minutes ago." She pulled out a small, thin, seemingly insignificant brown envelope.

Mark took it, and the two of them headed toward the exit without even stopping to speak further. Outside, the lights of Tokyo still shone as brightly as ever, but to them, the city had become a silent battlefield.

Once they were in the relative safety of an alley a few blocks from the hotel, Mark broke the seal on the envelope. Inside was a small USB drive and a handwritten note in Blake's handwriting.

"This is your pass to get out. But it won't be easy. Do as I say, and you might just survive."

Mark exchanged a glance with James, who needed no further explanation. They knew what was coming was not going to be easy.

"Time to move," Mark said, his voice gravelly.

Dr. James nodded, his mind already working on the next step. They couldn't afford to fail, not now. The stakes were too high.

The tension in the room continued to rise as Mark and Dr. James processed the chaos they found themselves in. Dr. James remained rooted to the spot in front of his computer, his mind racing, while Mark paced back and forth, unable to relax.

"We don't have time to dither," Mark said, breaking the silence that was starting to become suffocating.

Dr. James looked up, his eyes unfocused after spending too much time in front of the screen. Tiredness was hitting him hard, but he knew Mark was right. With every passing minute, Li Wei and BioCore were moving further away, taking with them the stolen nanotechnology. A development that could upset the global balance if it fell into the wrong hands, and all indications were that it already had.

"I know we don't have time, but we need to make sure we don't make any mistakes. One wrong move and this whole thing could fall apart," James replied, closing his eyes for a second to try to clear his thoughts.

"We're already in a disastrous situation," Mark growled, stopping in front of the window with a scowl. "General Cortez is over my head, and now we're involved with a company that could be weaponizing our own technology against us. We can't trust anyone, not even the system."

Dr. James nodded slowly, understanding the gravity of the situation. He knew that nanotechnology wasn't just another tool. It was a revolutionary advancement that, if manipulated for warlike purposes, could forever change the way wars were fought. Invisible, lethal, and worst of all, untraceable weapons.

"Li Wei has deep connections to BioCore and the Chinese government," James murmured, looking back at the image of the man on the screen. "If we can find a way to get close to him, maybe we can get him to release something he doesn't want. There's always a weakness."

Mark looked at him, considering the idea. He knew James was right, but he also knew they were treading into dangerous territory. Li Wei was not an easy man to handle, and any mistake could cost them much more than information. It could cost them their lives.

"Okay," Mark finally said, with a sigh of resignation. "Let's do it, but carefully. We can't afford to be careless."

James nodded and began working on his plan. The idea of approaching Li Wei was risky, but they saw no other way out. The hardest part would be getting Li Wei to agree to a meeting. Mark was sure someone like him wouldn't be easy to access without raising suspicion. But James had his own contacts, and he knew there were ways to approach people like Li Wei, as long as you offered something of sufficient value.

"I'm going to try to contact some acquaintances," James said as he typed rapidly on his computer. "There are a couple of people in Tokyo who might be able to facilitate the meeting. People who don't ask too many questions, but have the right connections."

Mark watched silently as James worked. He knew he was in the hands of someone with a sharp intellect, but that didn't lessen the anxiety he felt knowing that everything depended on something as fragile as an agreement between people they barely knew.

A few minutes later, Dr. James stopped and looked at Mark.

"I got a meeting with someone who can make the connection to Li Wei," he said, though his tone was tense. "Tomorrow morning in Roppongi."

Mark raised an eyebrow. Roppongi, the most chaotic and bustling district in Tokyo, was the ideal place to hold a discreet meeting without attracting attention, but it was also known for being the center of clandestine activities.

"Perfect," Mark murmured. "But we can't trust anyone. I'll be prepared for the worst."

Dr. James nodded, aware that any wrong move could prove fatal. As he put away his computer and closed his briefcase, his mind kept thinking about the step they were about to take. Everything seemed fragile, a simple lie could crumble the entire plan.

"Do you think we can make it?" James asked, looking directly at him for the first time in a while.

Mark looked back at him, firm but without promises.

"There is no other option," he answered simply.

Chapter 40

The next morning came faster than expected. Tokyo, in its usual frenzy of activity, offered no respite to those who tried to go unnoticed. Mark and James headed to Roppongi, a place where the mix of neon lights and dark alleys was complemented by the bustle of nightlife. They arrived at a small cafe, discreet but public enough not to raise suspicions.

"We'll be fine here," Mark whispered, observing the place. It seemed like a place of passage, the kind of place where no one asked questions.

Dr. James nodded as he adjusted his jacket, feeling uncomfortable in the situation, but knowing that he had to keep
He looked at his watch impatiently. There were only a few minutes left before his contact would arrive.

Not long after, a middle-aged man, dressed formally but with a nervous presence, entered the café and looked around before locating them. He made his way to their table with a slight nod.

"Mr. James, I'm Hiroshi. Nice to meet you," the man said, extending his hand.

James and Mark exchanged a quick glance before James shook the newcomer's hand.

"Thank you for coming, Hiroshi. We need your help in contacting Li Wei. We know you have the necessary connections," James said, getting straight to the point.

Hiroshi leaned forward, lowering his voice.

"Li Wei is a very difficult man to reach. But, I have an… arrangement with one of the companies he frequents in Tokyo. If you really want to get close to him, there will be conditions."

Mark narrowed his eyes, sensing that something else was coming.

"What kind of conditions?" "We'll get it," he asked, his tone slightly threatening.

Hiroshi remained calm.

"Money, of course. And discretion. If anything goes wrong, I won't be able to help you anymore."

Mark sighed. He knew this was about paying for information and access, and even though he didn't like it, they were up against a rock and a hard place.

"We'll get it," James said. "Tell us where and when."

Hiroshi nodded, handing them a paper with the details.

"Li Wei will be at a private reception tomorrow night. It's your best chance. But be careful. He's not someone you can easily fool."

Mark and James exchanged a glance, knowing the next day could be decisive.

"We'll be ready," Mark said, as Hiroshi stood up and bowed slightly.

The tension between them was palpable as they put the paper away. They knew what was coming would be a dangerous move, but they had no other options.

"Tomorrow, then," James murmured. It all depends on how we handle it.

"And we will handle it," Mark replied with determination. "There is no room for error."

****

The atmosphere in the BioCore conference room was as cold and calculated as the minds of those who inhabited it. Despite the palpable tension, the calm that enveloped each of the executives showed that they had been in difficult situations before. Mr. Hartman, the man in charge, sat at the head of the table with an unflappable look, but his fingers drummed on the table like an uncontrollable tic that betrayed his anxiety. The executives around him stared at the files stacked in front of them, waiting for the next move.

The sound of footsteps on the shiny floor broke the tense silence, and the door slowly opened. Everyone turned their heads toward the entrance, where a figure appeared with overflowing confidence. Emily, with a mischievous smile, walked calmly up to the table, unhurried but with firm purpose.

"Emily…" Mr. Hartman raised his voice, giving her a welcoming smile. "How nice of you to join us."

Emily sat down beside him, maintaining her confident demeanor, unfazed by the critical situation that had led to this meeting. Hartman's gaze hardened as he swept his eyes over the files in front of him, before settling back on her.

"We have a problem. We've learned that the Chinese military has stolen the nanotechnology before we could begin our bidding war. We thought everything was under control."

The other executives exchanged nervous glances, but Emily remained unfazed. Not a single muscle on her face betrayed concern.

"It's not a problem," Emily replied, keeping her voice cold and calculating. "It's an opportunity, Mr. Hartman."

Hartman frowned, confused by her nonchalant attitude.

"The research has been stolen, so excuse me if I'm not sure how this is an opportunity," he said in an incredulous tone, leaning forward.

The other executives looked at him with the same uncertainty. Emily, however, maintained her composure. She knew she had the key to turning a crisis into an advantage.

"They haven't stolen everything," Emily explained, her smile widening. "I let them keep the first part… let's call it a gift, a taste of what's to come. Something to whet their appetite."

Hartman crossed his arms, intrigued, and the executives leaned forward, interested in what Emily had to say.

"I'm listening," Hartman said, lowering his voice.

Emily continued calmly, as if it were all part of a master plan that only she knew about.

"The critical part of the research is still with us. Now they think they have it all, but soon they'll realize that they're missing the key to turning the technology into a full weapon."

The air in the room changed. The executives, who had been tense and worried before, began to exchange approving glances. Emily's strategy was taking shape in their minds, and they liked what they heard. Hartman tapped his fingers on the table lightly, impressed.

"So you set up the Chinese… to create demand from others," he said, clearly impressed. "Brilliant."

One of the executives, sitting to Hartman's left, nodded with a sly smile.

"They'll be desperate for the missing piece," he said, his eyes shining with an idea. "And we'll be in a position to sell it to the highest bidder."

Emily nodded, her confidence growing with each word.

"Exactly," she said. "The Chinese don't know what they're missing yet, but they will soon. And when they do, we'll have every major government lined up, ready to pay whatever it takes to control this technology."

The silence that followed was the kind of silence that only happened when everyone understood they were faced with a unique opportunity. The BioCore executives looked at

Emily with respect. She had turned an apparent defeat into a potential goldmine.

Hartman, wasting no time, rose from his seat and extended his hand to Emily, a clear sign of approval.

"You really know how to play the game, don't you?" he said with a smile. "We were worried when we heard about the theft, but you've turned this into a goldmine. Even though you couldn't bring Richard to us, you can still prove yourself a valuable asset."

Emily accepted the praise with a slight nod, but she wasn't done.

"There's more," she said, her eyes sharp as knives. "I also think we should prepare to show them how powerful this technology is. A test."

Mr. Hartman raised an eyebrow. The executives, intrigued, turned to him, looking for his answer. Hartman smiled slowly, a smile that indicated he was in complete agreement.

"A test?" Hartman repeated, his tone indicating he already knew exactly what kind of test Emily wanted.

Emily maintained her calculating smile.

"Just something small, just enough to attract the right attention. We know what this kind of technology can do."

"I can do it, but they need to see it to understand the true power they could have in their hands."

One of the executives, a tall, thin man with calculating eyes, spoke for the first time.

"And how do you propose to do this test, Emily?"

Emily leaned forward, her voice lowering in tone.

"There is a target in Japan that has been interfering with our progress. If we demonstrate what this nanotechnology can do there, we not only eliminate a threat, but we also demonstrate its effectiveness to potential buyers."

Hartman nodded slowly, clearly considering the idea.

"We will," he said finally. "Make the arrangements, but keep it discreet. We don't want to draw attention to ourselves too quickly."

Emily nodded, satisfied that her plan was in motion.

"Everything is under control," she said with unwavering confidence. "We will be ready when the bidders start coming to us."

Hartman shook her hand once more, clearly satisfied.

"Good job, Emily. Keep the pressure on." We'll let the bidders come to us and we'll make sure we make a profit no matter what.

Emily stood up from her seat, prepared to execute the plan that was now in motion. She knew that what was coming would not only change the dynamics of BioCore, but that of the entire world as well. As she walked out of the room, she couldn't help but think about what was coming next.

"A test," she thought to herself, "just the beginning of something much bigger."

With her mind sharpened and her next steps planned, Emily set out to prepare the test that would prove to the world the true power of BioCore's nanotechnology.

Emily walked out of the conference room with firm, determined steps. The meeting had been a success, but her work was just beginning. In her mind, the pieces were lining up; the Chinese believed they had won the game by stealing the nanotechnology, but they didn't know they only had one piece. And now, the real fight for control of the technological future was about to begin.

As she walked down the long hallway of BioCore, Emily mentally reviewed her next moves. She needed to act quickly and precisely. A small test, enough to demonstrate the power of the technology, but not big enough to raise immediate suspicion. A target in Japan seemed perfect. A country with a key influence on the economy and a close relationship with advanced technological research.

She pulled out her phone and dialed a number. On the other end of the line, a man's voice answered immediately.

"Yes?"

"Get ready," Emily said calmly. "We have a target in Tokyo. I need you to act quickly and discreetly."

"Understood," the man replied without asking any further questions. "Who is it?"

"Don't worry about the details. You'll get the information soon. Just make sure it all looks like an accident."

He hung up the phone and continued walking. Emily knew that the success of this move would determine the future of BioCore and her career within the company. The nanotechnology they controlled was not only a key piece in the biotechnology industry, but a potential global weapon. Controlling this technology was like having power over the fate of entire nations.

Arriving at her office, she turned on her computer and began working on the logistical details of the next step.

She knew the technology was ready to be tested, and what she needed now was the perfect time to prove it.

A few minutes later, an encrypted message appeared on her screen. It was from one of her contacts in Japan, a man with access to crucial information. The message was short but contained what Emily needed: the exact location of a clandestine laboratory in Tokyo, run by a small organization that was interfering with BioCore's plans. This lab was a perfect target. The attack might seem like an accident, but it would be a clear signal to everyone involved of what was at stake.

Chapter 41

Dr. James sat motionless in front of his laptop screen. His eyes remained focused on the message he had just received. Every word, every line of the attachment, cut through him like a dagger. Emily, the person he had trusted the most, had betrayed him in the most brutal way possible. She had been manipulating everyone from the very beginning, including him.

"Emily…" James whispered, almost not believing what he had just read.

Mark, who had been pacing the room, walked over and read the message over James' shoulder. When his eyes caught Emily's name, his expression went from confusion to shock and finally anger.

"She was always in control," Mark muttered, crossing his arms and frowning as he processed the revelation.

James slammed the laptop shut, the sound echoing in the silent room. The echo of the slam was the only thing heard for several seconds. His breathing was heavy, and his face was tense from the mix of emotions overwhelming him: anger, pain, betrayal.

"She set this all up… from the start," James said, his voice cracking but filled with growing determination.

"There's no point in meeting Wei now," Mark interjected. "It's not going to change anything."

But James wasn't listening anymore. His mind was racing, searching for the next step. He'd made the mistake of trusting Emily, and now everything he'd worked for, everything he'd believed in, was at risk. But he wasn't going to let her get away with it.

"I trusted her… and she used me," James continued, clenching his fists as he spoke. "But she's not going to get away with it."

Mark watched him silently. He knew James wouldn't let himself be carried away by desperation; if there was one thing he'd learned over the years working with him, it was that James was a man who always found a way out. But this time, things were different. They had been toying with them from the very beginning, and now they were caught in a web that went far beyond what they could control.

"What's the plan?" Mark finally asked, breaking the silence.

James looked up at him, and his expression had changed. He was no longer the scientist caught in chaos, but a man determined to regain control.

"We're going to expose her. We're going to bring all of this out into the open. If BioCore is willing to sell this technology to the highest bidder, we can't let it go ahead. And if Emily is behind this, she'll be the first to fall."

Mark nodded slowly. It wasn't a brilliant plan, nor was it extremely complex, but it was the only one they had. And the only viable option at the moment was to act before it was too late.

"And where do we start?" Mark asked, his eyes fixed on James.

"Reinhardt has more information. If he sent me this, it's because there's something we haven't seen yet. I need to get to him before BioCore or Emily do."

Mark walked over to the window, looking out at the lights of Tokyo that were beginning to come on as day fell. He knew that even though they were in enemy territory, they had no choice but to move forward. Emily's revelation had been a blow, but not the final blow. They still had time.

"Do you think Reinhardt will be willing to help us?" Mark asked, with a hint of skepticism.

"If he's still alive, yes," James replied coldly. "But we can't wait. We must move now."

Mark nodded and grabbed his jacket. He knew James was right. Every minute that passed brought them closer to a trap they didn't even know if they could avoid. If BioCore was willing to sell the nanotechnology to the highest bidder, time was the one thing they didn't have.

"What do you need?" Mark asked, checking his phone to coordinate the next step.

"First, direct contact with Reinhardt. I need to make sure they haven't found him yet." If he has more evidence, that could give us the advantage we need to stop BioCore. And then, we need a contingency plan. If this goes wrong, and we don't have enough evidence, we need to be prepared to disappear.

Mark looked at him with a raised eyebrow.

"Disappear?"

"If Emily knows we're close to discovering her plan, she won't stop until she eliminates us. And not just her, but all of BioCore. We can't risk standing still."

"Understood," Mark replied. "I'm going to make some calls. Let's see what we can move before it's too late."

James watched as his friend left the room. He knew they were in a tight spot, but he also knew he couldn't let Emily's betrayal go unpunished. She had played everyone, and now it was time to strike back.

Chapter 42

Hours later, in a small meeting room on the outskirts of Tokyo, Emily stood before her team again. Reports of the success of the initial operation were beginning to come in, and their plan was in motion. The sale of the nanotechnology
ology would be the final blow to securing BioCore's power, and once they achieved it, no one could stop them.

But something was bothering her. Despite the apparent victory, she knew she couldn't underestimate James. She had worked with him for years and knew his ability to survive even the most difficult situations. However, now it was different. She was in control, and James didn't know what was coming.

"The next step will be to make sure there are no surprises," Emily said, looking at the executives around her. "I want a full report of any unusual activity. No one can know what we're doing until it's too late."

One of the executives, an older man with a scar on his face, raised his hand.

"What about James?" he asked. "Don't you think he can interfere?"

Emily smiled coldly.

"James is already out of the game. He won't realize what we're doing until it's too late." By the time he finds out, he won't have the power or resources to stop us.

The man nodded, seemingly satisfied with the answer. Emily knew she couldn't show any sign of hesitation. If she wanted to stay in control, she had to demonstrate confidence at every step.

"Now, get ready," he ordered. "This is just beginning."

The meeting ended, and Emily watched her colleagues leave one by one. As the last door closed, she pulled out her phone and dialed a private number.

"Are you ready?" she asked, not bothering to say hello.

The voice on the other end of the phone answered firmly.

"Everything is under control."

"Perfect. I don't want any mistakes."

Emily hung up the phone and fell silent, staring at her reflection in the window. She knew she was playing a dangerous game, but there was no turning back.
The silence in the hotel room where James and Mark were staying was thick, only broken by the occasional sound of cars on the streets of Tokyo far below them. James had reopened his laptop, but this time not to check the files,

but to make sure he didn't leave any traces behind. If Emily was messing with them from the start, she had to assume they would be closely watched.

****

Mark returned with a worried expression, holding his mobile phone in one hand while the other ran through his hair in a gesture of frustration.

"Reinhardt isn't responding," he announced, not even waiting for James to ask.

James looked at him, his face grim. It wasn't a good sign. Reinhardt had been his most trusted contact, someone who had been inside the BioCore system and who, it seemed, had seen enough to turn against them. If he wasn't responding now, that only meant two things: either he had been discovered, or he was hiding to protect himself.

"Then we have to assume the worst," James said, not looking up from his screen. "If he doesn't respond, they may have already found him."

Mark slumped into a chair, letting out a frustrated sigh.

"This is a mess," he muttered. "We have no advantage now. Emily is in control, and BioCore is about to sell the technology to the highest bidder. If Reinhardt doesn't show up, we're done for."

James frowned, thinking about the situation. He had been confident that Reinhardt would be the key piece to dismantle the entire plot, but now everything seemed to be falling apart. But giving up was not an option.

"We're not done yet," he finally said, breaking the silence. "We still have one card up our sleeve."

Mark looked at him, confused.

"What card? What do we have left?"

James looked at his partner with a faint smile, a spark of determination shining in his eyes.

"Emily."

Mark frowned, still not understanding.

"What are you suggesting? Talk to her?"

James nodded slowly.

"Emily has always been ambitious, but she is also extremely calculating. She is playing with everyone, we know that. But what she may not have considered is that now we can play with her."

Mark looked at him silently, slowly understanding what James was trying to say.

"If we can make her believe that we have something that she doesn't have," James continued, "we could force her to act. And when she does, we can expose her."

Mark thought for a few seconds.

"And what exactly would we make her believe that we have? We don't have anything right now."

"We don't need it," James replied. "We just need her to believe it. Emily is in a position where the fear of losing what she has achieved can be her greatest weakness. If we plant the seed of doubt, if we make her think that we have obtained proof, we could make her make a mistake."

Mark let out a sigh, understanding the move but not yet completely convinced.

"It's risky, James. If she suspects we're playing her, she could end up sinking us before we even have a chance to do anything."

James nodded, acknowledging the danger.

"I know. But if we don't do anything, she wins anyway. We have to try."

****

Meanwhile, in the luxurious BioCore building, Emily walked through the halls with a firm step, confident and self-assured. She knew that each step brought her closer to complete control. She had worked too hard to get to this point and she wouldn't let anyone, not even James, interfere with her plan. Everything was in motion. Bidders had already begun sending signals of interest, and the bidding war she had orchestrated would become a resounding success.

Yet in the back of her mind, a small voice kept whispering doubts. She knew that James wouldn't give up easily. She knew him well enough to know that he would still try to fight, that he would look for a way to expose her. But she was prepared for that.

In fact, she had already given instructions to keep an eye on him. As soon as James or Mark made a wrong move, they would be ready to act. Nothing they tried would work. Nothing would save them.

Emily walked into her private office, closed the door, and sat at her desk, reviewing the latest reports. The sale of the nanotechnology was imminent. Within days, BioCore would be even more powerful, and she, the mastermind behind it all, would get her reward. But one persistent shadow kept clouding her mind: James.

She picked up her phone and dialed a private number. The call was answered on the first ring.

"Any news on James?" Emily asked, wasting no time on formalities.

The voice on the other end answered immediately.

"Nothing concrete. We're keeping an eye on him, but he hasn't made any moves yet that suggest he has anything that could harm you."

Emily frowned.

"Keep watching. I don't want any surprises. If he does anything suspicious, take him down."

She hung up the call and stared out the window, her face a mix of confidence and concern. He knew She was close to getting everything he wanted, but She couldn't afford to let her guard down now. James was still a risk.

Chapter 43

Hours later, James and Mark sat in the small hotel room, working out their plan. They both knew they didn't have many options, but they also knew the only way to beat Emily was to anticipate her moves.

"We have to get the information to her subtly," James said, typing frantically on his laptop. "We can't be obvious. If she suspects we're trying to set her up, she'll crush us before we can do anything."

Mark watched him, still somewhat skeptical, but aware they didn't have many other options.

"And how do you plan to do that?" Mark asked. "We can't just send her a message saying we have proof."

James smiled.

"No. We won't do it." We'll use someone else.

Mark looked at him, intrigued.

"Reinhardt?"

James shook his head.

"No. Someone she doesn't see coming. Someone who is in her circle, but not so close as to raise suspicions."

Mark frowned, beginning to understand.

"A BioCore executive?"

James nodded slowly.

"Exactly. Someone important enough to be close to Emily, but not so involved as to know everything. We'll make it look like that person has discovered something and is willing to betray her. Emily will react, and when she does, we'll be ready to expose her."

Mark let out a long sigh, taking in the plan.

"It's risky... but it could work."

"It's our only chance," James replied, his eyes filled with determination. "And I don't intend to waste it."

Mark nodded silently. he knew James' plan was dangerous, but she also knew it was her only chance to unravel the web of lies Emily had woven around her.

Chapter 44

The air in the BioCore conference room was thick with tension, as if every word Emily spoke was a silent shot echoing through the minds of those in attendance. The global officials, projected on screens in front of her, could barely conceal the mix of awe and anxiety on their faces. Emily held them in the palm of her hand. She knew that what they had just witnessed was only a taste of what nanotechnology could do, and its power felt almost tangible in the air.

Mr. Hartman, sitting at the end of the table, watched with a discreet smile, enjoying the control his company had gained. The other executives remained silent, all knowing that they were about to witness a historic event. The world as they knew it was about to change, and BioCore would be the epicenter of that change.

"Ladies and gentlemen, what you have just witnessed," Emily began, her voice firm but calm, "is only a fraction of the true power we possess."

She paused, allowing the gravity of her words to settle into the minds of each of the attendees.

"With this technology," she continued, "you don't just have the ability to control water sources. You hold the key to dominating entire civilizations. With a single command, you could destabilize economies, control governments, and change the global balance of power."

As she spoke, images of fading lakes and rivers continued on the screens, silent witnesses to the destructive power BioCore had developed. The officials didn't say a word, but their eyes revealed everything. They knew that what they had before them was a force with the ability to alter the course of history.

Emily smiled subtly. It was the smile of someone who knew that she had already won, that each of those officials was desperate to get their hands on that technology.

"As you know," she continued, "certain actors have attempted to appropriate fragments of our research. You can be assured that what they have obtained is not the complete product."

Li Wei, a high-ranking official on the screen from China, frowned.

"We have heard rumors," he said suspiciously, "that certain critical elements of the investigation are still beyond your reach. What about Dr. James? It is said that without him, your work is incomplete."

Emily remained calm under the question. She knew this question would come up at some point. She had been prepared for this.

"Dr. James is only one part of the process," she replied, her tone authoritative. "But rest assured, our technology is already fully operational, as we have just demonstrated. The missing components will be under our control before this auction ends."

Emily's words hung in the air, and the global officials remained silent, processing what it meant to be one step away from gaining such absolute power.

Mila Petrova, from her office in Moscow, raised an eyebrow skeptically.

"So you admit that they don't have everything yet?" she asked, her voice laced with cynicism.

Emily didn't flinch.

"That's right," she said, bluntly. "But as I've told you, that will change in less than forty-eight hours. And by then, those of you who decide to go ahead with the auction will be the first to get your hands on the most powerful geopolitical weapon ever created."

Katsuro Yamada, a representative from Japan, let out a short, cutting laugh.

"I'm not interested in empty promises," he said coldly. "If you don't have the whole package, this is a waste of time."

Emily maintained her composure. She knew this kind of pressure would come from a man like Yamada, one used to having everything under his control.

"Mr. Yamada," she said softly, "what you just saw is already enough to tip the balance of power. The ability to disintegrate a water source anywhere in the world... do you really think that's an empty promise?"

Yamada's eyes narrowed, but he didn't answer. He knew she was right.

Mr. Hartman, until then silent, leaned forward and nodded to Emily, motioning for her to continue with her presentation.

"Very well," Emily said, turning to the others in the room. "If there are no further questions or concerns, I suggest we begin with the auction."

The officials shifted in their seats, some exchanging glances, others quickly checking their devices. Emily could see nervousness slowly turning into greed. They were ready to fight for what she was offering, and they weren't leaving without making their bid.

"Bidding will begin in one hour," Emily announced. "You have until then to gather the funds and make sure you're ready to get into the game. This isn't just a financial transaction. This is history in the making, and you're at the forefront of it."

With a nod, Emily finished the bidding.

The meeting ended and the screens began to go dark one by one, leaving the BioCore executives alone in the room.

Hartman rose from his seat and approached Emily. There was a spark of admiration in his gaze, though also a certain wariness.

"Well done," he said, his voice low but firm. "You've got everyone eating out of the palm of your hand."

Emily nodded, grateful but not entirely relaxed.

"We're not done yet. James is still a problem. If we don't stop him before he moves his next piece, we could lose everything."

Hartman smiled arrogantly.

"Don't worry about James. We'll find him before he's a real problem. We've already taken steps to make sure he doesn't interfere with the auction."

Emily looked at him with a mix of skepticism and relief. She knew Hartman was a resourceful man, but she also knew James wasn't someone easy to stop.

"I hope you're right," she replied. Because if not, we could be playing a very dangerous game.

Hartman laughed softly.

"Don't worry. By the time this is over, James will be just a footnote in the story of our success."

Emily fell silent, watching Hartman walk away toward the door. She knew the game was far from over, and James, while a threat, was also her only weakness.

Chapter 45

The roar of engines filled the air as the plane touched down, its tires screeching against the tarmac. The lights of the airport illuminated the scene, creating long shadows beneath the plane as air traffic control operators directed each move. The familiar lights of the city loomed in the distance, a reminder that they were finally back in the States. For Mark Dawson, sitting in row 12 by the window, it was a bittersweet return.

"I can't believe we're back here after everything that happened in Tokyo," he murmured, breaking the silence he'd maintained for the last few hours of the flight.

Beside him, Dr. James barely looked up from his phone, once again scrolling through the files and emails he'd received before leaving Japan. His face showed signs of fatigue, but the tension was evident in his hands, which shook slightly as they held the device. He couldn't get the name that had appeared in Reinhardt's email out of his mind: Emily.

"I know," James replied dully, "but there was no other option. We couldn't stay there any longer."

Mark nodded, though something inside him still felt like they'd left something unresolved. They'd left Tokyo in a hurry, barely understanding the magnitude of what was at stake, but returning to the United States only amplified his concerns.

"What now?" Mark asked as the plane slowed, heading for the gate. "What's our next step?"

Dr. James put his phone in his jacket pocket and finally allowed himself a deep sigh.

"First we need to make sure what we have is safe. Reinhardt gave us the pieces we need to understand what's going on, but there are still loose ends. I can't… I don't want to believe Emily is behind all this."

Mark let out a bitter laugh.

"Do you really believe that? After what we saw? She sold us out, James." Everything we did at BioCore was part of her plan.

James pressed his lips together. He knew Mark was right, but accepting Emily's betrayal was a bigger blow than he was willing to acknowledge.

The plane finally came to a stop and passengers began to stand up, gathering their belongings from the overhead bins. Mark and James did the same quietly. The noise in the cabin intensified as the doors opened and travelers began to file out into the aisle.

"We have to move fast," Mark said as he slung his backpack over his shoulder. "We're not the only ones who know what's going on. Emily isn't going to wait for us to figure out her next move."

James nodded as they followed the flow of passengers toward the plane's exit. Each step he took felt heavy, as if a dark cloud was enveloping him more with each passing second. He had been a scientist all his life, a man of logic and reason. But now, logic was betraying him, and reasoning was no longer offering him the answers he needed.

When they finally got off the plane and into the airport terminal, the typical hustle and bustle of an American airport night greeted them. Families waiting, people rushing to their flights, employees bustling about. Despite all the chaos, James felt there was an eerie calm in the air, a stillness that didn't fit with his agitated mind.

"Is the contact here?" Mark asked as he looked around, searching for any sign of the person who was supposed to pick them up.

James checked his phone again, looking for the message he had received before boarding the plane. A name and a photo accompanied the message: "Gray. He will take care of getting you to a safe place. Wait for him at the arrivals gate."

"He must be nearby," James said, though his words lacked conviction.

Mark continued to search the crowd, his attention divided between the unfamiliar faces and the growing worry in his chest. He knew they were being watched. He had felt it ever since they left Japan. And even though they were back on American soil, he didn't feel safe.

Suddenly, a tall, sturdy figure approached, dressed in a long coat and a hat that covered part of his face. His movements were firm, calculated, and when he reached them, he raised his head just enough to reveal a pair of cold, calculating eyes.

"James. Dawson. I'm Gray," he said in a deep voice. "Come with me."

James and Mark exchanged quick glances before following him. Something about the way he moved and spoke told them that this man was not someone to be underestimated. As they followed him out of the terminal, the lights of the city shimmered in the distance, but the shadows seemed to lengthen around them.

Gray led them to a black SUV parked on a secluded corner of the terminal.

Airport. Wasting no time, he opened the back door and urged them inside. Once they were inside, he climbed into the driver's seat and started the engine.

"We don't have much time," he said as he quickly pulled out of the parking lot. "There are more people behind this than you think, and you're right in the middle of it all."

James frowned.

"What do you know about Emily?" he asked, unable to stop the name from slipping from his lips.

Gray didn't take his eyes off the road, but his jaw tightened.

"More than you'd like to know," he replied enigmatically. "She's not who you thought. But for now, the most important thing is to keep them alive. We'll talk more when we're safe."

Silence filled the vehicle as they made their way through the night streets. Mark leaned toward James, whispering in a serious tone.

"I don't like this. What if he works for Emily, too?"

James didn't respond immediately. Doubts were also crossing their minds, but at that moment, they didn't have many options.

"For now, we must trust him," he finally said. "We have no other choice."

Gray led them through the city, and as they went, the lights of the city faded, replaced by the darkness of the outskirts. Further and further away from the hustle and bustle, the landscape became eerie.

Finally, after what seemed like hours of driving, the SUV stopped in front of an abandoned industrial building. Gray turned off the engine and turned to them.

"This is our hiding place for now. You'll be safe here while we figure out the next step."

James and Mark exchanged glances, and although they knew they didn't have many options, they couldn't help but feel vulnerable. They were in a country they knew, but danger was still lurking, and every move they made brought them closer to the truth... and to Emily.

Dr. James got out of the vehicle, followed by Mark. They looked at the building in front of them, its grey walls and broken windows reflecting abandonment. It was the kind of place no one would look, which made it perfect… but also terrifying.

Gray stepped out of the SUV and, without another word, motioned for them to follow him into the building. Darkness enveloped them as they crossed the threshold, and with each step, they felt the danger around them grow more palpable.

Chapter 46

The interior of the building was gloomy and echoey. The walls were covered in graffiti and the air had a musty, abandoned smell. The light coming through the broken windows created eerie shadows on the floor. Mark looked around, feeling increasingly uneasy. It was the kind of place where one could disappear without a trace.

Gray led the way, moving confidently through the space. At the back, there was a door that led to what looked like a small makeshift laboratory. It was a tidier room than the rest of the building, with a work table full of equipment and documents scattered everywhere.

"This is where we can talk more calmly," Gray said as he closed the door behind them. Still staring at the equipment, he began to look through some files on the table.

James sat down in one of the chairs, while Mark stood, watching Gray intently. The tension was palpable. There were so many unanswered questions, and the uncertainty about Emily's role hung over them like a dark shadow.

"I need to know what you know about Emily," James said, breaking the silence. His voice was firm, though he could sense the anxiety within.

Gray looked up, sizing James up before speaking.

"She's cunning. Very cunning. She's manipulated everyone around her to achieve her goals. When you think she's on your side, she's actually playing a much bigger game. Her goal is control of nanotechnology, and she's been one step ahead of everyone."

Mark crossed his arms, frowning.

"But why? What's her motivation? Is it just money, or is there something else?"

Gray sighed, his expression becoming more serious.

"Nanotechnology has the potential to change the world, and Emily knows it. People are willing to do anything for power. She's not just after financial gain; she wants to be the one to control this new era." Imagine having the ability to alter the watcr supply, to manipulate natural resources. That gives you power on a global level.

Mark felt uneasy. There was something about the way Gray spoke that made him feel like they were in a trap, that every word was part of a game in which they were the pieces. But he had no choice but to listen.

"So what do we do now?" Mark asked. "How can we stop her?"

Gray walked over to a whiteboard where charts and notes were scattered about. He pointed to a map showing several key locations around the world.

"The first thing we need to do is understand where the technology is now and how it's being distributed. I've been tracking the movements of BioCore and its contacts. There's an auction group that several governments and organizations are participating in."

James leaned forward, interested.

"Auctions? What auctions?"

"Nanotechnology auctions," Gray replied. "Everyone wants a piece of the pie, and that means there's going to be a lot more activity in the coming days." The auction is set to end in less than a week, and Emily is at the center of it all.

Mark narrowed his eyes.

"So, we need to infiltrate. We need to get proof that she's behind this before it's too late."

Gray nodded, his expression grave.

"Exactly. But it won't be easy. Emily has unlimited resources at her disposal, and she's surrounded by loyal people. To get to her, we first have to dismantle her protection network."

James felt overwhelmed. There were so many moving pieces, so many variables. But there was one question that consumed him.

"And Reinhardt? How does he fit into all this? He knew enough to warn me."

Gray looked at him with a frown.

"Reinhardt is involved in a complicated way. He's a brilliant scientist, but he's been playing both sides. We need to find out what he knows and how he can help us. If we can get his help, we might have a chance."

Mark straightened, determined.

"So, what's the plan?" How do we locate Reinhardt?

Gray paused, watching the two men.

"There's one place we could find him. An old BioCore lab on the outskirts of town. If he's still there, he may have vital information."

James looked at Mark. It was risky, but they had no time to waste.

"Let's do it," James said, rising from his chair. "We can't let Emily win."

As they prepared to leave, a sense of urgency took hold of them. Every minute they spent in that hideout was a minute closer to Emily being able to act. Danger lurked, and they were determined to confront it.

Meanwhile, in an isolated cabin on the outskirts of town, Emily was sifting through documents scattered on a table. Shadows danced around her, and the only sound was the creaking of wood beneath her feet. She held a phone in her hand, nervous, knowing the situation was becoming increasingly dangerous.

"Is everything ready?" —she asked her contact on the screen.

The figure on the screen was a man with an imposing face, with an air of authority.

"We are ready to proceed. The auctions are scheduled for tomorrow and we have interested buyers," he replied, his voice deep. "But, Emily, you must be alert. There are rumors that James and his team are on the move."

Emily frowned.

"I can't let that stop me. I'm closer to getting what I want. If I secure the technology before they do, they won't be able to stop me."

The man on the screen leaned forward.

"Remember, Emily. Absolute power attracts attention. You must be careful."

She smiled, her gaze hardening.

"They won't stop me. I've worked too hard to let a couple of misfits get in my way."

****

The car sped down the road, the engine rumbling loudly as Mark kept his gaze fixed on the road. The dark night stretched out around them, broken only by the lights of the headlights. Dr. James was deep in thought, the weight of the situation weighing on his shoulders. Every message that came through on his phone reminded him that time was running out.

"Emily," he finally murmured, as if the name itself could conjure her up. "She's always one step ahead."

Mark turned his head, his expression grave.

"We can't let that stop us. If we can get the remaining data, we can have an advantage. But first, we need to get rid of her."

James looked at him, feeling a twist in his stomach.

"Are you talking about eliminating her? No, Mark, that's not what we need." If she figures out our plans…

"It's not just about her," Mark interrupted. "It's about stopping what BioCore has in mind. Nanotechnology in the wrong hands can be devastating."

James took a deep breath, taking in Mark's words. There was undeniable truth in what he was saying, but the moral dilemma plagued him.

"We need to find a way to disable her operation without causing her personal harm," he replied. "If we're going to do this, she needs to be smart."

Mark ran his hand through his hair, frustrated.

"I see your point, but we're in a race against time. We can't just stand there waiting."

James' phone vibrated again. Without thinking, he picked it up and saw that it was another message from Reinhardt.

"What if I answer her?" he asked, his voice nervous. "She could have vital information."

Mark stared at the road, not taking his eyes off the road.

"We could be giving him information about our movements."

James stared at the message, his fingers trembling over the screen. Reinhardt had sent details about a new location where a nanotech auction was taking place, and a couple of names that could be potential allies.

"I have no choice," he finally said. "If I want this plan to work, I must act now."

"Okay. But please be careful. We don't know who we can trust," Mark replied.

James nodded, feeling like every decision was crucial. He drafted a quick response to Reinhardt and sent it before he could change his mind.

James glanced at Mark, who kept his eyes fixed on the road.

"What do we do with the information we get from Reinhardt?" he asked, trying to plan.

"We'll use it to access the auction. Once there, we'll need to get the technology into our hands," Mark replied, gripping the steering wheel tightly.

James nodded, feeling the pressure mounting.

"If we manage to infiltrate and obtain the technology, we can prove that BioCore cannot be trusted."

"Right. And so, we may have a chance to alert the international community," Mark added. "But, to do that, we need to find a contact within the auction. Someone who can guide us."

"I'm going to check out the buyers. We need to identify those who might be willing to work with us," James said, pulling his laptop out of his backpack.

Mark watched as James began typing, concentrating on searching for information.

"You know what I'm thinking?" Mark asked, breaking the silence.

"What?" —James replied without taking his eyes off the screen.

'That this could be a trap. If Emily finds out about our plans, we could fall into a game we can't win'.

'James looked up, feeling a chill run down his spine'.

'You're right. But we can't stop now. I don't have the option to stop and back out'.

Chapter 47

Dr. Reinhardt's lab was plunged into near-total darkness, with only the weak light of a few monitors flickering in the corner. The air was heavy, charged with a palpable tension that both Dr. James and Mark felt as soon as they walked through the door.

"It can't be a coincidence," Mark whispered, his footsteps echoing on the tiled floor of the lab. He paused for a moment, taking in the chaos: papers scattered on the floor, an overturned chair, and Dr. Reinhardt's phone abandoned on the desk.

Mark knelt beside the overturned chair, examining the floor carefully. He saw small marks, scratches on the floor that didn't seem to make sense at first glance. But upon closer inspection, he understood what they meant: signs of a struggle.

"She didn't walk out of here," he said quietly, almost to himself.

Dr. James, across the room, took the phone from Dr. Reinhardt. His hand shook as he held it, his mind spiraling. He had worked with Reinhardt for years, and while he always suspected something like this could happen, he was never prepared for this moment. He felt cold sweat on his forehead, but he fought to keep it together. His breathing quickened as he tried to process the situation.

"They took him," Mark concluded, standing up and looking around the lab once more.

James opened his mouth to answer, but at that very moment, he felt the vibration in his pocket. His heart skipped a beat as he saw the name on his phone screen: "Emily." He knew answering that call meant facing what he feared most, but he had no other choice.

"Emily," he replied, his voice tense.

"Richard…" Emily's voice sounded strangely soft on the other end. "I missed you."

James exchanged a quick glance with Mark, who frowned at the name. Emily was no stranger to either of them.

"Where's Reinhardt?" James demanded, wasting no time.

"Oh, he's safe… for now," she replied, almost mockingly.

James felt anger rising within him, but he knew he had to remain calm. Emily always played with other people's emotions, and this time would be no different.

"What do you want?" Her voice came out harsher than he expected.

"I'll get to the point, I like that about you," Emily replied, her tone growing icy. "You want to know what I want, but you already know that, Richard. I've always wanted it. Power, control, money. And now, I'm closer to that than ever."

Mark moved closer, listening to the conversation intently, but keeping his eyes fixed on the shadows of the lab. Something didn't fit, something they were both overlooking.

"If you hurt him…" James began, but Emily cut him off with a soft laugh.

"Hurt him? I'm not a monster, Richard. Dr. Reinhardt is my trump card. Make sure you don't do anything stupid." Her voice grew sharper.

Mark waved his hand, pointing toward the back door of the lab, urging James to get moving. There was something else here, something they needed to figure out before it was too late.

"What's your ultimate goal, Emily?" James asked, trying to buy time.

There was a brief silence on the other end of the line. When Emily spoke again, her tone was cold, calculated, far more so than James had anticipated.

"I'm offering the world something it's never had before… control. Control over water, over life itself. Don't you see? This is bigger than all of us."

James felt his stomach turn. He knew Emily had always had dangerous ambitions, but this was beyond what he had imagined.

"You know where to find me when you're ready to join the winning team," Emily said before hanging up.

James stared at the phone in his hand as the line went dead, fury boiling inside him. Mark watched him silently, waiting for his partner to say something.

"What do we do now?" Mark finally asked, breaking the silence.

James took a deep breath, trying to get his emotions under control. He knew they couldn't just sit back and wait. Emily had Reinhardt, and that meant time was running out.

"We have to find her before it's too late," James finally said. "But first, I want to know what Reinhardt found before he was kidnapped. Something in this lab must tell us what he was working on."

Mark nodded, and the two of them began searching the lab for any clues. They knew Emily wouldn't stop, and the stakes were bigger than they could imagine

While Mark focused on sifting through the papers scattered on the floor, James walked over to a computer terminal that was still on. The system appeared to have been shut down hastily, but James had some tricks.

s up her sleeve. With quick hands, she began entering a series of commands, attempting to restore recent files that might have been deleted or locked.

Mark, for his part, picked up one of the papers and studied it. The diagrams were complex, filled with chemical formulas that were familiar to him only on a superficial level.

"This isn't just any research," Mark muttered, grimacing. "This looks like something involving nanotechnology."

James nodded as he continued to work on the computer. Finally, after a few tense minutes, the screen showed a series of files. Reinhardt had been working on something big, something involving the manipulation of nanomaterials at the cellular level. And according to the files that appeared, Emily wasn't exaggerating in her call. If they controlled this technology, they would have the power to change the balance of the world. Control over water, over life itself, just as she had said.

James leaned over the screen, eyes fixed on the open files. The silence in the lab grew deeper as the pieces began to fit together in his mind. The graphs showed data indicating how nanomaterials could integrate with living tissue, capable of altering essential biological functions. If Emily managed to control this technology, she would have the power to rewrite the rules of life itself.

"This… this is crazy," Mark muttered from across the room, still sifting through the papers. He held up one in particular that contained an intricate equation that eluded his understanding. "Do you really think Emily has control over something so… dangerous?"

James gritted his teeth, barely nodding. He knew Emily too well. They had worked together before, years ago, when all of this was nothing more than an idea. But something had changed in her, something that had led her down a dark and twisted path. Her ambition had always been relentless, but now, with Reinhardt gone, that ambition was on the verge of becoming a global catastrophe.

"What worries me is not whether she has control now," James replied, his tone more somber, "but how much time she has left before she completely gets it."

Mark dropped the papers on the table and approached James, watching the screen with growing unease.

"So, what's our next step?" he asked. "We can't go after her without knowing exactly what she's planning."

James looked at him seriously.

"Emily left a clue. 'You know where to find me when you're ready.' That means she wants us to go after her."

"Sounds like a trap." Mark crossed his arms, clearly uncomfortable. "But we don't have much of a choice, do we?"

James shook his head. They had no choice.

"No, we don't. And the longer we wait, the closer Emily will get to her ultimate goal." We need to move fast.

Mark nodded, aware of the danger involved. But they couldn't afford to hesitate. James stood up from the desk, gripping the phone tightly in his hand.

"I know a few places where Emily could be hiding," James said, walking towards the door. "Come on. If she has Reinhardt, then there's no time to waste."

The streets were dark and empty as James and Mark's car sped through the buildings. The normally vibrant city now felt strangely desolate, as if sensing the chaos looming over it. The car's engine roared as they took the turns, and the tension inside the vehicle was palpable.

Mark stared out the window, losing himself in thought for a moment, as the city lights flickered past them. Something about the conversation with Emily continued to unsettle him.

"What do you plan to do if we find Emily?" "Mark asked suddenly, breaking the silence that enveloped them.

James didn't take his eyes off the road, but his jaw tightened. The truth was, he didn't have a clear answer. He knew Emily was dangerous, but she was also someone he had once considered close to. The line between duty and personal feelings was blurred, and that only made things more complicated.

"First, make sure Reinhardt is safe," James replied firmly. "After that, we'll do whatever it takes to stop her."

"Even if it means…?"

"Even if it means going all the way, Mark."

Mark looked at him, searching for any sign of doubt, but all he found in James was cold determination, a resolve he hadn't seen in him in a long time. Dr. James was known for his patience and analytical skills, but now, it was clear that something else was driving him. The personal danger Emily represented, mixed with her boundless ambition, had ignited something in him.

The car turned onto a side street, stopping in front of an abandoned industrial building. The lights inside were off, but James knew this was one of the places Emily might be operating. She had been here before, years ago, when it had all started.

"Are you sure about this?" Mark leaned forward, looking at the dark building.

"I am," James replied, turning off the car's engine.

They both got out of the vehicle in silence. The night felt colder than usual, and the wind whistled through the building's broken windows. There was no sign of life inside, but that didn't mean they were alone.

James stepped forward, walking to the front door with cautious steps. Mark followed close behind, his hand ready to draw his gun in case things got messy. The plan was simple: get in, find Emily and Reinhardt, and get out before things got ugly. But they knew that in situations like this, things rarely went as planned.

The interior of the building was completely abandoned. The walls, covered in graffiti and damp stains, gave the place an air of desolation. The floor creaked under their feet, and the echo of their footsteps resonated in the wide empty space.

James moved forward with determination, but his mind was on alert. He knew that Emily was too smart to leave obvious clues. Every corner, every shadow could hide a trap. Mark was right behind, his eyes attentive.

"Are you sure she's here?" Mark asked quietly.

"If she's not here, we won't be far from finding her," James replied.

The air in the office was heavy, charged with pent-up tension. Mark Dawson rubbed his temples in frustration as he paced the room.

"They took him," he said, his voice shaky, but filled with rage.

Dr. Richard James didn't have time to respond. His phone vibrated in his pocket, cutting through the silence. He pulled it out and his heart skipped a beat when he saw the name on the screen. "Emily." Why now?

"Emily," he replied, trying to stay calm, though his mind was already in a thousand directions.

Emily's soft voice sounded on the other end of the line, a mix of nostalgia and something darker.

"Richard… I missed you."

Dr. James pressed his lips together, feeling the weight of each word. The last time they spoke, it had all ended in a verbal battle, with broken promises and painful truths. But that wasn't the priority now.

"Where's Reinhardt?" "He asked, direct, without beating around the bush.

"Oh, he's safe… for now," Emily replied, her tone playful, only further igniting Dr. James's uneasiness.

Mark stopped and stared at him intently, waiting for a sign, a clue as to what was going on. James exchanged a tense look with him before turning his attention back to the call.

"What do you want, Emily?"

There was a small silence, then a light laugh.

"Always so direct, Richard. I like that about you. You know exactly what I want. Power, control, money. The usual. And now I'm closer to it than ever."

"If you hurt him…" Dr. James began, his tone threatening, but he was interrupted.

"Hurt him? Please, I'm not a monster, Richard. Dr. Reinhardt is the key to making sure you don't try anything foolish. Don't underestimate me."

Mark moved closer, his ears attentive to every word. Frustration and fear were evident on her face, but Emily's voice remained cold and calculating.

"What is your ultimate goal, Emily?" he asked, knowing the answer would cost him sleep that night.

The line was silent for a moment before Emily's voice came back, this time icier, more distant.

"I'm offering the world something they've never had before: control. Control over water, over life itself. Don't you see, Richard? This is bigger than you, than me, than all of us. But don't worry, you still have an open invitation to join the winning team. You know where to find me when you're ready."

The "click" on the phone echoed in Dr. James' mind like a sentence. Emily had hung up. He looked at the phone in his hand, the glow of the screen slowly fading as anger began to burn within him.

"What did She say to you?" Mark asked anxiously, moving closer.

Dr. James set the phone down on the table and took a deep breath.

"She has Reinhardt. And she's not going to stop."

Mark slammed his fist against the wall, his frustration about to explode.

"I knew this was going to happen. I knew it ever since this whole damn project started falling apart. Emily has always been two steps ahead."

"The worst part is that she's right," Dr. James said, almost resignedly. "She's in control, and we're trapped."

Mark turned away, frowning.

"We can't let her get away with this. If she gets the control she seeks… there's no stopping her."

"I know," James said, his voice thick with tension. "But the first thing we have to do is find Reinhardt."

Mark nodded, his eyes burning with determination.

"We've got a lead now. She can't be far away."

Both men knew that every minute counted, and the more time passed, the more control Emily would have over the board. It wasn't just a matter of saving Reinhardt, but of keeping the world from falling into the wrong hands.

****

Night fell quickly, but tiredness didn't set in. Dr. James found himself in his study, surrounded by papers, reports, and analysis that no longer made sense. His mind was elsewhere, on every word Emily had said, on Reinhardt's safety, and on what it all meant. It was like being caught in a web he himself helped weave.

Mark returned after making a few calls, his footsteps echoing in the quiet hallway.

"I've talked to a few people. We have someone looking into Reinhardt's latest locations, but it won't be easy. Emily's been very careful," Mark said, sitting down in a chair across from James.

"She always has been," James replied, not taking his eyes off the papers on his desk. "She knew exactly how to get us to this point."

Mark clenched his fists. —What I didn't expect was that we were willing to fight.

James looked up and nodded slowly. —No, I didn't expect that.

Silence settled between them, only broken by the soft hum of the desk lamp's fan. They both knew they couldn't afford any mistakes. Reinhardt's life was at stake, and with him,

Emily's cabin was just a dot on the map compared to the Biocore location. A sleek glass and steel building stood in the darkness, lit by bright lights and surrounded by luxury cars.

Emily stepped out of her car, looking around with satisfaction. She had worked hard to get to this point, and she wasn't going to let anyone get in her way.

"Everything is in its place," she said, approaching the entrance, where security guards were checking out the attendees. "Let the show begin."

Chapter 48

The sound of the engine echoed through the night as Mark's car sped away from the parking lot. The lights of the city flickered on the horizon, but for Dr. James, the beauty of the scene was overshadowed by growing anxiety. The thought that Dr. Reinhardt might be in danger kept him on his toes.

"We need to think clearly," James said, staring out the window, his mind occupied with the possible scenarios that could have led to his colleague's disappearance. "If they've gone looking for him, that means they know more than we think."

Mark frowned as he maneuvered through the dark streets.

"Exactly. And if BioCore is behind this, they're one step ahead. We need to act fast."

James took a deep breath, trying to calm his thoughts.

"The last I heard of Reinhardt, he had been working on something important. A new version of nanotechnology that could change everything," he said, his voice breaking. "If that has fallen into the wrong hands…"

"We can't let that happen," Mark interrupted. "Let's go to his lab and find out what's going on. There may be clues to his whereabouts."

James nodded, feeling his determination growing.

****

The vehicle stopped in front of an old building, its windows covered in dust and neglect. A barely visible sign announced the lab. The door was ajar, and a shadow moved inside.

"Do you see it?" Mark asked, pointing to the open door. "Come on."

James got out of the car, his heart pounding. They approached the entrance, cautiously.

The scene inside the lab was bleak. Equipment was scattered, and papers were strewn across the floor. James felt a knot in his stomach at the sight of the place like this.

"Reinhardt…" he called, his voice echoing in the silence. "Reinhardt!"

Mark moved quickly to one of the workstations, scanning the turned-off monitors.

"There's no sign of a struggle, but this doesn't look right," Mark said, his tone grave. "Something here doesn't add up."

James bent down to pick up a crumpled document that was near the door.

"Look at this," he said, holding it up to Mark. "They're notes on nanotechnology, but they seem incomplete. Reinhardt was about to make a breakthrough."

****

In the parking lot, a dark car pulled up to the corner, and two hooded figures watched from a distance, waiting for the right moment.

****

Mark was still checking the computers.

"If we find the latest version of his data, maybe we can understand why they were looking for him," he said, gritting his teeth in concentration.

"The lab interface should be on his main computer," James replied. "Let's go find it."

Both men moved quickly, searching every corner of the lab, but soon noticed that the computers were turned off and inaccessible.

"There's no power," Mark said, frustrated. "We need a way to turn this on."

****

The figures in the dark car looked at each other, recognizing the opportunity they had.

"What do we do?" one asked nervously.

"We wait." If they're here, they're probably taking us to Reinhardt.

****

James found a backup generator in a corner.

"Here!" he shouted. "Maybe this will work."

He hurriedly turned on the generator, and slowly, the lights began to flicker and then stabilize.

"Perfect. Now let's see if we can access the main computer," Mark said, heading for the console.

James walked over, feeling relief beginning to set in.

"Here it is. Logging in," he said, typing frantically.

The figures, seeing the lights turn on in the lab, smiled at each other.

"Come on," one said. "Time to act."

Mark looked at James, anxious.

"What does it say? What did he find?"

"It seems Reinhardt was working on a security protocol. Something to do with nanotechnology control," James replied, his fingers moving quickly over the keyboard. "There it is. I got it!"

Suddenly, the sound of glass breaking rang through the air. Both men turned, their hearts pounding.

"What was that?" Mark asked, his voice filled with tension.

"I don't know. We should go check," James said, feeling the adrenaline flowing through his veins.

The hooded figures crept up to the back door of the lab, their faces covered in shadow.

"We're in," one of them said, holding a gun,

Mark and James left the lab, following the sound.

"Someone's here," James whispered, sensing the tension in the air. "We have to be careful."

Mark nodded, and they both moved toward the source of the sound. As they moved forward, the atmosphere felt increasingly tense.

A resonant echo led them into the hall, where they found more broken glass. Shadows seemed to move, and the atmosphere became dark.

"Is there anyone here?" James called, his voice firm.

There was no response.

"It's a trap, I know it," Mark said, looking around suspiciously. "Let's back up."

****

The hooded figures entered the lab, armed and ready for whatever came next.

"The nanotechnology must be here," one said. "Search everywhere."

****

James and Mark found themselves back at the back of the lab, looking for a way out.

"We need to get out of here. There's more than we expected," James said, feeling a mounting pressure.

"We can't let them catch us," Mark replied, looking toward the door. "We need a plan."

Both men felt the air grow heavy. At that moment, the sound of footsteps echoed through the hallway.

"Quick," Mark whispered. "This way!"

****

They ran toward the back of the building. Meanwhile, the hooded figures began to surround the main entrance.

"Where are we going?" James asked, looking into the darkness.

"To the street. We need to get a vehicle," Mark said, running into a nearby alley.

****

The hooded figures looked through the lab window.

"Where are they?" one asked, frustrated.

"Let's go find them," the leader said, ordering them out.

****

James and Mark stopped in the alley, looking for a vehicle.

"There," Mark pointed to a parked car. "Come on."

They both ran to the car, and as they tried to open the door, they heard the sound of footsteps approaching.

"Hurry!" James shouted, struggling with the lock.

Finally, they managed to open the door and threw themselves inside. Mark started the engine, the sound of the starter echoing through the night.

"Come on, come on!" James said, looking out the window as a hooded figure appeared in the doorway of the lab.

****

The car shot out of the alley, and both men felt momentary relief.

"We made it," Mark said, accelerating. "But we can't let our guard down."

James turned

to Mark, his expression worried.

"What do we do now? We have no idea where Reinhardt is."

"We'll contact Interpol. They might have information," Mark replied, his face hardened with determination.

****

James' phone vibrated on the seat. He glanced at the screen. It was a message from Interpol.

"Looks like we have news," he said, opening the message. "We've been alerted to unusual movement in several labs. It could be related to BioCore."

'So, wherever we go, we must be prepared' Mark said, feeling the tension rising again.

****

The lab was enveloped in a tense silence. Dr. Li Wang, a renowned Chinese scientist, walked slowly down the hallway, going over reports of the latest experiments. He knew something wasn't right, but the prestige of his research kept him moving, ignoring the warning signs. Inside the testing room, the subjects were confined to their capsules, plunged into semi-darkness.

"Everything seems to be under control," Li Wang muttered to himself as he scanned a screen filled with fluctuating biological data. But he couldn't ignore the uneasiness in his stomach. The tests had begun to show unstable results days ago, and his superiors were growing impatient. The pressure to speed up the experiments was intensifying.

Suddenly, a subtle knocking sound came from the other side of the lab. Li Wang looked up, his eyes darting to the capsules. One of the subjects, a stocky, vacant-looking man, began to move, his fists pounding on the glass that kept him trapped. Li Wang frowned, adjusting the controls to sedate him.

"This shouldn't be happening," he whispered. Yet when he pressed the buttons, nothing changed. The subject thrashed harder, his eyes bloodshot.

"Damn it! Why isn't it responding?" Wang shouted, running to the main console. As he tried to reset the systems, another pod began to shake. Then another.

The man in the dark suit, who had been watching from the security booth, leaned forward, his eyes fixed on the monitors. He didn't move an inch, his hands clasped in front of him, as if he were waiting for the inevitable disaster.

"Dr. Wang," his assistant's voice came over the intercom. "Containments are not responding. Subjects are breaking restraints."

Before Wang could respond, the nearest pod exploded with a metallic crack. The man inside emerged covered in sweat and blood, his face contorted with anger and pain. He lunged at Wang with inhuman speed.

"No!" Wang screamed, backing away, but it was no use. The subject caught up with him, his hands closing around his neck with brutal force.

The man in the dark suit continued to watch, impassive, as chaos erupted in the testing room. The other test subjects broke their capsules one after another, advancing towards the limp body of Dr. Li Wang with unstoppable fury. The scene was fast and bloody, an uncontrollable violence that could only have been seen coming if the warnings had been heeded in time.

The man in the dark suit calmly took his phone, still watching the images of the massacre unfold before his eyes. He dialed a number and waited for the other end to answer.

"The test subjects have gone out of control. Dr. Li Wang is dead," he said emotionlessly, as if he were reporting something routine. "We need immediate intervention. Inform the Chinese authorities."

He hung up without waiting for a reply, his eyes fixed on the screens that now showed the test subjects, free and uncontrolled, moving like predators inside the lab.

The chaos that followed was absolute. The guards tried to stop the subjects, but they responded with inexplicable brutality. Meanwhile, the authorities received the alert sent by the man in the dark suit, quickly mobilizing their forces.

The clock on the wall marked the passage of time, but at that moment it seemed as if everything was suspended. Every second counted as the destruction continued, and lives were taken in a place that was once a bastion of science and progress.

The man in the dark suit stood up from his seat, calmly adjusting his tie. As the guards stormed into the lab to try to control the situation, he had already left the observation room. He knew this would not stop here.

Chapter 49

The Biocore conference room was almost dim, the city lights reflecting off the huge windows that offered a panoramic view of the skyscrapers. The dim blue light projected from the video screen illuminated the face of Emily Carter, who sat in one of the long chairs at the conference table, her expression unmistakably satisfied. It was as if the world was on the verge of a transformation, one she herself had meticulously planned.

In front of her on the screen appeared the calm but calculating face of Li Wei, the Chinese tycoon who had invested millions in the research they now controlled. His soft voice contrasted with the tension in the air.

"Mrs. Carter," Li Wei said in a neutral tone, "when can I expect to receive the rest of the technology? And by that, of course, I mean Dr. James."

Emily let out a calculated smile, one that showed more power than any words could convey. She knew perfectly well what Li Wei wanted, and she knew she had the situation in her hands.

"Don't worry, Mr. Li. Everything is in place. Dr. James will be taken care of," she said, leaning back slightly in her chair, projecting confidence. "It's just a matter of time."

Li Wei nodded, but he didn't seem completely satisfied.

"I need all the technology in our hands, Emily." His voice hardened a little, letting her know that patience wasn't his strong suit. "You promised I would have everything, and now that I've paid a substantial amount, I expect to receive what I paid for."

Emily didn't let his tone intimidate her. She leaned forward, resting her elbows on the table, keeping an enigmatic smile on her face.

"I understand perfectly, but remember, you already stole some of the technology… so let's not play coy." But rest assured, I already have a team in China that is ready to give you another example of the power of nanotechnology." She paused dramatically before continuing. "And if all goes as planned, you will have two doctors for the price of one."

Li Wei seemed to think about it for a few seconds before nodding slightly.

"Two doctors and the full research. I like where this is going."

Emily's smile widened. She knew she had convinced Li Wei to remain calm. The promise of more technology and power was a language he understood better than anyone.

She leaned back in her chair, crossing her legs with the confidence of someone in absolute control.

"You will have everything you need, Mr. Li. The future of this technology is in your hands, as we agreed. And I am sure you will make the most of it."

Li Wei narrowed his eyes, a barely perceptible nod of approval.

"It seems I will. It has been a pleasure doing business with you, Mrs. Carter." Tell Mr. Hartman that I appreciate him and that he has done an outstanding job.

"The pleasure is mine," Emily replied softly. "I look forward to seeing how this plays out."

Li Wei smiled for the first time, a smile that did not reach her eyes.

"I will be waiting for the doctors. Tomorrow, then."

Emily nodded slowly. "You will have them."

Li Wei watched her for a moment longer before adding in a more somber tone,

"See that you fulfill what you promised. We will be monitoring your every move. The slightest failure will not be tolerated."

"There will be no failure, Mr. Li. You have my word."

Silence settled between them for a few seconds, before Li Wei's image flickered and the screen went dark. Emily sat for a moment, staring at the emptiness on the screen. She felt the weight of what she had just assured. It was a risky move, but she was used to moving in that kind of territory. She knew that everything depended on execution.

Suddenly, the doors to the conference room swung open and Mr. Hartman, her right-hand man, entered with a look that alternated between satisfaction and concern. His ever-upright posture reflected a mix of arrogance and preparation.

"Anything new?" he asked, without preamble.

Emily didn't look up, still processing the conversation with Li Wei.

"Mr. Li is a little unsure, but I convinced him to stay calm. I assured him that he will have the doctors by tomorrow at the latest," she replied calmly, although inside her the pressure was palpable.

Hartman smiled, satisfied.

"Excellent work, Emily. You've done well."

Emily gave a mischievous smile as she leaned back once more. Hartman approached the empty screen, staring at the reflection of his own face, as if he were already seeing the future.

"Tomorrow we'll know," Hartman murmured, almost to himself. If everything goes as planned, tomorrow will be the beginning of a new era.

Emily nodded, but something inside her was not completely at peace. She knew there were more players in this game, and one of them was Dr. Richard James. If they didn't get

If she could neutralize him soon, the whole plan was in jeopardy. As confident as she was, Dr. James was not someone to be underestimated.

Chapter 50

The vast, dark waters of the Pacific Ocean stretched out beneath the night sky, a shroud of mystery that hid deep secrets. The distant sound of helicopter blades grew louder, reverberating through the night. A helicopter bearing the BioCore logo streaked across the sky, its bright lights casting beams across the dark water.

Inside the aircraft, the masked operator peered out of the side door. His heart pounded as he held a small case in his hands. He opened the case, revealing several glowing vials that emitted an eerie glow. It was the latest technology developed by Biocore, a breakthrough that promised to change the course of humanity, but also had the potential to become a destructive weapon.

Without hesitation, the operator began to toss the vials into the ocean one by one. Each one sank into the water, shining like stars lost in the darkness. The helicopter, satisfied with its work, was moving away, disappearing into the night, leaving behind only the echo of its blades and the ephemeral glow of the vials.

****

The city lights flickered through the large windows, creating an eerie contrast to the tense atmosphere of the room. Emily stood firmly by the window, her mind

489

working at full speed. Mr. Hartman, at the head of the table, was checking numbers on his tablet, his face showing a mix of satisfaction and disdain.

"The offers are already coming in," Hartman said, looking up. "We control the technology now. All that remains is to close the deal."

Emily took a step forward, her gaze fixed on the horizon, as if searching for answers in the distance.

"We're not done yet," she replied, her tone calm but firm.

Hartman arched an eyebrow, amused by Emily's apparent concern.

"We're not done yet? The Chinese, the Russians, the Japanese… They're all making moves to get the last piece." Once the deal is done, it's over. There's nothing else to worry about.

Emily finally turned away from the window and walked over to the table, her expression impassive.

"I want Richard," she said determinedly.

Hartman let out a mocking laugh, setting his tablet aside.

"Richard? You think he's going to go into BioCore after all? That would be the dumbest thing he could do."

Emily kept her gaze locked on Hartman.

"Richard has a big heart. He's always trying to play the hero and help his friends. And that's where he's wrong. He won't stop, not as long as he thinks he can save the day."

Hartman tilted his head, his interest piqued.

"And you're counting on that?"

Before Emily could respond, the doors to the room opened with a soft hiss. Antonio and JJ entered, their faces cold and professional. Between them was Dr. Reinhardt, bound and gagged, his face frightened. His face showed signs of having been beaten.

"Of course," Emily said, her voice now laced with subtle menace. "He thinks there's still a way out of this. But he's already lost. He'll come here believing he can stop the auction, save Reinhardt, and maybe convince me to switch sides, because that's what he is."

Hartman crossed his arms, amused.

"He'd have to be delusional."

Emily moved closer to Dr. Reinhardt, crouching down to look him in the eye. The lack of compassion in his gaze was palpable.

"You should have known. But there's still time to choose the winning side."

Dr. Reinhardt tried to speak through the gag, his voice muffled by the panic that was washing over him. Emily continued, her tone soft but menacing.

"You could have left, John. But now you'll be the reason Richard comes running, and then, we'll have you both."

Hartman stood up, approaching Emily, intrigued but wary.

"You're pretty sure you think Richard is coming here to save someone he barely knows."

Emily stood up, facing Hartman with a smirk.

"He can't help it. He is who he is. He'll try to save Reinhardt, and when he does, we'll make sure he's in no position to do anything but take our side, giving us the perfect team to make the technology the best it can be."

Hartman frowned thoughtfully.

"We can form our own team."

Emily shook her head, impatient.

"No. I want Richard. I need to see the look on his face when he realizes he's out of options."

Hartman nodded slowly, understanding the complexity of the game they were playing.

Emily looked at Antonio and JJ, giving them a silent signal. Antonio smiled slightly, pleased with the nonverbal command.

"Make sure he stays quiet." When Richard comes, we'll give him exactly what he wants... for a price.

Antonio nodded, dragging Dr. Reinhardt out of the room, JJ following close behind. The door closed with a soft click, leaving Emily and Hartman alone, their plan now fully in motion.

The phone rang on the table, breaking the silence of the conference room. Emily, sitting in a chair, answered the call without hesitation.

"Yes? 92," she said, her voice firm.

"It's done," a voice answered on the other end.

A slight smile curved Emily's lips as she watched Mr. Hartman, who was looking through documents. She ended the call and stood up, crossing the room to where Hartman sat.

"They've made the launch," she announced, her enthusiasm barely contained.

"We've got everything set in motion. Now, all that's left is to see how it plays out," Mr. Hartman replied, not taking his eyes off the papers.

Emily walked away from Hartman, feeling a mix of pride and anticipation. They knew they had taken another step towards controlling the future, but deep inside them there was a spark of unease.

The control room was lit by flickering screens displaying real-time data. Emily and her team were working quickly. Suddenly, an alarm sounded, breaking their concentration.

"Security alert!" shouted Alex, a young technician who had been monitoring the systems. "It seems something is not right!"

Emily quickly approached the console, observing the screens.

"What is going on?" she asked, her voice tense.

"The systems are failing, but I don't know why. We need to reboot everything," Alex replied, her face pale with worry.

A loud crash echoed through the hallway, sending them both into a tense silence. Emily's breathing stopped and worried glances were exchanged.

"Did you hear that?" Alex whispered, her eyes wide.

"Yes," she replied, feeling her heart pounding. "Stay alert. We don't know what's going on."

As they worked, tension rose and the noise of chaos outside grew. Emily couldn't shake the feeling that they were on the verge of something much bigger than they had anticipated.

After what seemed like an eternity, the systems began to stabilize. Emily let out a sigh of relief, but it was short-lived as a new alert appeared on the screen.

"Warning: A breach has been detected in Sector C!" the automated voice echoed, sending shivers down Emily's spine.

"A breach? How is that possible?" Alex exclaimed, her voice filled with disbelief.

"I don't know," Emily replied, her mind racing. "We need to alert the security team. This could be serious."

"I'm on it!" Alex said, already punching the security line. Emily focused back on the control panel, the weight of the situation crushing her.

As they waited for an answer, Emily paced back and forth, her mind racing with possibilities. Suddenly, the door swung open, and a security officer burst in, his face pale.

"We have a situation!" he shouted, breathing heavily. "There's an intruder in Sector C, and we can't locate him!"

"What do you mean you can't locate him?" Emily demanded, adrenaline surging through her. "We need to contain this now!"

"We're trying! But the cameras went off after the alarm went off, and there's been no communication from the sector!" the officer replied, his voice tense.

The weight of responsibility settled on Emily's shoulders.

"We need to go there," she said, her voice firm despite the fear that filled her.

"Are you crazy?" Alex protested, grabbing her arm. "What if they're armed?"

"We can't let them compromise everything we've worked for," Emily insisted, breaking free from his grip. "We must act, now!"

"Okay," the security officer said, her resolve strengthening. "We'll go together. But we need to be careful."

The three of them moved cautiously down the dimly lit hallway leading to Sector C, tension crackling in the air. Emily's heart pounded as they approached the door, the hum of the lights providing the only sound.

"Ready?" the security officer whispered, glancing at Emily.

"Let's do it," she replied, determination shining in her eyes.

She nodded, and they pushed open the door, stepping into the unknown.

Inside, the air felt heavier, charged with a palpable sense of danger. Emily scanned the room, her instincts on edge. Shadows danced along the walls, and she could hear the slightest sound of movement.

"Stay close," she instructed, her voice low.

As they moved deeper into the area, they found chaos. Overturned equipment, papers strewn across the floor, and the atmosphere grew thicker. Emily's heart sank.

"This isn't good," she muttered, fear creeping into her voice.

Suddenly, a loud crash echoed from the back, causing them to jump.

"What was that?" Alex whispered, her voice barely audible.

"I don't know, but we need to investigate," Emily urged, feeling panic beginning to set in.

They crept closer, adrenaline coursing through their veins. As they rounded a corner, they came face to face with a figure, a shadowy silhouette moving between the teams.

"Hey!" the security officer shouted, reaching for his gun.

But before she could react, the figure darted away, disappearing through an exit door on the other side of the room.

"Stop!" Emily shouted, immediately leaping in pursuit.

They ran after the intruder, the sound of their footsteps echoing in the empty hallway. Emily's breathing came fast as they ran through the maze of equipment and shadows.

"This way!" the officer shouted, veering to the left. Emily followed, her mind racing with questions. Who was this person? What did they want?

Around another corner, they saw the figure slip into a maintenance hatch. Without thinking, Emily lunged forward, but the hatch closed just before she could reach it.

"Damn it!" she exclaimed, frustration welling up in her.

"What now?" Alex asked, panting beside her.

Emily backed away, her mind working at full speed.

"We can't let him get away. There must be a way to track him."

"We could check the security footage," the officer suggested, his voice firm.

"Let's do it!" Emily agreed, feeling a renewed urgency.

They rushed back to the control room, adrenaline coursing through their veins. Screens flickered, and Emily quickly pulled up the security footage from Sector C.

"Come on, come on…" she muttered, her fingers flying over the keyboard.

The video came to life, showing the chaos from moments before. Emily's heart was pounding as she scanned the footage, looking for any sign of the intruder.

"There!" she pointed at the screen, watching as the figure appeared, its movements quick and agile. "What are they doing?"

The footage revealed the intruder rummaging through the equipment, seemingly looking for something specific. Suddenly, it stopped, looking towards the door, as if it sensed they were being watched.

"What do they want?" Alex asked, confused.

Emily leaned closer to the screen, her heart pounding.

"I don't know, but we need to find out."

Just then, the screen flickered and the recording abruptly cut off. Emily's breath caught in her throat.

"No! What happened?" she exclaimed, pressing buttons frantically.

"Looks like the system went down," the officer said, desperation beginning to creep into his voice.

"We need backup," Emily decided,

knowing they had to act fast. "We can't let this continue."

She picked up the phone, her mind focusing on the task at hand as she dialed the security number.

"This is an emergency! We need backup in Sector C immediately," she ordered, her voice clear and firm.

As she waited for a response, Emily looked at Alex and the officer, who shared worried glances.

"What if we don't get there in time?" Alex asked, her voice shaking slightly.

"We can't think like that. We need to be prepared for anything," Emily said, feeling the pressure rising in her chest.

Finally, the sound of footsteps echoed down the hallway as reinforcements arrived. Emily took a deep breath, relieved to see her team.

"What do we have?" one of the officers asked, pushing the door open with determination.

"An intruder has entered Sector C and disabled the systems," Emily explained quickly. "We need to catch him before he causes more trouble."

"Understood," the officer said, his gaze fixed on Emily. "Where was he last seen?"

"He came in through here," he stated, pointing at the video before it cut off. "We need to search all areas for him."

As they organized themselves, Emily felt a mix of fear and determination. She knew there was more at stake than just her job; they were fighting for her future and that of BioCore.

The group split up, checking every corner of the lab, but Emily couldn't stop thinking about the figure she'd seen on the recording. Who was it? What were they looking for? It felt like there was a puzzle in her hands, but the pieces didn't fit.

"We found something!" an officer shouted from the back, drawing everyone's attention.

Emily ran to him, her heart pounding. There, on the work table, was an unknown device, glowing with flashing lights.

"What's that?" she asked, her voice a whisper.

The atmosphere in the control room felt tense, but the victory over the intruder had given them some relief. Emily, still with her heart racing, watched the control panel. The screen flickered with data she could barely process. The lights had stabilized, but the feeling of alertness did not disappear.

"What do we do now?" Alex asked, his eyes fixed on Emily.

"We must investigate who is behind this attack," she answered, feeling a heavy burden settle on her shoulders.

"But how? We don't have much time. They could return at any moment," said one of the officers.

Emily turned to the screen, searching for answers. Suddenly, an idea popped into her mind.

"Let's look at the security camera recordings from the beginning of their entry. Maybe we can find a clue," she suggested.

Everyone approached the monitor, and the specialist began to rewind the recordings. The image of the control room faded away, revealing a maze of dark hallways and shadowy corners.

The recording showed the intruder walking cautiously, looking over his shoulder, like a predator stalking his prey. Suddenly, he stopped and checked something on his wrist.

"What is that?" Emily asked, pointing at the screen.

The specialist adjusted the image, moving closer. On the intruder's wrist was a glowing device that emitted a blinking light just like the one they discovered on the table..

"It looks like a tracker or communication device," the specialist said, frowning. "That could be our key."

Emily turned to the group.

"We need to get that device back. If we can access its information, we might be able to figure out who's behind this and their intentions."

"How do you plan to do that?" —Alex asked, with a mix of admiration and concern.

'We'll follow up through the recordings. We need to see where he snuck off to. Maybe we can anticipate his next moves—Emily explained, determinedly.

With a new sense of purpose, they began to review the recordings, time running against them. As the images flashed by, Emily couldn't help but feel like the pressure was mounting. Not only did they have to catch the intruder, but BioCore's safety depended on it.

The recordings showed the intruder walking away from the lab, taking a path towards the storage area. Emily jumped up.

'Come on! —she said, heading for the door—. He could be trying to get something else.

The group moved quickly, footsteps echoing in the empty hallway. Emily led, her mind racing in different directions. Every second that passed seemed like a bigger challenge, like they were playing with fire.

Upon reaching the storage area, Emily paused, looking at the shelves filled with equipment and materials.

"Check every corner. He can't have gone far," she ordered, feeling the adrenaline rush through her body.

Everyone scattered, checking the shelves, looking for clues. Emily focused, scanning the room with her eyes. Then, suddenly, she heard a subtle noise behind one of the shelves.

"There!" she shouted, pointing to where she had heard the sound.

Everyone quickly approached, but when they arrived, the shelf was empty. Emily frowned, frustrated.

"He can't have left. This place is a mousetrap," one of the officers said, his voice tense.

But just as Emily turned around, she noticed something on the floor. A small device, similar to the one she had seen on the recording. She bent down and picked it up.

"Look at this!" she exclaimed, holding up the device. "It's a communicator. He was here."

"What does it mean?" Alex asked, looking at the object curiously.

"It means we could track his signals. If we connect it, we could have a direct line to him," the specialist replied, her mind already working on the possibilities.

They returned to the control room, and the specialist got to work immediately. Emily watched intently, each click of the keyboard echoing in the air, as their hearts beat in unison.

"I'm going to try to establish a connection," the specialist said, her gaze fixed on the screen. "This might take a moment."

Emily felt anxiety building in her chest. Every second felt like an eternity, and the fear of what could happen if they failed kept her on her toes.

"What if he notices?" Alex asked, her voice filled with concern.

"That's a risk we have to take," Emily replied, feeling more and more determined. They couldn't give up now.

Finally, the specialist looked up.

Chapter 51

The imposing BioCore building looms before them like a monster in the night. Its glass walls reflect the moonlight and the flickering city lights, giving it an eerie air. As Dr. James and Mark Dawson step out of the vehicle, they both feel the weight of tension in the air. They are aware that they are walking into a trap.

"This is it. There is no turning back," Mark says, his voice low, almost a whisper.

Dr. James nods, his thoughts scrambled. He pauses for a moment, staring at the building looming over them.

"Are you sure about this?" Mark asks, concern palpable in his voice.

"I have no choice," Dr. James replies, taking a deep breath as he prepares for what is coming. His gaze is steady, but his eyes reflect doubt. "Come on."

****

As they enter, the lobby feels eerily quiet. The dim light barely illuminates the men's faces, making the atmosphere feel even more oppressive.

"A little too quiet for me," Mark mutters, his eyes scanning the space warily.

"They're waiting for us, so they must try to stop us," Dr. James replies, quickening his pace toward the elevator. They're not worried about the silence; at this point, they know danger is imminent.

Inside the elevator, they both examine a floor plan of the offices they've secured. Mark pauses, pointing to the "Conference Room."

"I assume this is where they'll be," he says, his finger pointing firmly.

"It's on the fifteenth floor," Dr. James replies, his mind already projecting possible scenarios.

Mark presses the elevator button, and the doors close behind them with a dull thud.

****

As the elevator begins to ascend, a slight hum fills the space. The tension between them could be cut with a knife. Mark looks at Dr. James, searching for some sign of trust.

"What if we fail?" Mark asks, his voice barely a whisper in the enclosed environment.

"We can't afford to think about that," Dr. James replies, his gaze fixed on the doors. "If we fail, the future of BioCore and many others is at stake."

Mark nods, understanding the gravity of the situation. The conversation pauses, and both men sink into their thoughts, analyzing the decisions that have brought them here.

****

As the elevator doors open, a cold air greets them. The hallway is deserted, flickering lights barely illuminating the way.

"It's time for this game to end," Mark says, as they move forward with a determined stride.

Dr. James pulls a small flashlight from his pocket, illuminating the path ahead. As they walk, a feeling of unease creeps over them. Every shadow seems to move, every sound amplified.

"Do you have the device?" Mark asks, remembering the small gadget they could use in an emergency.

"I have it," Dr. James replies, nervously patting his pocket. "We won't use it unless absolutely necessary."

They both approach the door to the conference room. The door is ajar, and Dr. James pauses, listening quietly.

"Do you hear that?" he whispers.

Mark nods, listening. A low murmur filters from within. The tension intensifies.

****

The men peer cautiously in. The room is dimly lit, and several figures are gathered around a table. Apparently, they have been awaiting their arrival.

"Damn, they're here," Mark mutters, backing away slightly.

"We can't turn back now," Dr. James replies, his voice firm.

The two of them enter the room, and the figures turn toward them. One of the men, Mr. Li wei, stands up with a smile that doesn't reach his eyes.

"Dr. James, Mark, what a pleasant surprise," he says, his tone not hiding his disdain. "What brings you here at this hour?"

"We know what you're planning, Li," Dr. James replies, keeping his gaze steady. "We won't let you continue."

Mr. Li Wei laughs, a cold laugh that reverberates off the walls.

"Do you really think you can stop me?" "He asks, crossing his arms. "This is all bigger than you can imagine."

Mark frowns. The atmosphere becomes more tense as the other men in the room take up attack positions.

"You're playing with fire, Li. Many people's lives are at stake," Dr. James warns, not looking away.

"So what?" Li Wei replies, his voice full of arrogance. "Deep down, we're all pawns in this game. And you, James? Do you really think your intentions are pure?"

Mark feels the tension reaching its peak. The situation is volatile.

til, and any wrong move could trigger an explosion.

"We're here to stop you," Mark says, stepping forward. "You have no idea what you're doing."

Li Wei's men move in, surrounding them. Dr. James feels his heart pounding.

"What are you planning to do?" Li Wei asks, challenging his courage. "Are you going to fight?"

"We're not going to fight, but we are going to do the right thing," Dr. James replies, holding up the device in his pocket. "This can stop everything you've planned."

Hartman laughs again, his smile turning into a smirk.

"That won't work. Your threats don't scare me, James. I'm already too far into this game."

Mark feels time stop. The tension in the room is palpable, and every man is ready for action.

"Make no mistake, Li Wei," Mark interjects. No matter how far away you think you are, there is always a way back.

Li Wei's gaze hardens, and he nods to one of his men. Without warning, the room transforms into a battlefield. Screams and quick movements fill the air.

Mark lunges to the side, while Dr. James stands in the center, trying to connect the device. The noise of the struggle intensifies, and adrenaline courses through his veins.

"Quick!" Mark shouts, punching one of Li Wei's men.

Dr. James concentrates, fighting the panic that threatens to overtake him. His fingers move quickly over the device, trying to tune it.

"Cover me!" Dr. James orders, looking at Mark.

Mark lunges at the nearest man, dodging one blow while blocking another. Sweat runs down his brow as he realizes they cannot lose.

The fight continues, and Hartman's men seem to multiply, like shadows in the gloom. Dr. James, however, does not give in to despair.

"I've almost got it!" he shouts, the device flashing in his hand.

With a last-ditch effort, Dr. James manages to establish the connection. A bright light floods the room, and a high-pitched beep resounds, catching everyone's attention.

"Stop!" Hartman shouts, his face distorted by anger.

Dr. James does not stop. The light seems to absorb the tension from the room, and Hartman's men stop, paralyzed.

"Now, you're all in trouble," Dr. James says, raising his voice. "This device has the ability to disable any BioCore equipment."

Mark moves next to him, making sure none of Hartman's men dare come closer.

"I won't let you continue with this. Your game is up," Mark says, his voice firm.

Hartman looks at them with disdain, but something in his gaze indicates that he has underestimated the determination of the two men.

"Do you really think this can stop me?"

he says, his voice shaking between rage and fear.

Dr. James, without taking his eyes off Hartman, answers confidently.

"I don't know, but today we are going to fight for what is right. If you have any humanity in you, it is time for you to speak up."

Silence falls in the room, and the air feels tense. Everyone knows they have reached a critical point. The light on the device continues to flash, a clear warning that Li Wei's actions will have consequences.

"You leave me no choice," Li Wei replies, his voice full of frustration. "But what you don't know is that this is beyond me."

Dr. James feels the tension turn into an electric current. This is the moment when the future is defined, an instant that could change everything.

"So, explain to me," he says. "What are you really looking for?"

Li Wei falls silent, his eyes distilling a mix of fury and despair. He doesn't answer them, and Dr. James knows they've struck a nerve.

"You can't keep running away from your decisions, Li. It's time for you to take responsibility," Mark intervenes, his tone determined.

Finally, Li Wei lowers his gaze, as if realizing that the time has come to face his past.

"There are things you don't understand. This is bigger than you imagine," he whispers.

"This is it. Let's go," Mark whispers, his voice deep and determined.

They approach the door, but suddenly, Antonio and JJ turn the corner, their faces showing surprise and determination.

"About time you two showed up!" Antonio shouts, a cocky grin crossing his face.

Adrenaline floods through Mark. Without thinking, he lunges forward and tackles Antonio to the ground. The fight begins in an instant. JJ jumps on Mark's back, trying to get him off of him, and the ground becomes a chaotic scene of blows and screams.

Dr. James watches with concern, an internal conflict throbbing in his chest. Should he intervene or let Mark defend himself?

"Let's go! I'll take care of this!" Mark shouts, struggling with Antonio as he tries to free himself from JJ.

Dr. James nods, his heart pounding as he turns and runs to the conference room door. With a determined push, he pushes the door open, stepping into the unknown.

The room is dark, lit only by the flickering lights of the city filtering through the windows. Dr. James pauses for a moment, taking in the atmosphere. In the center, a long, empty table reminds him of the importance of his mission.

Outside the room, the fight continues. Mark manages to knock JJ down with a swift kick just as Antonio, now on his feet, grabs Mark from behind in a bear hug, slamming him into the wall. The sound of the impact echoes through the hallway.

Mark, feeling the pressure, pushes his foot against the wall, using the force to twist and push Antonio the other way. Antonio grunts as he hits the wall, and Mark takes the opportunity to elbow him twice in the stomach, breaking free for a brief moment.

"You have to get out of here!" Mark yells, watching as JJ stands up and begins to move to help Antonio.

With one swift movement, Mark throws Antonio into JJ, sending them both to the ground. But victory is short-lived. In an instant, Mark feels a tug at his waist: Antonio has regained his balance and catches him in a powerful grip.

Dr. James, from the doorway, watches as the fight intensifies. Uncertainty consumes him. He must do something. If they don't hurry, time will run out.

"Mark!" Dr. James shouts, his voice echoing in the empty space. "We need to get out of here!"

Mark, feeling the pressure of Antonio's grip, finds new resolve. Through a series of quick strikes and strategic moves, he manages to free himself and stands up just in time to see JJ, who approaches again with the intent to attack.

With renewed speed, Mark pulls a gun from behind his back. He holds it firmly, pointing it at both of them.

"Get back!" —he orders, his voice full of authority.

Antonio and JJ freeze, their eyes widening in surprise. The atmosphere becomes thick with the echo of tension.

"I don't want to do this," Mark says, his voice calmer, but still firm. "But I have no choice."

Dr. James is relieved that Mark has taken control of the situation, but he knows that the calm is fleeting. The tension between the four men is palpable.

"Mark, you don't have to do this," JJ interjects, trying to appeal to reason. "We can talk."

"Talk?" Mark replies, without lowering his gun. "You've crossed the line. I can't trust any of you."

Antonio realizes that the situation has changed. The arrogance on his face morphs into something darker.

"What are you going to do with that gun?" he asks, his voice defiant.

'Stop them, if necessary —Mark replies—. Now, back off. I don't want to hurt anyone, but I won't hesitate to do so.

Dr. James feels his heart pounding, knowing that every second counts. The exit door feels ever further away. He knows they must act fast.

The silence is broken when Antonio moves slightly to the side, trying to divert Mark's attention.

'Don't be scared, buddy —he says with a smirk—. This is just a game.

'It's not a game —Dr. James replies,

"They're playing with their lives."

Antonio's eyes narrow, and Mark senses the situation escalating. He can't afford to waver. The balance between violence and negotiation is tipping toward threat.

"I want answers. What are they really up to?" Mark demands, his gaze fixed on Antonio and JJ.

Antonio laughs, a cold, mirthless sound.

"That depends. What are you willing to do to get them?"

Dr. James, feeling the pressure, steps forward.

"This isn't about threats. This is about saving lives. Can you understand that, Antonio?"

The tension feels electric. Mark keeps his gun raised, but there's something in Antonio's voice that makes him hesitate.

"What if I told you your efforts are in vain?" Antonio says, the sarcasm in his tone revealing his defiance. BioCore is beyond what you can imagine.

Mark exchanges a glance with Dr. James. Uncertainty looms over them, and they must decide whether to continue the confrontation or find another way to obtain the truth.

"What does that mean?" Mark asks, lowering his gun slightly, seeking to understand.

"It means there are forces at play that you don't understand," Antonio replies, his tone changing slightly, as if deep down he feels the weight of the situation. "This is beyond personal."

Mark feels the atmosphere shift. Maybe there is more at stake than he thought. Dr. James watches, eager for an answer.

"What forces?" he asks quietly, trying to catch Antonio's attention.

Antonio looks at Mark, his arrogance beginning to fade, revealing a spark of concern.

"Are you willing to listen?" Antonio asks, his eyes assessing the situation.

"I'm willing to do whatever it takes," Mark replies, determination in his eyes.

"Then listen," Antonio says, his voice taking on a more serious tone. "There's something we must do. Something that can change everything."

Mark feels the truth on the verge of being revealed, and his instinct tells him to listen. But the danger is still present. The fight is not over yet.

"What do you have in mind?" Dr. James asks, his voice tense.

Antonio is silent for a moment, as if weighing his words. Finally, he lets out a bitter laugh.

"I can't tell you everything now. But you have to know that you are not alone in this. There are others involved. Others who have their own plans."

The revelation leaves Mark and Dr. James stunned. This is not a simple power play; it is a web of intrigue that extends beyond them.

The atmosphere grows even more tense. Mark feels the anguish rising in his chest. He knows they have to act fast.

"So what do we do?" Mark asks, his voice determined.

"First, you have to get out of here," Antonio replies, looking at them seriously. "You can't stay. You're in danger."

"Why should we trust you?" Dr. James interjects, his distrust evident.

Antonio sighs, frustrated.

"Because otherwise, you'll be on the list of next targets. You don't understand what you've unleashed."

Mark and Dr. James exchange glances. The feeling of time running out is intense. If you're in danger, you must act quickly.

"So what's the plan?" Mark asks, the gun still in his hand, but now with an air of uncertainty.

Antonio looks at Mark and Dr. James, a glint of desperation crossing his face.

"The plan is simple: get out of here and find the truth. But we need to work together."

"Together?" Mark asks, skeptical. "After everything that's happened, why should we trust you?"

Antonio steps forward, his gaze intense.

"Because I'm not here to fight. I'm here to survive, just like you."

Dr. James feels torn. Antonio's desperation is palpable, but the distrust still lingers.

"We don't have time to waste," he insists. "If there are bigger forces at play, we need to come together and find a way to stop them."

Mark nods, sensing the urgency pushing them to make a decision.

"Okay. We'll work together, but with conditions," Mark declares, maintaining his firm stance.

Antonio nods, knowing he has no other choice.

"So, we need to get out of here first," Dr. James says, looking around for a way to escape.

Mark lowers his gun slowly, sensing that the situation may be taking an unexpected turn.

"Where?" he asks, his voice full of determination.

"Down the back hallway," Antonio answers. "There's an emergency exit. No one should be in that area."

Dr. James and Mark look at each other, feeling that maybe, just maybe, they've found an ally in the team.

Chapter 52

Night had fallen over BioCore, and the elegant building glowed with an eerie light. The conference room, once a symbol of innovation and progress, had now become an emotional battleground. Emily and Mr. Hartman stood at the end of the table, smiles reflecting their satisfaction at what they were about to accomplish.

The door slammed open and Dr. James entered, his gaze burning with anger.

"It's over, Emily!" he shouted, his voice echoing in the room.

Emily turned slowly, her expression cold and calculating. Hartman stood still, enjoying the spectacle.

"It's too late, Doctor," Hartman replied with a sinister smile.

James approached, each step heavy with suppressed fury.

"You can't get away with this. Government officials have already been notified. They know what's going on here."

Emily's smile didn't falter. With a step forward, her voice became soothing, like a siren song.

"Oh, Richard, you're still the hero. I remember that. You don't have to fight this. You can join us. Imagine what we could accomplish together. Think of the money and the power. You won't be working in a sleazy dentist's office anymore; you'll be able to work on your own terms. We offer you that."

Dr. James hesitated, the temptation of his words weighing on him. Emily, sensing his hesitation, stepped closer, her tone overflowing with charm.

"You know this technology will change the world. Why fight progress when you could lead it?"

James clenched his fists, his voice shaking with rage.

"You know I could never be a part of this."

"I thought you'd say that," Emily said, her face hardening. The sweetness in her voice turned venomous. "Then you'll live the rest of your life always wondering what could have been!"

Suddenly, the door swung open again and Mark rushed in, panting, his eyes fixed on Emily and Hartman.

"The officers are on their way," he announced, his voice full of urgency.

Emily looked at Hartman and gave him a curt nod.

"Looks like you have another decision to make, Richard. Stop us or find Dr. Reinhardt."

Smiling wryly, Emily paced the room, her confidence unwavering.

"You see, I always have a backup plan. And deep down, I knew you wouldn't join us, so I took appropriate measures."

She stopped and cast a cold glance at Dr. James.

"This whole building is going to collapse when we get out of here. So, that means the old Doctor is going to collapse, too. Tick, tock, Richard. Tick… tock."

Mr. Hartman grabbed his briefcase and tablet, walking out of the room with an eerie confidence, followed by Emily.

"Go find Reinhardt. I'll take care of them," Mark said, determined, his protective instincts kicking in.

Dr. James hesitated, the decision tearing at him. He looked at Mark, knowing his partner was right.

"Go!" Mark exclaimed.

James, feeling the weight of urgency, nodded and ran for the exit, his heart pounding as he thought of Dr. Reinhardt.

Mark, now alone, faced reality. The room was silent, but the tension was palpable. James' choice to go after Reinhardt could cost them dearly. With a deep sigh, he darted in Hartman and Emily's direction, feeling every second count.

Mark ran down the hall, his mind racing with each step. The flickering lights created ominous shadows on the walls, as if the building itself was trying to warn him of impending danger. He knew that every corner could hide guards, but his determination kept him going.

As he turned a corner, he heard distant murmurs. He stopped, crouching behind a pillar. There stood Emily and Hartman, talking in low voices, their gestures quick and worried.

"We can't let him stop him. If he finds Reinhardt, he could ruin everything," Emily said, her voice heavy with tension.

Hartman nodded, his face grave.

"Not only that. The technology we have is too advanced. If it falls into the wrong hands…"

Mark knew he couldn't wait any longer. If Hartman and Emily were about to do something drastic, he had to act.

With a quick movement, he emerged from his hiding place and lunged at them.

"Don't move!" he shouted, pointing his gun at Hartman.

They both turned around, surprised. Emily's gaze turned cold.

"You think you can stop us, Mark?" she asked scornfully.

"I'm not here to play. I just want to make sure they don't do anything stupid," Mark replied, his voice firm.

The tension in the air intensified. Emily smiled, a flash of defiance in her eyes.

"You'd be surprised what people are capable of when they feel like they're losing. Maybe you should join us, Mark."

"Never," Mark replied, the anger in his chest burning.

But inside, a Doubt plagued him. What if there was a way to save Reinhardt and stop Emily at the same time? His mind searched for answers, but he knew time was running out.

"I have no intention of letting this end badly. I don't want any more deaths!" he shouted, the echo of his voice resonating in the empty hallway.

Meanwhile, Dr. James ran towards the lab, his mind in a whirl. The image of Emily and Hartman haunted him. The thought of the entire building being in danger made him feel like time was slipping through his fingers.

He reached the room where he believed Dr. Reinhardt was. Opening the door, he found chaos. Documents were scattered everywhere, and Dr. Reinhardt's computer was flickering erratically.

"Dr. Reinhardt?" he shouted, searching in the darkness.

There was no answer. The silence was deafening, and the feeling that something terrible was about to happen intensified. James walked over to the computer, trying to find some clue.

Suddenly, a subtle sound interrupted his concentration. A soft whisper. He turned around, and there was Reinhardt, covered in dust, hiding behind a table.

"Dr. James?" Reinhardt said, his voice shaking.

"Reinhardt!" James exclaimed, running towards him. "We must get out of here! Emily has activated a self-destruct protocol."

Reinhardt's eyes widened, fear reflected on his face.

"What? How do you know?"

James quickly explained the situation, time was of the essence. Reinhardt stood up, and together they headed towards the exit.

Mark was still aiming at Emily and Hartman, the tension in the air palpable.

"They have to surrender," Mark said, his voice almost a whisper.

"Never," Emily replied, her gaze defiant.

Mark knew his time was running out. The thought of the building about to collapse filled him with despair.

"Dr. Reinhardt must be safe. What they're doing could have disastrous consequences."

Hartman made a sudden movement, and Mark felt he had to act. With a shout, he launched himself at them.

But just then, Dr. James and Reinhardt appeared behind him.

"Mark!" James shouted. "Stop!"

Mark stopped dead, feeling the world crumble around him. Hartman turned around, his mocking expression turning to concern.

"I shouldn't be here, Richard," Hartman said, his eyes narrowed.

"And you shouldn't be alive," Dr. James replied, the rage in his voice palpable.

Time stood still. Decisions hung in the air. Mark, still with his gun raised, didn't know who to trust. There was a fine line between betrayal and loyalty, and they were about to cross it.

"This stops here," Mark said, his voice ringing with authority. "We're going to put an end to this, once and for all."

The atmosphere was thick, charged with uncertainty. The three men looked at each other, knowing.

Chapter 53

The dark night enveloped the BioCore building, a monument of ambition and secrets. Inside, footsteps echoed down the stairs. Emily and Hartman burst through the door, their faces alight with adrenaline.

"Come on, quick," Emily ordered, taking two steps at a time, closely followed by Hartman. The air was thick with tension, and they knew time was running out.

In the elevator lobby, Dr. James examined a map of the building. Every second counted. He had to find Dr. Reinhardt before it was too late. Beside him, in a dark corner, Antonio and JJ were tied back to back, their expressions a mix of frustration and fear.

"You'll never find him, Doctor," Antonio sneered, half-laughing.

Dr. James knelt down, his piercing gaze fixed on Antonio.

"This building is going to go down in flames as soon as Emily and Hartman get out of here. They don't care about you. They were both just pawns," he said, his voice firm.

Antonio, defiant, chuckled.

"Don't listen to him. He's lying," he muttered, trying to convince JJ.

Dr. James didn't flinch. He knew time was running out. He turned to JJ, who seemed to struggle internally.

"I'm not lying. If you tell me where the Doctor is, I'll make sure you get out of here alive. You'll probably still face charges, but you'll be alive."

JJ looked at Antonio, fear creeping across his face.

"What do we do?" he asked, his voice shaking.

After a long moment of indecision, Antonio nodded.

"He's in the basement," JJ confessed, his voice low but clear.

"Thank you," Dr. James replied, relieved to have the necessary information. He quickly stood up and headed for the elevator, pressing the button to go down. The elevator lights began to flicker, and the doors creaked open.

Meanwhile, Emily and Hartman reached the roof door, pushing it hard. The cool night breeze hit their faces, but they didn't stop. They needed a plan, and they needed to act fast.

"What do we do now?" Hartman asked, looking around.

Emily gave a confident smile.

"We'll get their attention. Once they're distracted, we can execute our plan. This building will be just the beginning."

Before Hartman could respond, a loud bang echoed inside the building. The fire alarm began to sound, filling the air with a high-pitched hum.

"It's time," Emily said, moving to the edge of the roof. "Get ready to act!"

Dr. James felt his heart pound as the elevator descended. The information he had gained from JJ was crucial, but time was not on his side. As the elevator lights flickered, he felt a surge of determination.

"I have to get to Reinhardt before they do," he muttered to himself.

The elevator doors swung open with a bang, revealing the basement. A cold, oppressive air emanated from the dark hallway. He peered in and saw a flickering light at the end. Without hesitation, he lunged forward.

As he moved forward, the tension rose. He knew everyone's lives were at stake. The closer he got, the more he could feel the weight of responsibility. As he turned a corner, he was met with a scene that shocked him: Dr. Reinhardt was tied to a chair, his face pale, but his eyes steady.

"Reinhardt!" Dr. James shouted, running towards him. "I'm here to get you out of here!"

Reinhardt raised his head, a mix of relief and concern.

"What's going on?" he asked, his voice weak.

"Emily and Hartman are planning to destroy this building. We need to get out now," James replied, cutting the ropes that kept him bound.

"I don't have much time," Reinhardt said, panting. He stood up, barely holding on.

Emily looked down, taking in the chaos they were causing. Police car lights reflected in the distance, a sign that time was running out. Hartman joined her, his gaze focused on the horizon.

"What if this goes wrong?" —he asked, doubt creeping into his voice.

Emily shot him a withering look.

—There is no "evil" option here. This is just the beginning, and if we fail, we lose everything.

James helped Reinhardt up, his gaze fixed on the basement door.

—We must move. If we don't make it to the exit, they will win, —James said, sensing the urgency in the air.

Reinhardt nodded, slowly regaining his strength. As they headed for the exit, a subtle, yet disturbing sound was heard behind them. They stopped dead in their tracks.

—What was that? —Reinhardt asked, his eyes wide.

James raised a hand, his instinct

He was telling her something was wrong.

"I don't know, but we can't stay here," she replied, moving forward cautiously.

Just as they reached the door, a shadow slipped between them. A man appeared, his face hidden under a hood. He was a BioCore security guard, and he was carrying a gun.

"Stop!" he shouted, raising the gun.

Dr. James acted fast. Without thinking, he pushed Reinhardt aside and lunged at the guard, attempting to disarm him.

****

Meanwhile, Emily and Hartman heard the commotion coming from the basement.

"What was that?" Hartman asked, his voice tense.

"It doesn't matter," Emily replied. "If they've found Reinhardt, it's time to act."

With determination, they headed for the stairs, ready to face whatever came their way.

****

Dr. James and the guard struggled. James, adrenaline pumping, managed to wrestle the guard's gun away, but not before the man activated his communicator.

"I need backup in the basement!" the guard shouted, as they struggled on the floor.

James gritted his teeth, feeling the pressure. He knew he needed to end this before more men arrived.

"Reinhardt, can you fight?" he asked, quickly looking at his partner.

Reinhardt, still shaking, nodded.

"Yes, but I have to be on my feet first."

*****

Emily and Hartman reached the basement door just in time to see Dr. James struggling. Without thinking, Emily launched herself inside.

"James!" she shouted, her voice echoing in the chaos.

Dr. James looked up, seeing the determination in Emily's eyes. Without hesitation, he took the chance.

"Help me!" he exclaimed, as he pushed the guard to the ground.

Emily lunged at the guard, helping James keep him on the ground. Hartman, looking at the scene, knew he had to do something.

"I'm going to get help," he said, quickly backing away towards the elevator.

Meanwhile, James and Emily fought the guard. Reinhardt, now standing, joined the fight, kicking the guard in the side. The man growled, feeling the impact.

"Let's get out of here!" James shouted, feeling time running out.

Just as they were about to escape, more guards appeared, blocking the exit.

"I won't let you go!" one of them shouted, raising his gun.

"Now!" —James shouted, launching himself towards the group of guards.

The whirring of helicopter blades filled the air as Emily and Hartman reached the roof. A BioCore helicopter waited, its blades spinning hard.

Mark emerged from the ladder, watching as Emily and Hartman approached. His heart sank as he realized he was too late. In an instant, Emily and Hartman climbed into the helicopter, the wind whipping at their faces.

Mark watched, frustrated, as the helicopter took off and flew away into the night sky. His entire being was clamoring for action,

Chapter 54

The whirring of the helicopter blades filled the air, creating a deafening noise that reverberated through the tense surroundings. Emily and Mr. Hartman ran to the edge of the roof, where the BioCore helicopter waited, its flashing lights illuminating the darkness of the night.

"Come on!" Hartman shouted, adjusting his jacket as the wind howled around them.

Emily smiled, feeling in control, like they were finally winning. Right behind them, Mark came running down the staircase, his footsteps echoing on the metal.

"Emily! Wait!" Mark shouted, but his voice was drowned out by the noise of the helicopter.

Emily turned briefly, her expression enigmatic. She knew there had to be a cost to her decision, but the idea of power was tempting. The helicopter took off, carrying them into the night sky. Mark stood on the roof, frustrated, watching them go.

"I can't believe they're leaving!" he muttered to himself, feeling helplessness wash over him. The truth was that he had lost the battle, and the war was just beginning.

****

Inside the helicopter, the air was tense but filled with a strange euphoria. Emily looked ahead, feeling the adrenaline surging through her.

"Are you ready for this, Hartman?" she asked, turning her gaze back to him.

"I've always been ready," Hartman replied, with a confident smile. "This is just the beginning."

As the helicopter ascended, Emily thought about everything they had left behind. The decisions they had made had brought them to this point, but there was no turning back. In her mind, the idea of what they could accomplish together was more powerful than any fear.

****

Mark felt empty as the helicopter disappeared into the darkness. His mind was racing. He knew he needed to find James and Reinhardt. They were the key to stopping Emily and Hartman.

"James!" he shouted, heading for the stairs again. "Reinhardt! I need your help!"

He quickly descended, feeling like every second counted.

****

As Mark ran down the stairs, he remembered James' words: "We can't let progress turn into destruction." He knew he had to be strong, that he couldn't give up. When he reached the basement floor, he found Antonio and JJ still tied up.

"Where's Dr. Reinhardt?" he asked them, sweat dripping down his forehead.

"He's gone," Antonio said, laughing scornfully. "He's gone, and you won't be able to stop them."

Mark approached them, determined.

"Where is he?" he repeated, his voice low and menacing.

****

Emily looked out at the rapidly receding landscape. The sky was clear, and the stars shone brightly. Her mind, however, was elsewhere.

"Where is Reinhardt?" she asked, her voice gravelly.

"It doesn't matter anymore," Hartman replied, with a confident smile. "With or without him, we're about to change the world."

Emily nodded, feeling the euphoria and anxiety in a dangerous mix. But there was a part of her that couldn't help but wonder. What would happen to Reinhardt? What would happen if he managed to stop them?

****

Mark turned to Antonio, his eyes burning with determination.

"Tell me where Reinhardt is, or I won't hesitate to leave you here," he threatened, fear flashing in his eyes.

JJ looked at Antonio, realizing they had to act fast.

"He's in the basement, but there's no time. They'll leave and you won't be able to do anything," JJ said, his voice shaking.

Mark frowned, but he knew he couldn't waste any more time.

"I'm going to find him, and you're going to untie yourself, do you hear me?" Mark shouted, but
Meanwhile, on the other side of the hideout, Dr. James and Mark. The news of Dr. Reinhardt's disappearance had hit them hard. The phone vibrated in James' pocket again. He pulled it out and saw the message from Gray, an Agent they met some hours ago.

"We have a lead on Reinhardt's whereabouts. But we need you both on the ground."

James took a deep breath. He knew this meant moving fast, much faster than he had anticipated.

He dialed.

"James," Gray's voice was direct, as always. "We have him."

"Where?"

Chapter 55

Dr. James ran through the lower levels of BioCore, his heart pounding as his mind tried to focus on the mission. Each footstep echoed in the cold, desolate hallway. Finally, he reached the basement. The flickering light barely illuminated the space, creating eerie shadows on the concrete walls.

In the background, a figure stood tied to a chair. It was Dr. Reinhardt, gagged but conscious. James felt a mix of relief and urgency.

"I got you!" Dr. James exclaimed, kneeling in front of him, his hands shaking from nervousness and adrenaline. "Now, let's get out of here."

Reinhardt, though weak, nodded with gratitude in his eyes. James quickly removed the gag that was constricting his mouth. Reinhardt coughed, taking in fresh air for the first time in hours.

"How did you… get here?" Reinhardt asked, his voice raspy.

"There's no time for that. BioCore's security is compromised. They have plans we can't allow," Dr. James replied, looking around for any threats.

Reinhardt shifted a bit, trying to restore his circulation. Dr. James quickly untied the ropes holding his colleague prisoner.

"You have to help me," James continued. "Emily and Hartman have escaped. We must stop them before they do any more damage."

"I knew you couldn't trust them," Reinhardt murmured, his face drawn but determined. "They have something that can change everything."

James looked at Reinhardt intently. There was something in his tone that piqued his interest.

"What exactly do they have?" he asked, impatiently.

"Nanomaterials," Reinhardt replied. They are capable of transforming human biology. They want to use it to control everything.

Dr. James felt his stomach twist. He knew what Reinhardt was saying was dangerous. With that technology, BioCore could manipulate people to their liking.
Dr. James and Reinhardt ran out of the basement, quickly climbing the stairs. Tension filled the air as their footsteps echoed off the metal.

"We can't let them escape," James said, his mind focusing on a plan of action. Reinhardt, at his side, was breathing heavily, but his eyes were shining with determination.

"Do you have a weapon?" "Reinhardt asked, looking at him.

James nodded, pulling a small revolver from his belt.

"Fine. If we confront them, I'll need you to cover me."

The two men reached the first floor, where the atmosphere changed drastically. Fluorescent light illuminated an empty hallway, and the silence felt eerie.

"Come on," James said, keeping his voice low. "Let's keep going."

Leaving the hallway, they found themselves in a long, dark hallway. James felt a cold current run down his spine.

"Do you think anyone else is here?" Reinhardt asked, his eyes scanning every shadow.

"If they are, they'll know," James replied, moving forward cautiously. His steps were firm, but every corner could bring surprises.

Suddenly, a noise echoed behind them. James turned around, revolver pointed in the direction of the sound.

"Who's there?" he shouted.

There was no response. The echo of his voice was lost in the silence. Reinhardt approached him, frightened.

"We may not be alone," he whispered.

Both men headed for the exit, adrenaline pumping through their veins. Every step they took was a step closer to danger.

Chapter 56

Dr. James and Dr. Reinhardt stood outside, surrounded by the blue and red lights of ambulances and police cars. The air was thick with tension. A group of doctors tended to Dr. Reinhardt, their faces serious as they assessed his condition.

Mark Dawson stood beside them, watching the chaos. He crossed his arms and looked up at the building, its facade covered in rubble.

"I guess the building collapsing was just a scare tactic," Mark commented, a smirk on his face.

Dr. James frowned, still worried.

"Another ploy by Emily. But at least we got Dr. Reinhardt. Still, we were too late. They got away, and the Chinese have what they need."

Mark chuckled, shaking his head.

"They got away… for now. But don't forget that the story isn't over."

Reinhardt, at his side, looked up, still weak, but with a spark of determination in his eyes.

"We can't stay here. We must act quickly. They won't rest until they use the technology."

James looked at Reinhardt, understanding the urgency of the situation.

"Do you have any idea where they might go?" he asked.

"Last I heard, they had connections at the port. There's a ship leaving tonight," Reinhardt replied, trying to stand up, but his strength deserted him.

Mark looked around, assessing the place.

"If we can get to the port before them, maybe we can stop the shipment."

Dr. James nodded, determined.

"Then, there's no time to waste. Mark, go to the police department and gather more men. Reinhardt and I will go to the port."

Mark raised an eyebrow, surprised.

"That fast?" Are you sure you're fit to do that?

Reinhardt stood up, a spark of defiance in his gaze.

"I can't stay here. They know my job. If we don't do something now, they could destroy everything I've created."

James looked at Reinhardt, sensing the determination in his voice.

"Okay, but if you feel bad, tell me."

Mark turned back to the building, preparing to make the call.

"Make sure they bring a team. This could get dangerous."

Dr. James drove through the dark city, his thoughts revolving around the mission. Reinhardt sat in the passenger seat, his face pale, but determined.

"We need to think about how to approach them," James said, breaking the silence.

Reinhardt looked at him, considering.

"If they've met with the Chinese, they're likely armed." We'll need a discreet approach. We can't let it slip away this time.

James nodded, keeping his eyes on the road.

"What do you know about the transaction?"

"What I've heard is that they're trading technology from our lab in exchange for access to resources we haven't even imagined," Reinhardt said, concern evident in his voice.

"That doesn't sound right. Not only are they after our technology, but they're also selling something in return."

Reinhardt sighed, anxiety clear on his face.

"It's a dangerous game. If they succeed, we could be looking at a future where that technology is used to control people."

James frowned.

"I can't let that happen. I won't."

The car pulled up in front of a series of docks. The flickering lights of the harbor illuminated the mist that drifted over the water.

"This is the place," Reinhardt said, looking around. "We need to be cautious."

Both men stepped out of the vehicle, looking around. The port was deserted, with only the sound of water lapping against the wooden pillars.

"Do you see anything?" James asked, revolver in hand.

Reinhardt shook his head.

"No, but that doesn't mean they aren't nearby."

They approached a cargo container that was loosely closed. James crouched down, peering inside.

"Nothing here. We need to keep moving," he said, feeling a growing sense of danger.

As they moved forward, a shadow moved at the end of the dock. James looked up.

"Did you see it?"

Reinhardt nodded, alert.

"Yes, it seems we're not alone."

Both men moved further into the dock, each step echoing in the silence. Tension grew as they approached the shadow.

"Stay alert. We don't know who they are," James warned.

The shadow moved again, and suddenly, a group of armed men appeared, surrounding James and Reinhardt.

"Surprise?" one of them said, with a smirk. He was a robust man, his gaze hard as steel.

James raised his gun, but Reinhardt stopped him.

"Wait. We don't want any more trouble."

"Too late for that," the man replied, raising his gun. "We're here for the technology."

Reinhardt straightened up, facing the man.

Okay Said the man. But you must get to them first!

James and Reinhardt looked at each other in surprise.

James and Reinhardt moved slowly, each footstep on the dock echoing in the tense night air. They barely looked at each other, their bodies firm and alert, knowing that danger lurked in the shadows.

Reinhardt stepped forward, his stance imposing. "What technology?" he asked, though he knew the answer. It was a game of timing, of gauging the situation.

The burly man tilted his head slightly. "You know exactly what I'm talking about. We've been following them, watching them… from the very beginning."

James frowned. "From the very beginning?" he repeated, processing the words.

"Ever since they set foot in this," one of the other men surrounding the pair said, his voice dripping with disdain. "All their research, every move. They thought they could escape our sight, but no. We're not that easy to fool."

Reinhardt narrowed his eyes. "So it was you who were sabotaging our work. Who are you working for?"

The burly man shrugged. "Who cares? What matters is that we're here now, and you have no way out."

The tension rose with every word, but Reinhardt, ever calculating, noticed something odd about the men around them. They weren't as organized as he thought, their movements were clumsy, and the way they handled their weapons seemed unnatural. It was clear that they weren't professionals.

"If you're so sure you have us trapped," Reinhardt said slowly, "then why haven't you done anything yet?"

The burly man smiled again, though this time with less confidence. "Because we want answers first," he admitted.

James exchanged a quick glance with Reinhardt. This was an opportunity, a respite. If these men wanted information, they could use that need to their advantage.

"Answers? To what questions?" James took a step forward, his tone challenging. "They've followed us, sabotaged us, harassed us. All for a technology they don't even understand. What do they really want?"

One of the gunmen frowned, clenching his jaw as if he were holding something back. "It's not just the technology," he confessed. "It's what it represents… the power it holds. We want to control that before someone else does."

Reinhardt stood his ground. "You have no idea what you're up against, do you?"

The burly leader dropped his smile, his expression hardening. "We know enough. More than you think."

"That's what should scare you the most," James said, his tone darker now. "You have no idea the risk you're taking."

Silence fell heavily over the group. The wind blew again, louder this time, as if the dock itself was holding its breath. One of the gunmen nervously shifted his foot, the dry sound of creaking wood echoing in the air.

"And what do you suggest?" the burly man finally asked, with a mix of frustration and curiosity.

Reinhardt turned slightly to James, thinking about their next moves. They knew that if they wanted to get out of this situation alive, they would have to play their cards right. And that meant buying time, manipulating the greed and uncertainty of their attackers.

"We can negotiate," Reinhardt said softly, measuring each word. "But you must understand that what you seek is not as simple as it seems."

The burly man let out a bitter laugh. "Negotiate? Do you think we are here to listen to your sales pitch?"

Reinhardt did not back down. "No, I do not think so. But if you kill us now, what you seek will be unattainable for you. There are things you cannot understand just by stealing them."

The burly man stared at him, weighing his words, while the other men exchanged nervous glances. The situation was becoming more unstable with each passing second.

James watched the tension on their faces and realized they were at a critical point. If they could sow enough doubt, maybe they would have a chance to escape or at least to turn the tide of the confrontation

"We know you've followed us," James continued, "but if you were really aware of everything, you wouldn't be standing here asking us questions. Clearly, you're missing something. And that's what we can offer you."

The gunmen looked at each other. The burly leader crossed his arms, clearly irritated, but intrigued.

"And what do you have to offer?" he finally asked, his tone somewhat less aggressive.

Reinhardt smiled slightly. He knew it was time to play his card.

"The answer to your problem," he said, "is bigger than you think. But if you want to know, you should listen."

The group of gunmen fell silent, waiting for the explanation. James and Reinhardt knew they wouldn't have much more of a chance, but if they played it right, they might just get out of this situation alive.

One of the other gunmen grew impatient, stepping forward. "Why are we still talking? We could end this right now and take what we need."

But the burly man held up a hand to stop him. "Not so fast. There's something we need to know before we take that step."

Reinhardt crossed his arms. arms, staying calm despite the danger. "And what exactly is it that you want to know?"

The burly man stared at him, evaluating every word that came out of his mouth. "We want to know how far they've gone. What they know, who they've involved. We want to make sure there are no loose ends when this is over."

James felt a chill run down his spine. The way he
The way he said it left no room for doubt. When they were done with them, there would be no witnesses left. They knew too much.

"And if we tell them what they know, what guarantee do we have that they will let us live?" Reinhardt asked, still holding his composure.

The burly man let out a low laugh. "That will depend on how much value their answers have."

Silence fell over the group for a long moment. The wind blew in from the harbor, raising the salty smell of the water, as James and Reinhardt weighed their options. Any wrong move could be their last.

Reinhardt, calculating as ever, knew they couldn't give up so easily. They had come too far in their investigation, and the truth they had uncovered was something the world needed to know, no matter how many wanted to silence it. But right now, their priority was to survive, and to do that, they had to play this game carefully.

"Fine," Reinhardt finally said, breaking the tense silence. "We will tell you what you know. But if you really want to understand what you have been chasing, you will need more than just our words."

James glanced at him, knowing that Reinhardt was preparing a play. But he remained silent, trusting his friend and companion.

The burly man narrowed his eyes, intrigued. "Anything else? What do you mean?"

Reinhardt smiled slightly. "What you are after is not just technology. It is a combination of what we discovered in our investigations and what others have been hiding for years. If you want to have full control, you will have to work with us. Or at least let us finish what we started."

One of the armed men frowned, clearly distrustful. "Why should we trust you?"

"Because if you kill us now, you will never find out what is really at stake," James replied, finally speaking after having remained silent.

The burly man watched them for a long moment, weighing his options. Finally, he lowered his gun, though the danger was not gone. "Very well. Let's talk."

The burly man lowered his weapon slowly, though tension still hung in the air. The other gunmen stood their ground, clearly ready to act if anything went wrong. James and Reinhardt exchanged a quick glance; they knew they had just bought themselves a bit of time, but it wasn't enough to relax.

"Talk," the leader demanded, taking a step closer. "I want to know everything you've discovered. And you better not try to play games with us."

Reinhardt nodded calmly, keeping his gaze locked on the man. "We understand well what's at stake here. What you don't understand is that this technology, this discovery, is not just a tool of power. It's not something you can control without consequences."

James continued, following his companion's lead. "At first, we too thought we were onto something revolutionary, something that would change the world in a positive way. But the deeper we dug, the darker it became. It's not just an advanced technology; it's a weapon, and the people behind it are willing to do whatever it takes to make sure it never reaches the public."

The burly man watched James closely, searching for any hint of lies in his words. "We already knew that. What we don't know is how far you guys have gone with that information."

Reinhardt crossed his arms, holding his ground. "We've discovered enough to endanger a lot of people, including those who pay you. We know that some of the people in positions of authority are involved. They're paid to keep watch and, when necessary, stop any developments that threaten their control."

The burly man frowned, and James saw a spark of surprise in his eyes. Maybe he hadn't expected them to know so much.

"So they have names," the man muttered, more to himself than to them. "That could be a problem."

"A problem for you, of course," James said, his tone beginning to challenge the leader's calm. "They've followed us from the beginning, trying to stop us, sabotaging our research, but what they don't understand is that it's too late now. What we know can't be undone so easily."

One of the gunmen, visibly impatient, stepped forward. "This is a waste of time. We must finish them off and move on. They have nothing of use to us."

The leader raised a hand again, silencing the impatient man. "They have something of use to us. And if they're telling the truth, it might be worth listening to them before doing anything." Then he looked directly at Reinhardt.

"Tell us. What makes this technology so dangerous? What did they find?"

Reinhardt took a breath before answering, knowing that his next words could determine his fate. "Technology is designed to evolve. It's not just a set of machines or programs; it's a network that grows, that adapts to its environment. And what makes it truly dangerous is that it can become self-sufficient. Left unchecked, it can make decisions on its own, decisions that no authority can reverse."

The stocky man seemed to process this information for a moment. Then, slowly, he turned to one of his companions, who had been watching everything from the shadows. "Is what they say true? Did you know anything about this?"

The other man, thinner and with a more reserved attitude, stepped forward. "What they're saying matches what we've heard. The project has always been experimental, but we never believed it could go this far. If what they say is true, they might be right. This goes beyond what any of us imagined."

The leader let out a heavy sigh, clearly displeased with the direction things were taking. "And who else knows about this?" Who else is on the list?"

****

The sun shone high over the luxurious office building in the heart of China. Inside, everything was tense. The large mahogany desk that presided over Li Wei's spacious office was a symbol of power, but today, that power hung in the balance. In front of him, Emily Carter and Mr. Hartman stood tensely. The atmosphere was charged, and the silence only amplified Li Wei's growing anger.

"You promised me the doctors, Emily," Li Wei said finally, her voice low but sharp. "You promised that Dr. James and Dr. Reinhardt would be mine. Now, where are they?"

Emily remained calm, though inside she felt the pressure. She stepped forward, her face impassive.

"I understand your frustration, Mr. Li," she replied, her tone controlled. "The situation was more complicated than we expected. But I assure you that we are working to assemble an even better team to continue the project."

Mr. Hartman shifted uncomfortably beside her, not saying a word. His eyes constantly shifted to Emily, as if he expected her to fix the problem, as she always did.

"I don't want substitutes," Li Wei replied, his voice now laced with irritation. "I wanted those doctors. That was the deal."

The air seemed heavier as Emily took a breath, ready to play her last card.

"I understand," she repeated. "And as a show of good faith, we are willing to offer a portion of the payment back."

Hartman snapped his head toward Emily, surprised.

"What?" he asked, his voice low but with a clear sign of alarm.

Emily did not look at him. There was no time for internal discussions. Control of the situation had to be maintained at all costs.

"Consider this a gesture of goodwill, Mr. Li," Emily continued, not losing her composure. "You have already gained much from the technology we have provided you." This is just to ensure that the trust between our organizations remains intact.

Li Wei fell silent, evaluating her words. His fingers drummed lightly on the desk, as if calculating every possibility. Finally, he spoke, his tone colder.

"You're walking a very dangerous line, Emily," he said. "But I've seen enough."

With a wave of his hand, he pressed a button on the desk, and a screen behind him came to life. The projected images showed the Pacific Ocean, with water levels visibly decreasing. The implications of those images were obvious, and the message was clear: the plan worked.

"The Pacific Ocean's water supply is already showing signs of depletion," Li Wei added, his eyes shining with ambition. "This will work… for now. But don't forget that you owe me those doctors."

Before Emily or Hartman could respond, the office door slammed open. A group of Interpol agents burst into the room, armed and determined.

"Li Wei, Emily Carter, Robert Hartman… you are under arrest!" the leader of the group exclaimed.

Li Wei's eyes widened in shock. He had not expected an ambush on his own territory. The agents quickly surrounded him, yanking him out of his chair and pushing him against the desk to handcuff him. As they subdued him, his gaze remained fixed on Emily, a mixture of hatred and surprise.

Emily, for her part, offered no resistance. Maintaining her calm facade, she allowed the agents to handcuff her without objection. Hartman, on the other hand, could not contain his fury.

"This is a mistake!" Hartman shouted as he tried to free himself from the agents' grip. "You have no idea what you are doing!"

Emily watched him briefly, knowing that fighting back would only make things worse. Everything seemed to be falling apart around her, but her mind kept working, calculating, searching for the next step.

"It's over, Hartman," she said, her voice calm but firm. "Don't fight this."

Li Wei, still held by the agents, turned to Emily with a venomous smile on his face.

"You've ruined everything," he spat with contempt. "But this isn't over."

Emily watched him as he was led away. Her outward calm did not reflect the inner turmoil she felt, but her eyes never stopped moving, searching for a way out of this mess. As the agents led her out of the office, she was already planning her next move. She knew the game wasn't over.

As Interpol's helicopters began to take off with their prisoners on board, the sky over China glowed with a red twilight, as if foreshadowing that the conflict had only just begun.

Chapter 57

Inside, the atmosphere is cozy, with soft lights creating an intimate setting. Booths are occupied by CUSTOMERS conversing in low voices, accompanied by the clink of glasses and bottles on the bar. In one of the booths at the back, Dr. James and Dr. Reinhardt sit with drinks in front of them. The conversation has been brief, but each word weighs heavy, laden with unspoken expectations.

Mark, a few steps away, finishes a phone call. His expression, satisfied, gives the impression that there is finally good news. He nods and smiles before returning to the table where the two doctors are waiting for him.

"That was General Cortez," Mark says, letting his calm voice fill the space between them. Emily, Hartman, and Li Wei were arrested in China by Interpol. They're in custody.

Dr. James lets out a deep sigh, relieved but still uneasy. He glances at his partner, Dr. Reinhardt, who shares that relief, though weariness is reflected in his eyes.

"Is it really over?" Dr. James asks, as if he can't believe what he's hearing.

Mark nods, taking a sip of his drink.

"Yeah. Interpol has them locked up. There's no way they're getting out of this."

Dr. James leans back, a slight smile playing on his lips, but the weight of worry still hangs over him.

"What about the ocean?" he asks after a pause. "The nanotechnology they dropped... the effects?"

Mark puts down his glass and leans forward, his expression more serious.

"They don't know yet. Water levels are being analyzed, but it will take time to determine the long-term impact." Steps are being taken, but it's a slow process.

Dr. Reinhardt, so far silent, finally speaks up.

"Let's hope it's not too late," his voice sounds grave. "The damage could be irreversible if it spreads too far."

Mark nods, though he tries to look on the bright side. He raises his glass, his optimism shining through.

"For now, we did what we could. We stopped it before it could get worse. That's something to celebrate, isn't it?"

Dr. James takes his glass, the smile on his face growing a little wider. He looks around the table, aware of the relief shared between them.

"You're right. It's over… and we're still here."

Dr. Reinhardt, also smiling, raises his glass.

"To getting through it."

"To moving on," Mark says.

Dr. James repeats, his tone determined:

"To moving on."

They clink their glasses, the sound echoing their silent victory. The weight of their journey, of the decisions they made and the consequences they faced, seems to be slowly easing off. For the first time in what seems like an eternity, they enjoy a moment of peace.

The bar continues to vibrate around them, oblivious to the gravity of what they just discussed. To the rest of the world, life goes on, but to them, this moment represents a conclusion, though they cannot yet foresee what the future will hold.

As the night progresses, the three men share more drinks, exchanging stories that fluctuate between the banal and the momentous. Dr. Reinhardt leans toward Mark at one point.

"Do you remember when all this started?" Reinhardt asks with a wistful smile. "I never thought we'd be here, in a bar celebrating that the world didn't fall apart."

Mark nods, a shadow crossing his face before disappearing.

"It's never easy to predict the outcome." "We're just doing what we can," he answers, his tone more thoughtful.

Dr. James steps in, his voice more relaxed now as the alcohol and relief slowly set in.

"So what's next?" he asks. "We know the nanotechnology is still there, and the ocean… well, we haven't figured that out yet. How long do you think it will take to get answers?"

Mark looks down at his glass, gently turning it in his hands before answering.

"It could be months, even years. The scientists are working, but you know how it is. We're not in full control. We can only hope the steps they're taking work."

The conversation drifts into the uncertain future, the tension that had permeated every one of their decisions still lingering in the back of their minds.

The night continues its course, and eventually, the bar begins to empty out. The three men, now a little more relaxed, stand up, preparing to leave. But just as they're about to leave, Mark's phone vibrates. He takes it from his pocket and, seeing the screen, his face hardens.

"It's General Cortez again," he says, his tone changing drastically.

Dr. James and Dr. Reinhardt exchange a quick glance before nodding. They both know things might not be that good.

The three men walked silently down the suburban street, the echo of their footsteps resonating in the quiet night. Despite the relief they had felt in the bar, worry had now returned. Mark stood in front, his gaze fixed on some unseen point on the horizon, while Dr. James and Dr. Reinhardt followed close behind.

The air was cool, and the streetlights flickered slightly, as if something in the night was not quite right. General Cortez's call had changed the mood, and what seemed like an ending was beginning to crumble.

"What exactly did the general say?" Dr. Reinhardt finally asked, breaking the silence that had accompanied them since they left the bar.

Mark stopped, turning to them with a frown.

"He said there was an unexpected development. Apparently Interpol has lost contact with the team that was monitoring the area where the nanotechnology was released. They don't know what happened, but reports indicate abnormal activity."

"Abnormal activity?" "Dr. James repeated, his tone filled with disbelief. "What kind of activity?"

Mark pursed his lips before answering.

"They don't have any concrete details yet, but they fear that the water levels around the area are fluctuating erratically. It's possible that the nanotechnology is doing something more than they expected."

Dr. Reinhardt let out a long sigh, his face tightening.

"This can't be happening. If nanotechnology is out of control, we could be facing a global-scale environmental catastrophe."

Dr. James nodded, but tried to remain calm.

"We still don't know for sure what's happening. Maybe it's just a misunderstanding."

"A misunderstanding?" Reinhardt narrowed his eyes at him. "James, we've been at this too long to ignore the signs. If something has gone wrong, we can't afford to be optimistic."

Mark remained silent, watching the discussion between his colleagues. He knew Reinhardt was right, but he didn't want to jump to conclusions. There were still too many unknowns, and the situation could get worse if they lost their cool.

"We have to go back," Mark finally said, his tone determined. "We can't just stand here speculating. If what the general said is true, we need to be in the control room."

The other two nodded, without further ado. They knew that, despite their doubts, they had no choice but to return to base.

****

The trip back to the operations center wasn't long, but it felt like an eternity. Each of them was deep in thought, trying to process what could be happening. When they arrived, the atmosphere at the base was tense. Screens displayed charts and maps, and personnel moved quickly, speaking in urgent whispers.

Mark, Dr. James, and Dr. Reinhardt were greeted by a ranking officer, who led them straight to the control room. There, General Cortez was waiting for them, his expression grave.

575

"Thank you for coming so quickly," the general said, wasting no time in formal greetings. "The situation has changed dramatically in the last few hours."

Mark stepped forward, wasting no time.

"What's going on?"

General Cortez pointed to one of the larger screens, which showed a satellite view of the affected area.

"The team monitoring the launch site has disappeared. We haven't had contact with them in over four hours. And this…" he paused, zooming in on the image, "is what's been happening in the ocean."

On the screen, the water around the site seemed to be in constant motion, as if something beneath the surface was stirring up the currents. The graphs showed unusual readings, and the sensors registered fluctuations that couldn't be explained.

"The currents are changing direction at an alarming rate," the general continued. "It's not natural behavior."

Dr. Reinhardt stepped forward, looking at the data with concern.

"What about nanotechnology? Have you been able to track what it's doing?"

The general shook his head.

"It's complicated. Preliminary analysis indicates that nanotechnology could be interacting with the marine ecosystem in ways we didn't anticipate. But more worrying is that there's been an increase in energy levels near the site."

"Energy?" Dr. James asked, frowning. "What kind of energy?"

"We don't know for sure, but it seems that nanotechnology is absorbing or releasing some kind of energy that affects the environment. So far, we haven't seen any adverse effects on marine life, but that could change at any moment."

Mark took a deep breath, processing the information.

"What do you propose we do?"

General Cortez looked at him seriously.

"We need a team on the ground. The only way to know what's going on is to send someone to investigate. The problem is that we don't know what's going on.

The team quickly prepared. The emergency lights in the operating room cast long shadows on the walls as technicians adjusted equipment and radio operators checked frequencies. Specialized suits, designed to withstand exposure to nanotechnology, were lined up next to analysis cases and tablets loaded with real-time data. Mark, Dr. James, and Dr. Reinhardt were about to embark on a dangerous mission that could decide the fate of more than just them.

"I can't believe we're doing this," Dr. James muttered, adjusting the zipper of his protective suit.

"You have to get used to the unexpected in this job," Mark replied as he finished checking the communication equipment. His tone was serious, but there was a hint of determination in his voice that instilled some confidence in his colleagues.

Dr. Reinhardt, always meticulous, checked and rechecked the equipment they would be carrying. He knew they couldn't afford any mistakes.

"If something goes wrong out there, we won't get a second chance," he said without looking up, adjusting the glove on his suit.

Mark glanced at him briefly and nodded.

"I know. But there's no one better prepared than us. We have the knowledge, the data, and the experience. And besides, we can't expect others to take risks for something that started with our decisions."

General Cortez, standing near the door, watched them with a mix of respect and concern. Despite his role as military leader, he knew that the real experts on this mission were these three men. Still, he couldn't help but feel the weight of uncertainty.

"The helicopter will be ready in five minutes," he reported, his tone stern but with a hint of empathy. "When you get to the site, you'll meet the containment team. They've already set up a secure perimeter, but they haven't gotten close enough to get detailed readings."

"Understood, General," Mark said firmly.

Dr. James and Dr. Reinhardt watched in silence, each grappling with their own inner fears, but also with a shared determination. They knew this was their duty, and though the risk was immense, they could not allow the disaster to spread without doing everything they could to stop it.

Chapter 58

The helicopter sliced through the dark sky, its rotors creating a noise that reverberated throughout the cabin. Below, the ocean waters shimmered faintly in the moonlight, but near the area where the nanotechnology had been released, something more disturbing was visible: a light grayish-blue mist rising from the water, pulsing with a strange glow.

"That doesn't look right," Dr. James muttered, watching the phenomenon from the helicopter window.

"It's not supposed to do that," Reinhardt said with a frown, analyzing the readings on his tablet. "We hadn't anticipated nanotechnology interacting with water like this."

"It could be a secondary reaction," Mark theorized. "Something we didn't detect in the first analyses."

"Or something completely unexpected," Dr. Reinhardt added, concern palpable in his voice.

The helicopter landed on a floating platform near the secure perimeter established by the containment team. The three men quickly got off, being greeted by the commander of the containment team, a tall woman with a stern expression.

"I'm Captain Rodriguez. We've secured the area as best we could, but we haven't been able to get any closer to the core of the phenomenon," she reported as she led them toward the command post. "The fog you see there isn't just a visual phenomenon. Our sensor equipment is detecting some sort of electromagnetic field around that area, something we've never seen before."

"What effects has it had on the personnel?" Mark asked as they walked.

Rodriguez nodded toward a group of soldiers who were sitting in the distance, visibly affected.

"Some of our men experienced dizziness, disorientation, even hallucinations. We have evacuated the worst affected. None of them were able to get within five hundred meters of the epicenter."

Dr. James exchanged a glance with Dr. Reinhardt. This was much worse than they had anticipated.

"We need to get closer," Dr. James said firmly.

Captain Rodriguez looked at them in disbelief.

"I can't allow it. If something happens to them in there, we will have no way to get them out quickly."

"We can't afford to stay here and watch the situation worsen," Mark intervened, keeping his tone calm but with firm resolve. "We know this is dangerous, but we are the only ones who can understand what is happening in there."

Rodriguez hesitated for a moment, but finally nodded in resignation.

"Okay. I will provide you with a backup team, but if the situation is not as good as it seems, we will have to wait until the end of the war."

The tension in the air immediately increased. Dr. James and Dr. Reinhardt looked in the direction Mark pointed, but the fog thickened, covering any possible movement. However, the feeling of something unknown and potentially dangerous was still there.

"It can't be," Dr. James muttered, adjusting the controls on his sensors. "There's no sign of life, just nanotechnology... but something is interfering with the signals."

Reinhardt leaned toward the equipment he was carrying, adjusting the readings and examining the data quickly.

"We're not picking up any biological signals, but there is something. A fluctuating electromagnetic field, as if the nanotechnology is interacting with the environment in a way we've never seen before."

Mark frowned, his eyes narrowed as he continued to watch the fog.

"Something's out there. And I don't think it's just runaway nanotechnology. We got too close, whatever's here has noticed it."

Dr. James gulped and looked around, his body tensing.

"Do you think it could be some kind of defense? Or worse, an evolutionary system that nanotechnology has developed?"

Mark didn't answer right away. What they were witnessing was something no simulation or rehearsal had prepared them to face. Finally, he decided.

"We can't retreat now. If nanotechnology has developed some kind of defense mechanism, we need to find out before it becomes uncontrollable."

Reinhardt nodded, though his expression showed more fear than conviction. As they moved forward, the feeling of oppression increased. It was as if the fog not only blocked vision, but also affected space itself, creating a strange distortion in the air.

Suddenly, the fog seemed to part before them, revealing a dark structure at the center of the entire phenomenon. It looked like some kind of organic mass, twisted and pulsating, made up of shiny, intertwining metallic filaments. It was constantly moving, as if it were breathing.

"What the hell is that?" "Dr. James said in a whisper, his voice laced with horror.

Mark approached cautiously, taking readings with his device.

"This is… incredible. It's nanotechnology, but it's taken on a physical form… almost biological."

Reinhardt knelt near the structure, keeping a safe distance as he recorded data.

"It's evolving faster than we imagined. It's like it's achieved rudimentary consciousness, or at least the ability to self-organize. This was never meant to happen."

Mark clenched his fists as he assessed the situation. They knew nanotechnology had the potential to change and adapt, but this was a whole new level. A danger they couldn't have foreseen.

"We have to stop this before it spreads any further. If this thing reaches the ocean on a larger scale…" Mark left the sentence unfinished, but everyone knew what that meant. A global environmental disaster, perhaps irreversible.

Suddenly, an intense humming sound filled the air, and the structure in front of them began to glow brighter. Reinhardt's sensors went off, showing readings out of the ordinary.

"It's reacting to our presence!" he shouted, backing away immediately. "We have to get out of here."

Mark made a quick decision.

"Get back! We're going to need more support to contain this."

Just as they took the first step back, the ground beneath their feet began to shake. The glow of the structure intensified even more, and a low sound, like a distant roar, filled the air.

Dr. James stumbled, falling to his knees.

"What's going on?!"

Mark grabbed him by the arm, helping him up.

"It's the structure! It's releasing some kind of energy."

At that moment, the fog surrounding them began to move erratically, as if it was being pushed by an invisible force. And then they saw it. Amidst the fog, several shadows, human figures, began to emerge, walking towards them with strangely synchronized movements.

"Those are...?" Reinhardt began to ask, his eyes wide.

"No," Mark interrupted. "They're not human."

The figures, shrouded in fog and glowing faintly with the same blue light as the structure, had no definable features. They were shadows, simulacra created by nanotechnology, but their movements were precise, almost as if they were alive.

"It's replicating us!" Dr. James shouted, horrified. "Nanotechnology is creating versions of us."

Mark gritted his teeth.

"This is worse than we thought. We have to destroy it before these things spread!"

But before they could act, the figures began to move rapidly towards them. Their bodies made no sound as they advanced, but the threat was obvious. The simulacra had no peaceful intentions.

Real World Applications

Nano-robots can be introduced into water in a manner similar to how substances like fentanyl are integrated into drugs. Once the water becomes contaminated with these nano-robots, it can then be used for irrigation, potentially affecting the growth of crops such as fruits and vegetables.

Animals that eat or drink the contaminated water will become contaminated with biomolecular magnetic nanomaterial(nano-robots).

The second application involves aerial spraying, typically executed using small aircraft such as drones or light planes that operate at altitudes below 3,000 feet. This method utilizes technology where nano-robots replicate rapidly when exposed to water vapor in the air, which is influenced by human breath. This process enhances the effectiveness and efficiency of the spray, enabling precise delivery and faster replication of the nano-robots in the targeted environment.

The third application involves the use of a small canister, designed for controlled environments such as retail stores or indoor facilities. This technology enables precise deployment in confined spaces, ensuring optimal control and effectiveness within the specified area.

All applications can be remotely controlled via 5G or higher-speed Wi-Fi connections. These technologies are designed for covert operations, with the primary intent of executing precise, discreet actions (Murder).

How to protect your temple light from dimming and the potential dangers of emerging technologies and their unforeseen consequences. Higher quality water distillery and reduce technological advancement of signals.

Be well my friend. Your blessings are always my gratitude"

Thanks!